The Good News
of the Return of the King

The Good News
of the Return of the King

The Gospel in Middle-earth

MICHAEL T. JAHOSKY

WIPF & STOCK · Eugene, Oregon

THE GOOD NEWS OF THE RETURN OF THE KING
The Gospel in Middle-earth

Copyright © 2020 Michael T. Jahosky. All rights reserved. Except for brief quotations in critical publications or reviews, no part of this book may be reproduced in any manner without prior written permission from the publisher. Write: Permissions, Wipf and Stock Publishers, 199 W. 8th Ave., Suite 3, Eugene, OR 97401.

Wipf & Stock
An Imprint of Wipf and Stock Publishers
199 W. 8th Ave., Suite 3
Eugene, OR 97401

www.wipfandstock.com

PAPERBACK ISBN: 978-1-7252-6316-1
HARDCOVER ISBN: 978-1-7252-6313-0
EBOOK ISBN: 978-1-7252-6314-7

Manufactured in the U.S.A. 09/28/20

Sarah: Your daily sacrifices and loving support over the last five plus years have made this book possible. Your Christlike love and sacrifice has fueled this book and it is dedicated to you and our two beautiful children, Lucas and Annabelle.

Contents

Permissions		ix
Preface: My "Road into Jerusalem"		xi
Acknowledgments		xxi
Introduction		1
1	*The Lord of the Rings* as Parable	48
2	Parables Are Good News Stories	74
3	*The Lord of the Rings* Is Good News	94
4	The King Beneath the Mountain	133
5	"Estel"	158
Endnotes		193
Bibliography		211

Permissions

Christian Reflections by CS Lewis ©copyright CS Lewis Pte Ltd 1967, 1980

God in the Dock by CS Lewis ©copyright CS Lewis Pte Ltd 1970

On Stories and Other Essays by CS Lewis ©copyright CS Lewis Pte Ltd

3 Ways of Writing for Children by CS Lewis ©copyright CS Lewis Pte Ltd

Selected Literature Essays by CS Lewis ©copyright CS Lewis Pte Ltd 1969

Surprised by Joy by CS Lewis ©copyright CS Lewis Pte Ltd 1955

Pilgrims Regress by CS Lewis ©copyright CS Lewis Pte Ltd 1933

Letters to Children by CS Lewis ©copyright CS Lewis Pte Ltd 1985

The Problem of Pain by CS Lewis ©copyright CS Lewis Pte Ltd 1940

Letters of CS Lewis Vol III by CS Lewis ©copyright CS Lewis Pte Ltd 2006

Mere Christianity by CS Lewis ©copyright CS Lewis Pte Ltd 1942, 1943, 1944, 1952

Reflections on the Psalms by CS Lewis ©copyright CS Lewis Pte Ltd 1958

The Great Divorce by CS Lewis ©copyright CS Lewis Pte Ltd 1946

Excerpts from THE PEOPLES OF MIDDLE-EARTH: The History of Middle-earth, Volume XII by J.R.R. Tolkien, Copyright ©1996 by Frank Richard Williamson and Christopher Reuel Tolkien as Executors of the Estate of J.R.R. Tolkien. Reprinted by permission of Houghton Mifflin Harcourt Publishing Company. All rights reserved.

Excerpts from UNFINISHED TALES OF NUMENOR AND MIDDLE-EARTH by J.R.R. Tolkien, Copyright ©1980 by J.R.R. Tolkien Copyright Trust. Reprinted by permission of Houghton Mifflin Harcourt Publishing Company. All rights reserved.

Excerpts from THE SILMARILLION by J.R.R. Tolkien, edited by Christopher Tolkien Copyright ©1977 by J.R.R. Tolkien Copyright Trust and Christopher Reuel Tolkien. Reprinted by permission of Houghton Mifflin Harcourt Publishing Company. All rights reserved.

Excerpts from MORGOTH'S RING: The Later Silmarillion by J.R.R. Tolkien, Copyright ©1993 by Frank Richard Williamson and Christopher Reuel Tolkien as Executors of the Estate of J.R.R. Tolkien. Reprinted by permission of Houghton Mifflin Harcourt Publishing Company. All rights reserved.

Excerpts from "Mythopoeia" from TREE AND LEAF by J.R.R. Tolkien. Copyright© 1964 by George Allen & Unwin Ltd. Renewed 1992 by John F.R. Tolkien, Christopher R. Tolkien, and Priscilla M.A.R. Tolkien, Copyright ©1988 by The Tolkien Trust. Reprinted by permission of Houghton Mifflin Harcourt Publishing Company. All rights reserved.

Excerpts from "Beowulf: The Monsters and the Critics" from THE MONSTERS AND THE CRITICS by J.R.R. Tolkien. Copyright © 1983 by Frank Richard Williamson and Christopher Reuel Tolkien as Executors of the Estate of J.R.R. Tolkien. Reprinted by permission of Houghton Mifflin Harcourt Publishing Company. All rights reserved.

Excerpts from "On Fairy Stories" from THE MONSTERS AND THE CRITICS by J.R.R. Tolkien. Copyright © 1983 by Frank Richard Williamson and Christopher Reuel Tolkien as Executors of the Estate of J.R.R. Tolkien. Reprinted by permission of Houghton Mifflin Harcourt Publishing Company. All rights reserved.

Excerpts from THE HOBBIT by J.R.R. Tolkien. Copyright © 1937, 1951, 1966, 1978, 1995 by the J.R.R. Tolkien Copyright Trust. Reprinted by permission of Houghton Mifflin Harcourt Publishing Company. All rights reserved.

Excerpts from THE LORD OF THE RINGS by J.R.R. Tolkien, edited by Christopher Tolkien, Copyright © 1954, 1955, 1956, 1965, 1966 by J.R.R. Tolkien. Copyright © Renewed 1982, 1983 by Christopher R. Tolkien, Michael H.R. Tolkien, John F.R. Tolkien, and M.A.R. Tolkien. Copyright © Renewed 1993, 1994, by Christopher R. Tolkien, John F.R. Tolkien, and Priscilla M.A.R. Tolkien. Reprinted by permission of Houghton Mifflin Harcourt Publishing Company. All rights reserved.

Excerpts from THE LETTERS OF J.R.R. Tolkien, edited by Humphrey Carpenter with the assistance of Christopher Tolkien. Copyright © 1981 by George Allen & Unwin (Publishers) Ltd. Reprinted by permission of Houghton Mifflin Harcourt Publishing Company. All rights reserved.

Preface: My "Road into Jerusalem"

Although I did not know it at the time, this book began to take shape when I was sixteen years old. The year 2001 was an important year for me for two reasons. First, it was the year I decided to seriously reconsider Christianity, and second, it was the first time I read *The Lord of the Rings*. Although it has taken several years for me to discover this, *The Lord of the Rings* restored my ability to read Scripture properly and hear it for what it is: good news. *The Lord of the Rings* re-mythologized and reenchanted the biblical narrative for me when I needed it most. Apparently, I am not the only person who has had this experience. Sandra Richter recounts: "The *first* gospel I heard was that of a king, exiled from his throne. One who, although the heir of Numenor, had taken the form of a vagabond and, being found in the appearance of a Ranger, lived out his life on the margins of his own lawful inheritance, tirelessly laboring to undermine the enemy that held his citizenry captive."[1] Myths—stories—act on us as concrete experiences and move us in ways propositional argument cannot. Perhaps it will be news to some of my readers to hear that Christianity is good news. I realize many books on this subject already exist, but I believe that I have uncovered something very special and worth reading about: *The Lord of the Rings* is a parable about what Jesus's parables are about, which is the very story of reality itself. Myth is so effective because it embodies the very message it seeks to communicate; the myth *is* the message. Parables are a special type of myth, or story, and in this book, I want to show that this is because they are *incarnational* stories. When God chose to disclose himself, he chose to do so mythically through parable.

So, who am I, why did I write this book, and what is this book about? I am a college humanities professor who specializes in history, philosophy, religion, mythology, and the fine arts. I currently teach at St. Petersburg College and regularly include J. R. R. Tolkien and C. S. Lewis in my Introduction to Humanities curriculums. Although I am not a biblical scholar per se, it is an area that I have spent most of my academic career researching, writing, and teaching in. Although I am not a professional Tolkien scholar, I have spent much of my career in higher education researching, writing, and talking about Tolkien and his books. My humanities training allows me to bring an interdisciplinary perspective to what is very much an interdisciplinary subject. Although I am only a "cradle Catholic" and not a lifelong Catholic like Tolkien was, I am familiar enough with Catholic theology and history to bring an "insider" as well as an "outsider" perspective to this subject. After being baptized and receiving first communion in the Catholic Church, I wandered away from it for many years, until recently I decided to return, this time with my wife and two children. Researching and writing about a lifelong Catholic like Tolkien played a significant role in this decision. During the interim, I was a member of a Presbyterian church for many years where I taught classes on apologetics. As such, I believe I bring a unique perspective to the subject of this book.

Why did I write this book? I wrote this book because I wanted to share how *The Lord of the Rings*, as Christian literature, has helped me understand Christianity better. Let me be clear: this is not because *The Lord of the Rings* is a carbon copy of the story we can read in the Bible. Instead, it feels like an extension of the biblical story. Somehow, *The Lord of the Rings* feels like an addition to the biblical epic. It expands the biblical story and can give us new insights. What do I mean by that? In this book, I argue that *The Lord of the Rings* functions like one of Jesus's parables, a kind of mythical "what if?" of the gospel. C. S. Lewis called this type of story a "supposal," which I believe is essentially the same as a parable. What is a parable? From two Greek words that mean "to cast alongside," parables are comparative narratives that bring together the mundane and the transcendent, the abstract and concrete. They are imaginative stories that re-mythologize and reenchant reality by putting the transcendence back into the world that the modern rational, materialistic worldview has taken out of it. Many of us, you see, have lost the ability to see that reality has a transcendent dimension to it, or we have become jaded about it, so it isn't as real to our hearts and minds as it ought to be. Parables put the "real" back in reality. Parables, as a form of mythology, show us that truth is not narrowly defined by what human reason, the senses, and science can prove. According to John Piper, parables work by harnessing the power of "likening." According to Piper, the key of likening is this: "Likening some aspect of reality to what it is not can reveal more of what it is."[2]

What is a "supposal"? According to the Christian apologist and C. S. Lewis scholar Alister McGrath, a supposal is "an invitation to try seeing things in another way, and imagine how things would work out if this were true."[3] Lewis himself coined this term and used it to describe the literary genre of *The Chronicles of Narnia*. A "supposal" draws us into a mythical narrative and then challenges us to view reality sacramentally again. Lewis himself wrote of the "supposal" that the Incarnation of Christ "is an invention giving an imaginary answer to the question, 'what might Christ become like if there really were a world like Narnia and He chose to be incarnate and die and rise again in *that* world as He actually has done in ours?'"[4] This, I learned from Lewis, is not the same as allegory. One way of defining an allegory is a type of story which renders concrete experience into purely abstract terms. Allegoresis, the art of interpreting literature as allegory, is also potentially problematic. Yet no literature is self-interpreting, and we cannot completely avoid doing this. J. R. R. Tolkien indicated this when he wrote, "Any attempt to explain the purport of myth or fairytale must use allegorical language."[5] Elsewhere in his essay on *Beowulf*, Tolkien wrote that "myth is alive at once and in all its parts, and dies before it can be dissected."[6] We cannot help but use allegorical language when examining a myth, and yet when we do, the myth dies. What is the solution? Once again, Tolkien provides the answer. Myth, he wrote, "is at its best when it is presented by a poet who feels rather than makes explicit what his theme portends; who presents it as incarnate in the world of history and geography."[7] This is an incredibly important insight for the present book, so please take note of it. So, what does Tolkien mean? He means that when we let the myth remain what it is—a story—then "we are experiencing a principle concretely." Myth is a special kind of concrete experience, and we can only enjoy that experience when we let the myth be a myth. According to Charlie W. Starr, "only when we put the experience into words does the principle become abstract."[8] A parable is a special kind of concrete experience which communicates reality to us via the imagination first and then to our rational mind. In other words, parables, as a type of myth, sneak past the rational mind which wants to define truth as only what can be proven rationally and scientifically. *The Lord of the Rings* is not a fictional version of the biblical story; it is a story *about* what the biblical story is about: the story of reality itself.

This revelation took well over a decade for me to fully discover, but when it became clear how *The Lord of the Rings* helped me understand Christianity better, I decided that I wanted to share this with others. While researching this book, I was very surprised—and comforted—to learn that I was not the only person to come to this conclusion. However, I gradually felt that the books that explained how *The Lord of the Rings* does what I suspect it was doing to me were incomplete, unsatisfactory, or both. In 2015, I had the honor of being part of a Tolkien studies panel at a conference in New Orleans where I presented an early form of what is now one of the chapters of this book. I was galvanized by the responses I received from people about my paper and presentation and decided to approach a publisher's booth at the conference and pitch my idea. A few weeks later, this pitch turned into an offer and a request for a proposal and the adventure began. Then, after a peer review process at my first publisher, it became clear that the book had taken on a life of its own and gone in a direction that was, it seems, too Christian for that publishing house. The last few months of 2019 were very stressful and discouraging as I eagerly sought a Christian publisher who would be interested in publishing this book.

Then, a few weeks before Christmas 2019, I received an offer from Wipf and Stock. I know it may sound cliché, but I truly believe God wants this book to reach people, and I am certain that without his knowledge of people's hearts and gracious assistance, this book would have never seen publication. Early in the writing process, I decided not to take an exclusively Catholic approach to writing the book, despite my background. Neither did I feel knowledgeable enough to write from a specific Protestant point of view. The perspective I try very hard to take in this book is closest in spirit to C. S. Lewis's "mere Christianity," which is historical and interdenominational.[9] The difficulty with this is, of course, that not everyone agrees on what "historic" Christianity or "interdenominational" Christianity looks like. I have worked very hard to write in the same vein as today's leading Christian scholars such as N. T. Wright, Timothy Keller, Paul Gould, and Alister McGrath, just to name a few. All these scholars argue that in order to write from the perspective of "mere Christianity" one must write about Jesus and Christianity in its original Jewish context, so that is what I have done in this book. My hope is that the book appeals to Christians of *all* denominations and to those seekers outside the church desiring an approximation of "mere Christianity." Nevertheless, I want to disclose to my readers that the Catholic tradition has shaped my understanding of Christianity the most significantly.

One of the most exciting influences on my academic career and this book has been the two study abroad trips which I have led in Israel. When I returned from my second trip in the Summer of 2016, I discovered an essay written by Lewis entitled "Christianity and Culture." In it, he talks about the role that culture may or may not play in a person's conversion to Christianity. Throughout the essay, he discusses the various views that Christian theologians have held about culture over the last two millennia. Many Christians—for good reason—have mixed feelings about culture outside the church. A Christian's relationship with culture is an important topic and there are many pitfalls to avoid. For example, Christians ought not to be strictly against culture, because there is much within culture outside the church that is worth reading, watching, and listening to. Fragments of

Christ exist everywhere truth is discovered. On the other hand, indiscriminately embracing every cultural trend or movement, for example, is unwise. It seems a Christian's relationship with culture is much more nuanced and paradoxical than I think many Christians believe. While reading Lewis's essay, I came across a passage where he states: "Imitation may pass into initiation. For some it is a good beginning. For others it is not; culture is not everyone's road into Jerusalem, and for some it is a road out."[10] What Lewis is trying to say is this: Christians believe that after God created everything, he blessed it as *tov meod* (Hebrew for "exceedingly good") which—importantly—includes what Christians sometimes derisively call "the world." "Culture," or "the world," contains many pointers which, when discovered, may subsequently lead someone on the "road into Jerusalem" toward Christ. And sometimes it may not. Sometimes, culture (or the church!) provides people with opportunities that may pave a road away from Jerusalem. By "road into Jerusalem" Lewis meant one's journey to—or away from—Christ and Christianity. Reading this essay after walking the Via Dolorosa really impacted my faith. Now, as I contemplate Lewis's essay and my memory of walking the Via Dolorosa, I realize that *The Lord of the Rings* has been my "road into Jerusalem."[11]

As a young boy, I not only lost touch with my Catholic upbringing, but with Christianity in general. Then, at sixteen years old, I began to seriously reconsider Christianity again. Why? One reason was due to watching how my mother's life was profoundly transformed by Jesus. The second reason was because of *The Lord of the Rings*. At that time, I did not consciously realize there was a providential connection between these two things. Peter Jackson's film adaptation of *The Fellowship of the Ring* arrived in theaters in 2001. I began to read *The Fellowship* with my brother before the film came out and then soon found myself reading Tolkien's entire mythology. Around this time, I also began to read the Bible daily, but I did not attend church or engage in any serious academic study of Christianity. As a matter of fact, I often felt lost and struggled with what it meant to be Christian. A lot of converts feel this way today; after baptism, many wonder what the next step is. Over the years, I have realized that learning to be a disciple of Jesus is much more important than having a conversion moment and story. I do not want this to sound the wrong way, but I enjoyed spending more time in Middle-earth than in my Bible. Eventually I realized, many years later, that I was hearing the gospel in Middle-earth, even though I did not know it at the time. Tolkien's story made me feel like I had somewhere I belonged and that I was part of an epic story; at first, I did not think this was something the Bible could provide. Everything in Middle-earth felt incredibly real and urgent, and I wanted my "real life" as a Christian to feel like that. Everywhere I went, something in life reminded me of something in *The Lord of the Rings*. Little did I know, I was experiencing the power of parable.

When I first started reading Tolkien's books as a sixteen-year-old, I only wanted to understand and appreciate the story itself. I did not think there was any meaning beyond the story. Later, throughout my college years, I began a tradition where I would read *The Lord of the Rings* every fall semester, which continues to be a tradition for me to this day. With each new annual reading, I began to feel that the story lingered with me in an indescribable way, but I could not put my finger on why. I realize now why it is: I truly heard the gospel first in Middle-earth. The story of Aragorn in particular affected me profoundly. He seemed familiar, but I did not know how or why. Years later when I began research for this book, I came across one of Peter Kreeft's books entitled *The Philosophy of Tolkien* where he says, "Though we do not have kings in America, or want them, our unconscious mind both has them and wants them. We all know what a true king is, a real king, an ideal king, an archetypal king . . . something in us longs to give him our loyalty and fealty and service and obedience. He is lost but longed for and will someday return."[12] After reading this, I began to feel slightly less crazy. Kreeft's insight brought me comfort and helped me make sense of why Aragorn's story specifically affected me so profoundly. And then I discovered N. T. Wright's book *Simply Jesus*. Reading this book was like finding the missing piece to the puzzle. Wright's interpretation of Christianity—that it is the story of "how God became king"—reminded me of a story I had already heard: the story of the return of the king.[13] Suddenly, I realized that Tolkien's mythology was a story about what Jesus's stories are about: The good news of the return of the king.

You hold in your hands the story of the journey that led to this understanding. *The Lord of the Rings* is not "about" Jesus's parables or the Bible in general, it is about what Jesus's parables and the larger biblical story is about: the good news! I now realize that this revelation was my "conversion experience." The sense of adventure I have always felt in reading *The Lord of the Rings* and my love of Jesus and the Bible have converged in this book. The biggest obstacle has been the issue of allegory, which I will be addressing in the Introduction and chapter 1. My argument in this book is that in *The Lord of the Rings*, Tolkien has given us a *parable* of the gospel that not only can restore our understanding and appreciation of Jesus's parables and the Bible, but can also show us how parables can reenchant reality.

Who is this book for? Although it does have some academic sections, I have written those sections as clearly as possible so that laypersons can also benefit from them. The book does assume some knowledge of the characters and plot of Tolkien's three main books: *The Silmarillion*, *The Hobbit*, and

The Lord of the Rings. I do not provide detailed plot or character analyses, save a few exceptions. If you have not read any of Tolkien's books, however, "spoiler alert"! If you want the best experience possible, only read the Preface through chapter 2 of this book, since starting in chapter 3, I begin an analysis of Tolkien's books. The best stories invite us to read them again and again. We call them classics because they are always relevant and true to reality. My hope is that Christians and non-Christians, laypersons and academics, as well as fans of and newcomers to Tolkien's books may find this book accessible, interesting, and enriching. I have a special hope that people who are either skeptical of Christianity or religion in general and people who are in spiritual dry periods will give this book a chance, because I truly understand where you are coming from. As a Christian humanities professor, I have studied many different cultures and religions, and this experience has sometimes caused me to doubt and ask questions about my own worldview. If your story resembles mine, then I believe you can benefit from reading this book. Indeed, we can all benefit from what Tolkien called "recovery" and "escape." Tolkien believes that "We need . . . to clean our windows; so that the things seen clearly may be freed from the drab blur of triteness or familiarity—from possessiveness."[14]

In this book, I present Tolkien as an apologist, a "defender," of the Christian worldview. Although this book is not a "how-to" manual of how to use Tolkien's literature as an apologetic for the gospel, there is plenty of apologetic "mithril" here for Christians to mine. While apologetics is not the same as an evangelism, the former goes together with the latter. Because the two often get confused, I want to offer a brief explanation here. The Greek word *apologia* means "to give a defense" (see 1 Peter 3:15-16) of the Christian *worldview*. What is a worldview? A worldview is a "pattern of ideas, beliefs, convictions, and habits" from a specific point of view.[15] Of the Christian worldview Dorothy L. Sayers once said that she felt she had "fallen in love with an intellectual pattern."[16] Worldviews are not merely patterns of propositional statements about reality, however. Scholars such as Alister McGrath have explained that worldviews are usually expressed through "myths," an ancient Greek word which originally meant "true story." According to McGrath, Tolkien frequently used the term "myth" in his letters and essays. Indeed, Tolkien's views on myth proved to be the decisive factor in Lewis's return to Christianity in 1931 (more on this in the Introduction). According to McGrath, the Greek word *mythos* did not originally mean "false story" but "grand narrative" or "narrated worldview."[17] I will show in this book that Tolkien believed that the most effective apologetic combined *mythos* and its propositional counterpart *logos*, and that this belief was rooted in an intimate understanding and appreciation of the apologetic approach of Jesus and his parables. Jesus presented and defended the gospel primarily through parables, a type of *mythos*. According to Klyne Snodgrass, parables are a form of "indirect communication" that creates "an imaginary world that reflects reality."[18]

Although presenting an apologetic for Christianity was not Tolkien's primary goal in writing *The Lord of the Rings*, it was a by-product of writing a "fundamentally religious and Catholic work" which he "deliberately" crafted out of certain religious ideas.[19] Parables are a type of story wherein one's worldview is expressed as incarnate in the narrative. Indeed, the Greek word *parabole* means to "cast alongside" or to "throw from the side."[20] In other words, parables are effective for people who wish to "tell it slant," in the words of Emily Dickinson.[21] For Tolkien, an explicit apologetic of the Christian worldview would have been a violation of what he felt was an effective apologetic of the Christian worldview. Why? Because an explicit, heavy-handed approach to proclaiming the gospel was not Jesus's way and does not conform to the "art of the parable."[22] Parables are a type of indirect communication that communicates its content through its form. In other words, *what* a parable says is inseparable from *how* it is said. Robert Funk has argued that the "gospel tends to make explicit what is only implicit in the parable; and thus violates the intention of what may be the dominant mode of discourse in which Jesus taught."[23] Jesus's parables, then, may be the closest we can get to authentic Christianity. Jesus primarily relied on parables to communicate the gospel, and so a Christian's theology should be parable-centric. According to Gisela H. Kreglinger, parables make up approximately one-third of the gospels.[24] Tolkien himself had a knack for speaking "parabolically" about *The Lord of the Rings*, a fact which is clear to anyone who has read his letters. Tolkien's back and forth about whether *The Lord of the Rings* is or is not a Christian story and is or is not an allegory is well-known among Tolkien scholars. But what does this mean? At base, parables are a type of metaphorical speech. What is a metaphor? According to Gisela Kreglinger, "metaphor is . . . speaking about one thing in terms that are seen to be *suggestive* of another."[25] All this will be explained in more detail in the present book. Tolkien was not confused about allegory, but we may be, and so we will take a deep dive into this subject in the Introduction and chapter 1. If we want to understand why Tolkien appeared ambivalent about *The Lord of the Rings* being a Christian story, we will need to better understand myth, allegory, metaphor, and parable.

Tolkien was very ambivalent when he spoke about the Christianness of his books. Why might that be? I believe there are two reasons. First, because he wanted readers to *focus on the story*. Second, because as we will learn, this is how Jesus spoke about the gospel and himself. Jesus placed a strong emphasis on stories in coming to belief. According to Gisela Kreglinger, "true revelation only happens when one participates in the meaning of the story."[26] The only way we will be able to discover what the story is "about" is by staying focused on the story itself. Parables show us that something about Christian discipleship can only be imparted through narrative. God revealed himself to Israel primarily through narrative, not proposition. *The Lord of the Rings*, like Jesus's parables, is ultimately a story about the importance of stories in coming to belief in Jesus Christ.

As stated above, I believe Tolkien often spoke ambivalently because *Jesus himself spoke this way*. The way of the parable is to "tell it slant," and a good metaphor—regardless of its brevity or length—"will emphasize one aspect of a thing while hiding others."[27] I believe that Tolkien's proclivity for paradox was due to his love of and devotion to Jesus and his parables. He was not confused about whether *The Lord of the Rings* was a Christian story; we have failed to understand *how* it is a Christian story. Although a bit more complicated, neither was Tolkien confused about whether *The Lord of the Rings* was an allegory or not. In a letter to Joanna de Bortadano in 1956 Tolkien wrote, "Of course my story is not an allegory of Atomic power, but of *Power* (exerted for Domination)."[28] On the other hand, Tolkien *also* said, "I cordially dislike allegory in all of its manifestations."[29] Is *The Lord of the Rings* an allegory in one sense but not in another? There has been an incredible amount of confusion about this issue in Tolkien studies. One of the main goals of this book is to demonstrate that this apparent contradiction can be resolved through a proper understanding of parables. Tolkien's letters also reveal an intense reverence for the miracle of the incarnation, which will be crucially relevant to our discussion about parables. I am indebted to Holly Ordway's book *Apologetics and the Christian Imagination* specifically for the connection between the incarnation, story, and apologetics. Many Tolkien scholars have taken some of the comments he made about the incarnation in his letters to mean that either *The Lord of the Rings* is not a Christian story or that it is, but it contains no incarnation.[30] Neither theory is correct because both stem from a theology that is not rooted in the parables.

Jesus spoke in parables to challenge and gently lure his audience into discipleship, not to coerce them into a conversion. Jesus relied on metaphorical language not because it was another way of saying what could have been said literally, or to deceive people, or to make an emotional impact, but because *what he wanted to say was inseparable from the way he was saying it*.[31] Any understanding of the Christian worldview which fails to keep parables at its center must, I am convinced, be revised. According to Sallie McFague, "if the parable (and its close cousins, story and confession) are seen as primary forms for theology, then the content of theology might well be different than it has been in the past."³² Since Jesus spent the greater part of his ministry speaking in parables, a non-parabolic theology will miss too much. As we will see, this is a topic that not only Tolkien himself understood and took seriously, but a subject which Father Robert Murray—one of Tolkien's close friends—delivered a sermon about during the Tolkien Centenary in 1992.

If our understanding of Christian theology is grounded in Jesus's parables three things become clear not only about Tolkien and his mythology, but about Christianity as well. First, as his 1939 lecture "On Fairy Stories" and his friend Murray's sermon "J. R. R. Tolkien and the Art of the Parable" will both make clear, Tolkien's theology was indeed grounded in Jesus's parables, an important fact which subsequently shaped the way he understood "fairy stories." Second, we will see that Tolkien's reverence for the miracle of the Incarnation stemmed from his parabolic theology. In other words, Tolkien recognized that there is a relationship between the incarnation and Jesus's parables. Parables are, in short, *incarnational myths*. Parables are the best means of communicating the reality of the incarnation because their form *is* incarnational. Thirdly and finally, as we will learn in the Introduction, Jewish parables are *monarchic*. The root word for "parable" in Hebrew, which is *mashal*, originally meant "shadow" or "rule." This is a reflection of the way Semitic kingship was understood in the ancient world. God's "shadow" on earth was the king, who was also his "son" or "image." The king also *ruled* on earth as God's steward.³³ As N. T. Wright has said, "the very *form* of the parable thus embodies the *content* it is trying to communicate: heaven appearing on earth."³⁴ As a corollary of this, I hope to show that Tolkien was a very profound and effective Christian apologist *because* of his intimate understanding of parables. Once again, I realize calling Tolkien an apologist may take some Tolkien scholars by surprise since Tolkien was quiet and guarded in his witness, but as we will see, there is abundant evidence to suggest that he was as great an apologist as Lewis was. My hope is that this book will reveal that Tolkien's books, especially *The Lord of the Rings*, comprise a beautiful literary apologetic for Jesus Christ and the gospel. In the words of C. S. Lewis, I hope this book is like "red beef and strong beer" for your "road into Jerusalem."³⁵

Acknowledgments

I have told my wife, Sarah, that after this book is finished, I would like to go see mountains again, like Bilbo told Gandalf at the beginning of *The Fellowship of the Ring*: "I want to see mountains again, Gandalf—*mountains*; and then find somewhere where I can *rest*."[36] This book has been a joy to write, but it has been a long and weary road. Writing this book has been one of the biggest challenges of my life, and I have been helped by many people that I would now like to thank. Sarah, my wife, has been by my side every step of the way from the conception of the book to its completion, and without her love, support, and companionship, this book would have never been finished. I have had to write this book without any time off from a full-time teaching position over many years, and so Sarah graciously helped me find the time to make sure I could reach the finish line. I want to thank Paul Gould who decided to answer an email from a stressed-out humanities professor whom he did not know and then graciously connected me to people who in turn helped me find a home for my book at Wipf and Stock. Paul, thank you for taking a chance on me and for your guidance and support. I am also indebted to many members of my family, most of all Mom and Dad, who encouraged and supported me constantly. The opportunities you provided me with over the last two decades have led to the creation of this book; thank you, I love you both very much. I am also grateful to my in-laws, especially Kelly, who read portions of this manuscript and gave me wise advice over the years. Last, but not least, I want to thank my sister, Jan Jahosky, for helping me market this book, and Matthew Wimer at Wipf and Stock for his support.

ENDNOTES

[1] Sandra Richter, "Response to Chapter 1," in Ryken, *Messiah Comes to Middle-Earth*, 35–36.
[2] Piper, "C. S. Lewis, Romantic Rationalist," 32.
[3] McGrath, *C. S. Lewis: A Life*, 277.

[4] Lewis, "Letter to Arthur Greeves from the Kilns, 18 October 1931," in Lewis and Hooper, *Letters*, 366–68.
[5] Tolkien, *Letters of J. R. R. Tolkien*, Letter 131.
[6] Tolkien, "Beowulf," 113.
[7] Tolkien, "Beowulf," 113.
[8] Starr, *Faun's Bookshelf*, ch. 10, sect. "Myth, Reality, and Truth," loc. 1936.
[9] In his essay "On the Reading of Old Books" (which is in the *God in the Dock* essay collection), Lewis says that "Mere Christianity turns out to be no insipid inter-denominational transparency, but something positive, self-consistent, and inexhaustible" (p. 203).
[10] Lewis, "Christianity and Culture," in Hooper, *Christian Reflections*, 28.
[11] Lewis, "Christianity and Culture," in Hooper, *Christian Reflections*.
[12] Kreeft, *The Philosophy of Tolkien*, ch. 1, loc. 575.
[13] Wright, *Simply Jesus*. Wright uses the phrase "how God became king" in this and many of his other books.
[14] Tolkien, "On Fairy Stories," sect. "Recovery, Escape, Consolation," para. 1.
[15] Myers and Noebel, *Understanding the Times*, 5.
[16] Sayers, *The Letters*, "Letter to the Archbishop of Canterbury, 1943."
[17] McGrath, *Lunch with C. S. Lewis*, 63.
[18] Snodgrass, *Stories with Intent*, 7.
[19] Tolkien, *Letters of J. R. R. Tolkien*, Letters 142 and 211.
[20] Kreglinger, *Storied Revelations*, 15.
[21] Dickinson, *Poems of Emily Dickinson*, poem 1129, p. 41.
[22] Murray, "J. R. R. Tolkien and the Art of the Parable," in Pearce, *Tolkien: A Celebration*, 40–52.
[23] Funk, "Parables: A Fragmentary Agenda," in Funk, *Funk on Parables*, 300.
[24] Kreglinger, *Storied Revelations*, 22.
[25] Kreglinger, *Storied Revelations*, 22.
[26] Kreglinger, *Storied Revelations*, 368.
[27] Kreglinger, *Storied Revelations*, ch. 2.
[28] Tolkien, *Letters of J. R. R. Tolkien*, Letter 186.
[29] Tolkien, *Lord of the Rings*, Foreword.
[30] Tolkien, *Letters of J. R. R. Tolkien*, Letter 181.
[31] Kreglinger, *Storied Revelations*, ch. 2.
[32] McFague, *Speaking in Parables*, ch. 4.
[33] Young, *The Parables*, Introduction.
[34] Wright, *Simply Jesus*, 93.
[35] Lewis, *Surprised by Joy*, 166.
[36] Tolkien, *The Lord of the Rings*, 32.

Introduction

THE STORY OF REALITY

What is it about *The Lord of the Rings* that people love so much? I think it is because the story, indeed, the entire world of Middle-earth, feels *real*. How can a story featuring hobbits, dwarves, elves, dragons, and other fantastical creatures feel real? By being *Christian*. I am fully aware that this statement will raise objections, but please stay with me. How does the realism of Tolkien's novel have anything to do with it being Christian? I propose that the key to understanding this is a proper understanding of what both a myth and historic, orthodox Christianity is. This may initially appear to compound the problem: Isn't a myth an untrue story? Is there really such a thing as "mere Christianity"? Many people view the biblical story the same way they view *The Lord of the Rings*, but I believe this is because they have forgotten the true meaning of words like "myth," "truth," and "reality." Believe it or not, a proper understanding of what a myth is can help us better understand Christianity. A myth is essentially a story about the way things are (reality). In philosophical terms, that means that myths at least have the potential to be stories with truth in them. I am sure by now you may be wondering, "What do you mean by truth?" I promise that I have much more to say about myth, reality, and truth further in, but this point I'm about to make will suffice for now: the biblical story—that is, the Christian story—claims to be the story of reality itself. This raises another important question, but this time about Christianity and the Bible: isn't the biblical story a very culturally specific story? In other words, maybe the Bible is only a book for Jews and Christians, or for people who believe in the biblical God. Consequently, if *The Lord of the Rings* is a Christian novel, then it also follows that it is only a book for those people, right? Nothing could be further from the truth. Israel was called by God to be a blessing to *all* nations (Gen 22:18) and was tasked with drawing *all* nations to herself (Zech 8:23; Isa 49:6). This claim, too, raises even more questions: How is the biblical story everyone's story? Isn't that intolerant to other religions? Aren't all religions equally true? In the first part of this Introduction, my hope is to address these and other important questions and demonstrate why it is the incarnate presence of the Christian worldview in *The Lord of the Rings* that is primarily responsible for the story's inner realism.

To accomplish this, we will also need to look more carefully at how myth, reality, and truth are interconnected and how these terms can help us get a better understanding of historic, orthodox Christianity. Very briefly, what would an understanding of "historic, orthodox Christianity" entail? First, it would include presenting Christianity, as it appears in the New Testament, as a Jewish religion. Of course, as scholars well know, there is a very specific point in time when the term "Christianity" began to be used, and it is important to point out that Jesus never used this term. Second, it would include an intimate familiarity with the Scriptures and story of Israel in the Old Testament. These first two points will help ensure we are getting as close as we can to an "orthodox" understanding of Christianity, for that Greek word means "correct belief." The only proper way to understand Christianity is to understand the theology of Second Temple Judaism first. Last, but not least, an understanding of *historic* Christianity would include awareness of the first century in which Christianity originated, and especially knowledge of the Jewish and Greco-Roman context within which nascent Christianity came into existence.

Since we are all familiar with the popular saying "a picture is worth a thousand words," that seems like a good place to begin. Claiming that the realism of Tolkien's novel is because of its inherent Christianness implies that the Christian worldview tells the story of reality itself. Consider the people and events of the Bible that you know for a moment: Adam and Eve in the garden of Eden; Noah and the great flood; Abraham entertaining angels; Abraham's near-sacrifice of Isaac; Jacob impersonating his brother, Esau, and stealing his brother's birthright; Joseph and his dreams; Moses and the burning bush; the construction of the tabernacle; David and Goliath; Solomon's Temple, and many others. In every one of these stories are what scholars call "types," from the Greek word *typos*, meaning "figure" or "model." Types are signposts or pointers that have been planted in reality that point toward an "antitype," the thing to which the type refers. According to Gerald R. McDermott, types "are things or events that God has set in place."[1] Yet the Bible tells us that types do not merely point to these realities; they participate in them. Thomas Aquinas used the sacraments such as baptism and the Eucharist as examples of types that point toward the antitypes of God's grace and fellowship with Jesus Christ. In both examples, it is the sensory experiences—immersion in water, eating and drinking—that enact or demonstrate what they mean to say. Images and sensory experiences are used to invite the individual into a sacramental reflection and experience of God's grace and presence. Rather than communicate these realities directly, God chooses to communicate them to us *indirectly*. This may not seem an important point, but it is crucial for understanding the arguments in the present book.

According to McDermott, God chooses this indirect, experiential, sensory, and imaginative way to speak to us because "God is infinite, and his creation is finite." After all, how could we fully comprehend God? Says McDermott, "God accommodates his truth to our finite understandings just as human adults change their manner of presentation when teaching children."[2] We learn best when abstract concepts are presented in narrative form because stories are concrete experiences which mimic real life. In the Bible, God primarily relies on types to communicate with us not only because we are epistemologically limited (more on that soon) by what we can know, but because it is a far more imaginiative and *beautiful* way to know as opposed to straightforward propositional argumentation. Moreover, it reveals something about the character of who God is. Christians believe that every inch of reality is filled with types. The question remains, however, what is the great antitype to which all these types point and in which they all participate? According to McDermott, throughout the centuries, the church has maintained that the great antitype is the Triune God of the Bible, especially the Second Person of the Trinity, Jesus Christ. Christians also believe that Jesus Christ and his kingdom is the great Archetype ("original model"). Moreover, Christians maintain the belief that Jesus Christ is the *only* Archetype in all of reality, and "that all the types draw their being and substance from this Archetype," albeit with one caveat: all types contain this archetypal substance in different degrees.[3] Lastly, Christians must rely on Jesus Christ and the Bible as the objective measuring sticks in their evaluation of which types contain such and such a degree of the archetypal substance. The Christian thinker Edward Pusey spoke of this as the "sacramental union" between the type and the Archetype of Jesus Christ.[4] This will prove an extremely important insight to keep in mind throughout the book, as part of my argument consists in showing that Jesus's parables are the perfect example of this "sacramental unity" of type and archetype.

Reflect on the parable of the lost coin from Luke 15:8–10 for a moment. In the parable, Jesus says that a woman has ten silver coins and loses one, but then proceeds to sweep the house diligently until she finds the lost coin. This is one of the shortest yet most powerful of Jesus's parables because it uses the *type and image* of a silver coin—an everyday object—to communicate a poignant truth about turning to God in repentance (and so much more). A picture is worth a thousand words, indeed. Why is this a good place to start our journey in understanding the Christian myth as the story of reality? Christianity teaches that creation is filled with types and that those types point to a great Archetype. These types not only point analogously toward the great Archetype, they also participate *in* that archetype. How so? If Jesus Christ, a historical person, is God, and God created reality and everything and everyone in it, then to say that these types participate in the great Archetype means that they participate in, and are fragments of hints about the person of Jesus Christ. Reality is filled with what James W. Sire has called "adumbrations" of Christ—shadows and signposts.[5] All the stories we tell about reality—most of all the biblical story—point to the great Archetype. The degree to which *The Lord of the Rings* is Christian depends on the kind of types contained in the story and their resemblance to the archetype.

My main argument is that *The Lord of the Rings* communicates truth in the same way that Jesus did through his parables. Moreover, I will argue that *The Lord of the Rings*, like Jesus's parables, is *incarnational*. These points, too, have to do with why *The Lord of the Rings* feels so real. Since I will be saying so much on this last point throughout the book, I will only say a few words about it here. Above, I mentioned that types do not only point to their antitypes and the great Archetype, but participate in them, and that this is what Pusey called the "sacramental union." That is precisely how the incarnation—the wonder of God becoming human—ought to be understood: a sacred unity of material and immaterial, concrete and abstract, type and antitype. God "has shared his being—in many different dimensions—with types in all of reality" so that we could seek him and find him.[6] Another way we might say this is that reality itself is incarnational because it was created *by* the incarnational God. Although this statement might seem difficult to understand at this early stage in the book, what I am trying to say is that the incarnation is the most real thing that ever existed. Literature in general, and parable specifically, is one of the most powerful and effective ways of discovering God because God himself is the great storyteller and reality is his story. If everything in reality in some way points to Jesus Christ—the incarnation—then the best possible way to communicate that would be through a type of communication that is in form what it wants to say in content (incarnational).

Serious consideration of the underlying philosophy of the Bible will demonstrate that the authors of the Bible, writing under the inspired authority of the Holy Spirit, sincerely believed that what God was doing through Israel, he would do for all humankind. In other words, the biblical storytellers, via revelation from God, are claiming that Israel's story is the story of the way things really are. This insight should challenge Christians to reevaluate how we tell the story that God is telling in the Bible. Israel and her people matter, and we cannot ignore her in our studies, though sadly, many Christians do. The biblical story, then, can never just be understood as only Israel's story, or only a story for people who believe in God. This insight should also shed light on how the church ought to do apologetics and evangelism. Perhaps instead of focusing on proving that Christianity is the only religion to contain truth (it is not), Christians ought to be showing how Christianity can make sense of reality comparatively better than other worldviews, a technique which Alister McGrath talks about in his recent book, *Narrative Apologetics*. This approach would honor the fact that non-Christian worldviews contain truth and demonstrate that God created all people with intuitions of the biblical narrative. It would also demonstrate that all human beings were created with an in-built proclivity to reach out to God through myth. Now, I will present evidence that does make a good case for Christianity as the true religion, but not as the only religion to contain truth. Perhaps instead of trying to prove that one religion is truer than others propositionally, Christians ought to strive to show how the Christian *story* makes comparatively better sense of the data of reality than its competitors.[7] By showing how Christianity does this, one *is* showing that Christianity is the true religion.

It is no coincidence that McGrath refers to J. R. R. Tolkien and C. S. Lewis frequently throughout his book to support this approach. Both Tolkien and Lewis used this method in explaining how the Christian myth—that is, "grand narrative"—relates to non-Christian myths through both their fiction and non-fiction writings. Christians believe that God is truth, and that he revealed himself to humankind in and through Jesus Christ, but no one has seen God the Father in all his glory face to face. In one sense, yes, humanity has seen God the Father through Jesus Christ, but "only a reflection as in a mirror." Christians believe that one day, a full revelation of God the Father will be disclosed through the return of Jesus Christ, but that day has not yet come. This is what Paul spoke of in 1 Corinthians 13:12 where he said, "For now we see only a reflection as in a mirror; then we shall see face to face. Now I know in part; then I shall know fully, even as I am fully known." No human being can prove that one religion is truer than the others *unless* that claim comes from outside humanity through revelation, which is exactly what Christianity claims. I say all this because it has been my experience that many Christians not only believe it to be their duty to prove Christianity is the only true religion, but that they *can* prove that it is the only true religion.

A religion ought to be judged by its ability to out-narrate its competitors, not its ability to be proven propositionally true 100 percent. As finite beings, we simply cannot do this—but God can. This is an insight that we will want to keep in mind as we move further into the book.

According to Roger E. Olson, the Bible has certain "hidden features" and "certain philosophical and theological truths" which are implied by the story.[8] As was pointed out above, Israel's story should be understood as a microcosm of humanity's story. One of the goals of this book is to explain, as Olson has in his book, those hidden philosophical and theological truths embedded in the *mythos* of the Bible. Only after we understand this story will we be able to discover it embedded within Tolkien's books. What, then, is a myth? *Mythos*, a Greek word, originally meant something like a "grand narrative" or even "true story," according to McGrath.[9] Today, many Christian philosophers are arguing that the best way to understand *mythos* is as a "narrated worldview," a story with embedded propositions and assumptions about the nature of reality.[10] From now on, when the word "myth" is used in this book it will mean "narrated worldview," unless otherwise specified. If a myth is a narrated worldview, then the next logical question is what is a worldview? Worldviews are comprehensive visions of reality which scholars often liken to a pair of glasses. According to Douglas Groothuis, a worldview is "a broad-ranging theory of everything, in that it tries to account for the nature and meaning of the universe and its inhabitants."[11] Philosophers believe that worldviews can—and should—be expressed *as* narratives, for it is through story that we arguably find our place in the bigger story of human life and society.

At first glance, it may seem controversial to claim that the reason why *The Lord of the Rings* feels incredibly true to reality is because of the presence of the Christian worldview in the novel. There are at least two reasons many people may find this thesis jolting. I have already hinted at these reasons above. First, this may imply that the Christian myth possesses the unique ability to complete, fulfill, and clarify all other myths. Is that not intolerant? A corollary of this is that *The Lord of the Rings* would also be seen as an intolerant, exclusive text because Christianity is seen as an intolerant, exclusive worldview. Bigoted? Yet that is exactly what Jesus and the Bible claim, so if one wants to disagree with it, one must first test it (which we will do). We test this claim by subjecting the Christian worldview to the "inference to the best explanation" method alluded to above. (Apologists measure the truth of the Christian worldview by how well it stands up to other criteria as well.) Some scholars have even (correctly) argued that there are other non-Christian religious influences in the novel, and that this disproves the thesis that Tolkien's is a Christian novel. Later I will show that the opposite is true: the presence of non-Christian religious influences only strengthens the thesis that *The Lord of the Rings* is a deeply Christian book. The presence of these other non-Christian worldviews also contributes to the novel's realism, but more on that later as well. Second, it may imply that there are Christian doctrines embedded and hidden within the pages of the novel, begging to be discovered. In other words, *The Lord of the Rings* is "just" a Christian allegory, and can be easily reduced to an imaginative sermon, if only we could "break the code" in the story. In this book, I am neither hunting for hidden doctrines nor exact parallels between the Bible and Tolkien's books, nor trying to claim Tolkien's books exclusively for the Christian community. Instead, I will demonstrate how *The Lord of the Rings*, *The Hobbit*, and *The Silmarillion* contain the same *mythos*—the same story of reality—as the Bible, and that it is a story for everyone. Furthermore, I will show that Tolkien's literary style was strongly influenced by the narrative art of Jesus's parables. Parables reflect truth very differently from the strict, conscious allegory which Tolkien disliked.

The way in which Tolkien chose to communicate truth through his books was very important to him, if the comments in his letters about this are any indication. I should quickly note that imparting some moral or lesson didactically was not Tolkien's primary goal. In this book, I have taken great pains to show that *The Lord of the Rings* in particular ought to be understood as a kind of parabolic novel.[12] Just like Jesus's parables, *The Lord of the Rings* can only be understood when situated within the bigger story which precedes it, so we will also be talking about *The Hobbit* and *The Silmarillion*. If one imagines *The Silmarillion* and *The Hobbit* as comprising a sort of "Middle-earth Old Testament," and *The Lord of the Rings* as a parable—itself a miniature announcement of the gospel—then the way the latter reflects truth can only be best understood through its relation to the former. By showing all this, I also hope that I demonstrate how narrative in general, and imaginative narrative specifically, can communicate the truth, goodness, and beauty of the Christian worldview in a unique way. Myth—that is, story—has a way of enfolding and presenting the propositional content of a worldview non-invasively. My hope is that by showing how all this works, Christians will gain a better understanding of how to present the gospel of Jesus Christ in a way that is not only deeply loyal to Jesus himself, but that is also imaginative, rational, existentially appealing, and most of all, persuasive—persuasive in the "inference to the best explanation" sense, as we discussed above. Tolkien's books, especially *The Lord of the Rings*, may be some of the best apologetics for the Christian worldview precisely because they do not seem like they would be. Most people's expectations when talking with Christians is that they will get a heavy-handed dose of theology and doctrine and an invitation to convert or face the eternal consequences. I hope to show that that just is not the way Jesus approached apologetics.

Unfortunately, there are some serious intellectual and existential obstacles that we must clear out of the way first before any of this becomes apparent, most of all, our culture's relativistic and pluralistic approach to religion. Religious pluralism, sometimes called metaphysical pluralism, is the view that all worldviews and myths are equally (objectively) true. On the pluralist's worldview, Christianity is only true for Christians, but not necessarily true for everyone else. Moreover, the religious pluralist will say that religions like Christiantiy are not "true" in any sense of the word, let alone realistic. They may be true "for you," but not "for me." By the way, when someone says, "that's just true for you," they really mean, "that's *objectively* true for you." The easiest way to prove this is to ask this question: "Is it really true that this is only really true for me"? The problem with this view is that the traditional philosophical understanding of these terms—"truth" and "reality"—is that a statement is true if it captures something meaningful about reality and if it corresponds and aligns with the way things are, and every viewpoint assumes this. As Lewis once wrote, "truth is always about something, but reality is that *about which* truth is."[13] For the pluralist, this sounds like a circular argument, assuming what it is trying to prove, but actually, the pluralist is in the same boat as the Christian. Both the pluralist and the Christian assume the definition of truth just mentioned. The problem is, they both cannot be right, so how do we proceed? By taking worldviews and plugging them into the data of reality to see which makes the most rational and existential sense of the facts of reality. If one does this, it will quickly become clear that religious pluralism is incoherent and contradictory. There is also the problem of narrowly defining truth as what one can prove through the senses, human reason, and the various scientific methodologies in existence. What is more, the belief that all religious narratives are equally valid, that they are all totally true in their own way, cannot possibly be true. How could that statement be true when religious narratives, beliefs, and practices contradict each other? One need only look at the major claims of the world's top three religions, Christianity, Islam, and Hinduism, to see how incredible the pluralist's claim is.

Let's return to my claim I made at the outset of the book that the reason why so many people love *The Lord of the Rings* is because it is a deeply, convincingly realistic story, and that it is so because it is a Christian story. Some scholars and readers may fear that this means saying that *The Lord of the Rings* is "just" a Christian story, which would imply that Christianity is "for Christians," and therefore not for others. This, in turn, implies that either all religions are only subjectively true, and that none of them are true for everybody, or that Christianity is the only true religion. Are our only two options either to conclude that Christianity is the only true religion or that all religions are equally true? Thankfully, no, there is a third option, which I have already presented ("inference to the best explanation"). According to McGrath, who has perhaps expressed this third option the most cogently and eloquently, "Christianity brings to fulfillment the echoes and shadows of the truth that result from human questing and yearning. Human 'myths' allow a glimpse of a fragment of that truth, not its totality . . . yet when the full and true story is told, it is able to bring to fulfillment all that was right and wise in those fragmentary visions of things."[14] Any worldview must be judged not only by its ability to fit in with reality, but by its ability to address our deepest human longings. There are many excellent books listed in the bibliography that one can consult to see the criteria which apologists have agreed make a worldview tenable. My point here is this: It can be shown that Christianity makes comparative better sense not only of reality and human longings, but of other competing worldviews. In one of McGrath's recent books, for example, he confesses that while "many today regard any totalizing narrative with suspicion, preferring to see such narratives as local and particular . . . the Christian metanarrative provides a robust and reliable framework of meaning, which can be enriched or given enhanced granularity through interacting with other stories." This insight is the "master key," if you like, for the rest of the book. McGrath's point is this: not only does Christianity "bring to fulfillment the echoes and shadows of the truth" from human myths, but by fulfilling them, and thus interacting with them, Christianity *itself* is made richer.[15] This understanding of the Christian worldview enhances one's appreciation of non-Christian worldviews rather than denigrating them.

This is the perfect moment to introduce the author at the heart of this book: J. R. R. Tolkien (1892–1973). As will become quickly apparent, everything that we have discussed thus far about worldview, myth, and Christianity can be found in Tolkien's essays and correspondence. This is especially true of his 1939 lecture and essay "On Fairy Stories" where he wrote, "The Gospels contain a fairy story, or a story of a larger kind which embraces all the essence of fairy-stories."[16] Elsewhere, in a letter, Tolkien indicated that the gospel is "the greatest" fairy story.[17] "Fairy stories" are a type of story which contain something like the whole quality of experience of reality within them. In other words, they are a particularly comprehensive type of *mythos*, chiefly because they are holistic, by which I mean that they do not just contain literal truth, but also non-literal truth as well. According to Matthew Dickerson and David O'Hara, "if man is indeed the spiritual animal, the creature who lives at once both in the world of the seen and the unseen, then those stories that take place in both worlds—that is, on the borders of

Faerie—will be far more relevant than stories that take place entirely in one world to the exclusion of the other."[18] Fairy stories are therefore particularly powerful and effective vehicles for communicating the content of the Christian worldview, since it contains both literal and non-literal truths. Primarily because they are holistic stories, they also bear a close resemblance to the New Testament parable. Neither fairy stories nor the parables they resemble are exclusive to the Judeo-Christian tradition—a fact which Tolkien implies in the quote above. However, he does claim that the Gospels contain a "story of a larger kind" which embraces "all" fairy stories, which seems to indicate that the gospel story is a very special type of fairy story.

Christian theology proposes that heaven and earth currently overlap, but that one day, heaven will fill all the earth. Ever since the fall of Adam and Eve, humankind has been estranged from God. This is a fact that Christians believe permeates all aspects of life, including our noetic (knowledge-based) and linguistic faculties. For example, we might say, as Charlie W. Starr has argued, that *mythos* and *logos*, literal and non-literal truth have also become estranged from each other due to the noetic effects of the fall. Indeed, in his book *The Faun's Bookshelf*, Starr argues that Owen Barfield, a friend and fellow Inkling to Lewis and Tolkien, believed that *mythos* and *logos* were unified in a kind of "original tongue" before the fall.[19] Interestingly, the Greek word for parable means "to cast alongside," suggesting the reunification of *mythos* and *logos* in one literary form. Perhaps one reason why stories communicate truth better to our hearts and minds is that they bring together these estranged aspects of reality. As we saw above, many people feel that the statement "Christianity is the only true religion" is unfair, intolerant, and bigoted. But what if we have misunderstood Jesus's words because we have forgotten how to think about the nature of truth? Christian philosophers and theologians believe that this is one of the noetic effects of the fall. Maybe parables/fairy stories are reminders of how humanity used to think and speak about reality, and that is why they are so effective. Sadly, experience has taught me that most Christians do not understand what it means to say that Christianity is the true religion. To claim that Christianity is the one true religion does not mean that Christianity is the only religion to contain truth, but the only religion to contain *complete*, total, objective truth.[20] Christians believe that Christianity is God's story about humanity and reality whereas other religions are humanity's stories about God, humanity, and reality. In other words, Christianity is a religion whose main claim does not depend on the discoveries and inventions of man, but the revelation of God. Ah, but Islam claims the same thing, you say. Yes, it does, and this is where McGrath's "inference to the best explanation" narrative apologetics approach shines. Christianity and Islam cannot both be true, for they have conflicting truth claims about Jesus Christ (among other things). Instead of getting logjammed in a theology debate, we should remind ourselves that there are many other aspects of reality and human experience that a worldview needs to explain efficiently in order to out-explain its competitors.

One of the first things I teach my students about are the terms "metaphysics" and "epistemology." This is a key step in understanding everything we have discussed thus far. Metaphysics is the study of what is ultimately real, true, and possible, whereas epistemology is the study of knowledge and truth and most importantly *how* we know truth. There is an inescapable circularity between these two: one's epistemology (theory of knowledge and truth), for example, must appeal to one's metaphysics (theory of what is ultimately real, true, and possible). How can one determine *how* we know something is true without already presupposing *what* we think is true? In other words, we all have certain assumptions, or presuppositions, about reality already. No one begins "neutrally" with a specific epistemology and then builds a case for what is real, true, and possible. And if you do, you are not being intellectually honest! Thus, to say that the Christian worldview is the only religion to contain total, complete, objective truth implies that truth can also be discovered *outside* the sacred tradition and holy Scripture. The Bible itself contains many passages that teach this. In the New Testament alone, I can think of Paul's visit to Athens in Acts 17 and the story of the Magi in Matthew 2 as two examples of what Christian theologians call "general revelation" or "common grace." Both of these Christian doctrines affirm that people outside the sacred tradition can know truth about the God of the Bible and that God's existence can be inferred from certain aspects of reality. As Greg Koukl summarizes in his excellent book *The Story of Reality*, "Christianity is a picture of reality. This is the Story of the way the world really is."[21] This means that of all the worldviews/myths in existence, the Christian myth makes the most sense of reality. This does not mean that other myths do not make sense of reality, but that to the extent that they do, they are unconsciously Christian. On the Christian view of things, this means that non-Christian worldviews contribute to and enrich the Christian way of seeing reality, which sees all true stories as part of the grand narrative revealed in the Bible.

In my college classrooms, I often hear, "Why does it have to be the Christian myth? Why can't it be Buddhism or Hinduism or Islam or atheism? Why does Christianity get this primary place among worldviews? Who says?" How can Christians today address these throughtful concerns, and how can fantasy literature help? Literature and myth, by their very nature, can address these concerns by inviting us to look at reality from a different perspective. Sometimes people need a story, not a philosophy lesson. Literature invites us to "try on" the worldview of the author and ask, "What if I looked at the world from this perspective?" We all base our lives on a narrative or live our lives according to some storyline or way of seeing things. If all worldviews are like hypotheses of reality, then we must choose the theory that makes the *best* sense of the data of reality. No one can prove anything with absolute certainty, so that means that we must choose a worldview/myth that has the most explanatory scope and power, the one that explains the facts of life best. So, if it is not Christianity, which worldview/myth will it be? What is the best story about reality and human experience? All of us must answer that question; we all live our lives within some worldview. To the person with the above objections and concerns, one should ask oneself, "One critierion a worldview must possess is the ability to make sense of other worldviews and their myths. Can Buddhism or Islam or atheism explain why something like Christianity exists? Can it make sense of its central tenets?" To this one might respond, "The view that all religions are equally valid is more inclusive than what Christianity teaches." But is this view as open-minded and tolerant as it claims to be? No indeed, this view *excludes* more people than it *includes* (it would certainly exclude Christianity, the world's largest religion). Besides, this claim that Christianity offers the best explanation of reality does not exclude *people*, but *ideas*. This is an important point, for in my experience, I believe many people reject what we have been arguing on the grounds that it is intolerant and bigoted towards people, but that is not true. Everyone excludes—including the so-called inclusive religious pluralist. In conclusion, then, *The Lord of the Rings* feels real because of the incarnate presence of the Christian worldview, which purports to be telling the story of reality itself. We have begun to answer some of the popular objections concerning this claim and refreshed our understanding of some important philosophical definitions. In the next section, I want to argue that the literary form of *The Lord of the Rings* is one of the pieces of evidence that tells us that it is a Christian story, and therefore why it is such a deeply realistic story.

"FAËRIE"

"Fairy stories" are a type of story that contain something like the whole quality of experience of reality. In his essay "On Fairy Stories," Tolkien describes the world of the fairy story as "Faërie." According to Tolkien, "Faërie contains many things besides elves and fays, and besides dwarfs, witches, trolls, giants, or dragons: it holds the seas, the sun, the moon, the sky; and the earth, and all things that are in it: tree and bird, water and stone, wine and bread, and ourselves, mortal men, when we are enchanted."[22] What is

"Faërie"? Tolkien says, "I will not attempt to define that, nor to describe it directly. It cannot be done. Faërie cannot be caught in a net of words; for it is one of its qualities to be indescribable, though not imperceptible."[23] The "Perilous Realm," as he also calls it, defies comprehensive explanation. Perhaps the reason why Tolkien was reluctant to fully define Faërie is not only that it cannot be done, but that it *should not* be done. Part of the power and effectiveness of fairy story and parable is their literary form. Since story acts upon us in a very different way than other experiences, we should try, whenever possible, not to dissect the experience. As was hinted earlier, however, this is impossible to avoid entirely, especially in a book like this. What Tolkien may have been saying is this: the real meaning of a story will first and foremost be the *story* itself. According to Starr, "if we were looking for abstract meanings in the myth, it would stop being a myth to us and become an allegory."[24] To review: Faërie not only includes real sense objects, but things that are real to the imagination, it is the name for an author's created story-world, and it defies reductionism.

In his book *Cultural Apologetics*, Paul Gould argues that we live in a "flattened" and "disenchanted" world, which is to say a world emptied of transcendence.[25] Combining this insight with Tolkien's description of Faërie, then, leads us to the conclusion that Faërie is how reality *ought* to be understood. It is a restored, reenchanted understanding of reality, not the materialistic, mechanistic, exclusively physical reality many believe we live in. It seems I did not go far enough in my initial statement about *The Lord of the Rings*: we love Tolkien's book because it feels *more real* than our everyday reality. I am not the first author to have discovered this. According to Peter Kreeft, "in a work of fiction, such as *The Lord of the Rings*, the characters and creatures and landscapes and histories can seem either 'fake' or 'real,' not by conforming to the physical world but by conforming to Platonic Ideas."[26] Plato's *eidoi*, "Forms" or "Ideas," are neither physical nor mental, but objective spiritual essences or archetypes that are standards for everything we experience. What Kreeft is saying, then, is that everything in *The Lord of the Rings* feels more real not because it conforms to physical things or our private, subjective thoughts, but because it conforms to the Forms. That is the metaphysical explanation for why *The Lord of the Rings* feels more real than our everyday reality. Faërie, then, is a *reenchanted* world, or reality as it ought to be. Fairy stories are stories which help us discover reality, not abscond from it. We love *The Lord of the Rings* because it reenchants us and drives us more deeply into a more capacious understanding of reality. And the extent to which *The Lord of the Rings* does this is the extent to which it is a Christian story, and so it is a very Christian story. In this book, I want to show you *how* Tolkien's novel does this, and how you can help others recover a reenchanted view of reality.

To do that, we will have to make sense of how the story of Israel ought to be viewed as the story of reality. I believe that Tolkien's books can actually help us do that. Some of the same images, characters, events, and themes (types) that we find in the Bible are found in Tolkien's books, but it is the juxtaposition of these familiar images alongside the unfamiliar setting of Middle-earth that help us to see reality clearly again. Tolkien was a devout Catholic his entire life, and his novel seems to reveal just how aligned his mind was with the Christian way of looking at things. The reason why Tolkien felt so confident in including Finnish, French, Old English, Middle English, Norse, Germanic, Slavic, Greek, and Celtic elements in his stories was precisely *because* of this understanding of Christianity that we have discussed thus far. In fact, I argue that it is because Tolkien understood the Christian myth as the story of reality that he included these other cultures and myths in his books to illustrate *how* the Christian myth "unifies and transcends" the "fragmentary and imperfect insights" of other myths.[27] This argument does not mean that there are not unique expressions of truth, goodness, and beauty in non-Christian myths. On the contrary, there are many ways to express the same truth, and the God of Christianity wants to say that each has its place in contributing to a total understanding that is completely disclosed in Jesus Christ. Indeed, neither Tolkien nor his friend C. S. Lewis wanted to give up reading the myths of other cultures for precisely this reason: there was truth, goodness, and beauty to be found in each of them. This includes fantasy literature as well. In his book *Making Sense of God*, Timothy Keller argues that "even though we know the tales are fiction, we have such a deep longing for these things that we get a unique satisfaction from immersing ourselves in the stories, particularly if they are well told."[28]

"MYTH BECAME FACT"

Scholars generally recognize that C. S. Lewis (1898–1963) was more active as a Christian apologist (Greek for "giving a defense") than his older friend Tolkien. While it is true that Tolkien did not publish popular theology prodigiously like Lewis did, Lewis was indebted to Tolkien for one of his profoundest ideas. That idea was implanted in Lewis on the night of September 20, 1931 while Tolkien, Lewis, and Hugo Dyson strolled along Addison's Walk on the grounds of Magdalen College in Oxford, England. Lewis had been a Christian as a young boy but, largely due to his mother's death and service in World War I, Lewis classified himself as an atheist from 1916 until about

1929. In 1929, he began to identify again as a theist but did not yet accept Jesus Christ. According to Lewis, all that changed after his talk with Tolkien and Dyson: "Now what Dyson and Tolkien showed me was this: that if I met the idea of sacrifice in a Pagan story I didn't mind it at all . . . provided I met it anywhere *except* the Gospels."[29] During their stroll, Lewis confessed to the other men that he struggled not only with the meaning of the gospel, but with the historical claims of Christianity as well. He could not understand how someone's death thousands of years ago could benefit him, let alone all of humanity. Lewis had no problem finding meaning in the pagan myths or in believing that Christianity was "nothing more than the Jewish version of the same old mythic archetype" present in those pagan myths.[30]

According to Tolkien's biographer, Humphrey Carpenter, his understanding was that Lewis confessed that the reason he could accept the pagan (or more broadly non-Christian) myths was because they were lies "breathed through silver."[31] For Lewis, myths may be beautiful and moving, but that doesn't necessarily make them true. Myths are always entertaining, maybe educational, but ultimately false narratives. With this comment, however, Lewis was confusing truth with factuality, which are not the same thing. No, perhaps the myths Lewis found to be moving were not all true in a factual, scientific sense, but they were realistic and faithful to certain facts about human life. We need to ask here what is meant by "truth." To answer that, we need to recall the distinction between metaphysics and epistemology. The implication of Lewis's statement—"lies breathed through silver"—is that the myths he enjoyed did not tell us the *rational, empirical*, and perhaps even *scientific* truth about reality, but they were, nevertheless, ultimately beautiful, which is to say, *true to reality*. In other words, these myths ultimately captured something of the beauty of humanity and reality, but they ultimately failed the truth test *as Lewis defined truth*. As I pointed out a moment ago, recalling the distinction between epistemology and metaphysics is helpful here. For Lewis, *epistemologically*, unless these myths told the truth along rational, empirical, and scientific lines, then these myths could ultimately not tell us anything about *reality*, as it really is. For Lewis, reality was only physical, not metaphysical. Lewis's philosophy assumes the thing it is trying to prove, which is that these myths are not true because they cannot be proven by human reason, logic, senses, and the sciences. One cannot assume that reason, the senses, and the scientific method are the only ways to know truth and then compile a picture of reality, because that view itself cannot be proven rationally, empirically, or scientifically.

According to Starr, "reality (or fact) is what *is*; truth is a proposition *about* fact."[32] Lewis's understanding of truth—and therefore reality—was reductionistic. Tolkien showed Lewis that, whether he realized it or not, he was himself living inside a myth which could not live up to its own philosophical standards. That is, Lewis was living within a storied explanation of reality that limited truth to what could be proven rationally, empirically, and scientifically. Lewis was living inside the myth of rationalism, empiricism, and materialism which says that truth is only what reason, our senses, and science can prove. Things proven in these ways are "the facts" (i.e., "reality"), and therefore truth equals rationalism, empiricism, and materialism. Was Lewis not living within a "lie breathed through silver" himself? Tolkien was not only able to show Lewis that the modern worldview is also a myth, but an impoverished and boring one at that. Ironically, the myths Lewis found beautiful but false were truer than the one he was living in. That is because myths—according to their ancient definition—are more faithful to reality because they include the existence of the supernatural. Myths, in other words, are *metaphysical* stories, stories about *all* of reality, not just what reason, the senses, and science can tell us.

And then there was the issue of the relationship between the pagan and Christian myths. "Perhaps," Lewis later wrote, "the reason Christ resembled so closely the myths of the pagans was that Christ was the myth that came true."[33] All true stories that human beings have told about God, reality, and themselves contain a glimpse of the theme—the incarnation—which is the plot of the story of reality. To understand this, we need to apply what we just discussed about myth, truth, and reality. Think about this: if all myths are stories about reality, and Jesus Christ claimed to be the most real thing to have ever existed, then it would logically follow that all myths are ultimately about Jesus Christ. If reality is truly metaphysical, and Jesus is God, and God is the creator of all things (seen and unseen), then it logically follows that the incarnation--God becoming man--would be the most real thing ever to exist because it is the coming together of the seen and the unseen. We intuitively sense the estrangement of the seen and unseen, by the way; just look at the way that we cannot epistemologically get outside ourselves enough and achieve total objectivity. This noetic gap, if you will, is one of the many pieces of evidence that suggests the alienation of the seen and unseen realms. In conclusion, if Jesus Christ is God *and* man, then it follows that he is the *really* real.

For Christianity to be the "myth that came true," it must have been revealed from outside history—from the unseen realm. All other myths are told from the epistemologically limited perspective of broken human beings, but because we are all made in God's image, then it would logically follow that our myths would capture something accurate about God and reality. Now some might object to this and say, oh, how convenient, Christianity is "revealed" from outside history and Buddhism was not. Yet no other religion except Islam really claims anything like Christianity does, so it is not that Christians are guilty of rigging the game, as it were. To really object to this, you would not only have to reject the existence of the supernatural, but also that a God, who exists outside the universe, *could* not do this. To test this hypothesis, one must look at the many lines of evidence that philosophers, theologians, and scientists have discovered that *does* seem to indicate such a God exists and *is* able to do this. Lewis could accept that the pagan myths moved him; from there, it is a small step to acknowledge that the Christian myth works on us in the same way as other myths. Indeed, a myth's ability to make sense of reality is what makes it a true story. After all, the original meaning of the Greek word *mythos* was "true story."[34] At first glance, this seems to be a ridiculous proposition: How can anyone say that the stories of Balder, Dionysus, or Osiris, are true? Dying and rising gods were, in Lewis's mind, beautiful metaphors—nothing more, nothing less. These are not real, factual people or events, Lewis thought, so how could anyone say they are true? Well, it is certainly true that when we phrase it that way, without all the philosophical explanation we just gave, it does sound quite ridiculous. Later in life, Lewis wrote an essay which explored the interconnectedness of myth, truth, meaning, and reality, saying, "What flows into you from myth is not truth but reality (truth is always about something, but reality is that *about which* truth is)."[35] It would be more correct to say that these aforementioned myths are *realistic*, but when we break down what that means, we come back to the conclusion that that means they are, in fact, *true*. According to Doug Groothuis, for a proposition to be true (or false), it must be meaningful: "It must stake out a share of reality conceptually and be intelligible."[36]

What Tolkien did next is evidence of his consummate skills as a Christian apologist: Tolkien challenged Lewis to imagine that the Christian myth acts upon us in the same way as men's myths. This is a very important insight: Christianity is, like all other religions, first and foremost a narrative about the way things are (a myth). Christianity has a rich store of metaphorical, supernatural elements, like so many other myths, but unlike most other myths, it does not *only* have these elements. Christianity is also a deeply *historical* myth. Myths are narratives that incarnate and communicate propositional truth imaginatively. This insight is evident in the word "mythology," which is a combination of two Greek words, *mythos* and *logos*. According to Karen Armstrong, in the premodern world, these were "two recognized ways of thinking, speaking, and acquiring knowledge."[37] By saying that myths were lies, or untrue stories, Lewis was exhibiting the typical modern, *logos*-based way of knowing or proving truth, as we discussed above. *Mythos* is the realm of metaphor, analogy, simile, and parable.

Metaphor, analogy, simile, and parable are the realm of non-literal truth, but they are not often seen to be because modern people insist on proving everything through *logos*. Importantly, *mythos* is emphatically *not* just another way of saying *logos*. In other words, metaphors are not things that just mean something else; the metaphor is the message. When Tolkien used the term "myth," he used it with respect to its original, premodern definition, which is analogous to the modern term "metanarrative." A metanarrative is a "grand story" about reality.[38] Furthermore, every myth, or metanarrative, is a narrative expression of one's "worldview." As we learned earlier, a worldview is a theological and philosophical view of all reality, a "way of 'seeing the world as.'"[39] According to Jeff Myers, a worldview is a "pattern of ideas, beliefs, convictions, and habits that help us make sense of God, the world, and our relationship to God and the world."[40] Scholars argue that worldviews address five ultimate questions human beings ask: origins, identity, meaning, morality, and destiny.[41] Where do we come from? Who are we? What is truth? Is there a real right and wrong? Where are we going? History shows that cultures have relied on storytelling to communicate their worldviews.

Up until his conversation with Tolkien, Lewis lived within the modern myth. Stories organize and give structure to our beliefs about reality, but they also reflect the universal human intuition that reality itself *is* a story. We tell stories because life itself has a narrative quality to it. Later, after Lewis had become a Christian again—which he credited to the talk with Tolkien and Dyson—he wrote exactly that in his review of *The Lord of the Rings*: "'But why,' (some ask), 'why, if you have a serious comment to make on the real life of men, must you do it by talking about a phantasmagoric never-never land of your own?' Because, I take it, one of the main things the author wants to say is that the real life of men is *of that mythical and heroic quality*."[42] Lewis came to believe that we cannot live without myth's ability to illuminate ultimately important aspects of reality and human experience. In saying that Christianity is the myth that came true, Tolkien was saying that Christianity is a narrated view of reality, but with one crucial difference: the Christian myth really happened; it is the really real. The Christian myth corresponds accurately with *all* of reality as humans experience it. It addresses our desire for rational and empirical proof and satisfies our existential yearnings, and its historical veracity is supported by a variety of different disciplines. So, by saying that Christianity really happened, Tolkien was claiming that Christianity is true on both levels of knowing truth (*mythos* and *logos*). During their 1931 stroll, Tolkien showed Lewis the bankruptcy of his reductionist view of reality and that becoming a Christian did not mean rejecting the truth, goodness, and beauty found in other myths.

By showing Lewis that the modern myth he was living in could not live up to its own philosophical standards, Lewis was compelled to reconsider Christianity. Now that his confidence in the modern myth had received a crippling blow, Lewis's primary objections to Christianity melted away. According to Starr, years later Lewis confessed that "he would not have become a Christian if it meant saying that other religions in the world were completely wrong."[43] Hearing this may put many of my readers at ease, for many of us have discovered truth, goodness, and beauty in other religions. It seems that Tolkien showed Lewis that to become a Christian did not mean that he had to leave these intuitions about other religions behind. If Christianity really is the true myth, then all myths with truth within them will be validated in the end. Perhaps that is why, in the very last line of his essay "On Fairy Stories," Tolkien wrote, "All tales may come true; and yet, at the last, redeemed, they may be as like and as unlike the forms that we give them as Man, finally redeemed, will be like and unlike the fallen that we know."[44] What Tolkien means is that if Christianity is the true myth, then all myths which have contained fragments of truth will, in the end, be validated. We will finally understand the reason why we found truth, goodness, and beauty in the myths we enjoyed: all myths reach out, in some degree, to the truth—to Christ. When the Christian story is consummated at the end of history, then all the interconnectedness of the myths we intuited will be fully revealed. Interestingly, on Tolkien's view, this also includes imaginative stories such as *The Lord of the Rings* and *The Chronicles of Narnia*.

It is troubling that so many Christians today feel that they must totally reject non-Christian worldviews and myths in order to remain faithful to Jesus. We miss so much of what God is trying to say about himself by neglecting to study other cultures, their sacred scriptures, and their art. The Bible itself gives the lie to this view that truth cannot be discovered outside the Christian tradition, as we will see a little later. By the end of their stroll, Tolkien's argument satisfied the rational *and* imaginative sides of Lewis and prompted him to return to Christianity. Later in life, the Christian Lewis reflected on what he learned from Tolkien that fateful night on September 20, 1931 saying, "The heart of Christianity is a myth which is also a fact. The old myth of the Dying God, *without ceasing to be myth*, comes down from the heaven of legend and imagination to the earth of history . . . by becoming fact it does not cease to be myth: that is the miracle."[45] Unfortunately, even many modern Christians have lost touch with or become ashamed of the "mythical radiance which rests upon our theology," and thus one of the most beautiful facts about God: he is a storyteller.[46] Yet Christians are not the only ones who have lost touch with the "mythical radiance" of Christianity. Non-Christians might be shocked and surprised to learn the implications of what we have just discussed. Tolkien believed that a proper understanding of the Christian worldview had the power to reenchant our view of reality. But how can such a recovery take place if believers and unbelievers alike struggle to abandon their preconceived notions about myth and Christianity? In the next section, we will take a closer look at who Tolkien was and what he believed. We will also work to establish a better understanding of what historic, orthodox Christianity looks like.

TOLKIEN AND HIS FAITH

Jonathan Ronald Reuel Tolkien was born in Bloemfontein, South Africa, on January 3, 1892, to parents Mabel and Arthur. After three years in South Africa, the family moved back to England because John became ill. In 1896, when he was only four, his father died. Tolkien's mother, Mabel, raised her two sons, John and Hilary (Tolkien's younger brother), as a single parent until, in June 1900, Mabel joined the Roman Catholic Church. Consequently, Mabel's family withdrew their financial support, which led, along with diabetes, to her untimely death in November 1904. Tolkien and his brother, Hilary, were placed in the care of Father Francis Morgan. Later in life, Tolkien was disappointed that few Catholic publications reviewed *The Lord of the Rings*. Why? Perhaps it is because God, whom Tolkien believed was the main character of his book—the "ever-present Person who is never absent and never named"—wasn't being recognized.[47] More specifically, Tolkien might have been disappointed because his Christian readers weren't recognizing the parabolic way in which God was being represented in the story. Judging by the number of times Tolkien responded to letters about the issue of allegory (more on this soon), it seems likely that many of Tolkien's Christian readers were expecting a more straightforward representation of God such as what one finds in John Bunyan's *Pilgrim's Progress*. John 5:39–40 tells us that Jesus faced a similar disappointment: "You study the Scriptures diligently because you think that in them you have eternal life. These are the very Scriptures that testify about me, yet you refuse to come to me to have life." Thus far, I have argued that our misunderstanding about the Christianness of *The Lord of the Rings* stems from misunderstanding myth and Christianity itself. In the previous sections, I built a case showing that these are intertwined issues and that many Christians are ashamed of the "mythical radiance" resting on Christian theology. Since we have already discussed myth, it is time to attend to the issue of understanding what historic, orthodox Christianity looks like. By the time we have finished, I hope that we will be in a better position to understand Christianity, and therefore

The Lord of the Rings. From a close reading of Tolkien's letters, it seems clear that a large part of his disappointment over certain interpretations of his books stemmed from what Joseph Pearce has called a "*myth*understanding" of Christianity (and thus, his books).[48] Is there perhaps a clue in the words and teachings of Jesus that might help us with our interpretation? Indeed, there is. Jesus tells us in Luke 24:27, "And beginning with Moses and all the Prophets, he explained to them what was said in all the Scriptures concerning himself." Jesus is saying that if we want to understand the Scriptures, then we must read the Scriptures backward with him in mind. To approach a historic, orthodox Christianity, we must look at the totality of scripture, not just the New Testament.

Earlier in the Introduction, I pointed out that one of the factors involved in understanding historic, orthodox Christianity consists of keeping Christianity in its Jewish context. I also pointed out that knowledge of the story of Israel is paramount, which is the essence of what Jesus is saying in Luke 24:27. If we want to understand how *The Lord of the Rings* is a Christian story, then we must first understand the Christian worldview, and to understand the Christian worldview, we must understand it through ancient Jewish eyes. Might we also better understand *The Lord of the Rings* as a Christian novel if we keep Jesus's words from Luke 24:27 in mind? Perhaps one of the ways we can understand *The Lord of the Rings* as a Christian story better is by reading Tolkien's mythology (all his Middle-earth books) *backwards*, just as we ought to read Scripture. Before we can do that, we must first attend to the issue of understanding what historic, orthodox Christianity looks like. Simply stated, Christianity is a first-century sect of what we now call "Judaism" (though that term did not exist in the first century). Christianity claims to be the *one true form of Judaism*, or Judaism brought to fulfillment. It helps to know that there were at least three other forms of "Judaism" during the first century. In this book, we are trying to come to an understanding of "mere" Christianity—which I believe to be Christianity in its earliest form. Is that possible? While a perfect understanding of the earliest form of Christianity is impossible, by keeping history, theology, and literature together, we can come close.[49] One thing that we cannot say with absolute certainty is whether Tolkien would agree with this book's argument for what historic, orthodox Christianity looks like. Tolkien was a lifelong Catholic, and it is quite possible he would disagree with my analysis of what historic, orthodox Christianity looks like.

One word on this last point before moving forward. Several excellent books already exist on the Catholic elements present in Tolkien's books. I do want to point out, however, that Catholicism is arguably much closer to earliest Christianity because of its historical and theological connection to biblical Judaism. According to Taylor R. Marshall, "sometimes the connection between biblical Judaism and Catholicism is direct (as in the connection between Passover and the Holy Sacrifice of the Mass)—at other times a certain element of Catholicism does not possess an organic link to biblical Judaism."[50] It should also be noted that Protestantism and Catholicism agree much more on theological issues than they disagree, but that is not a topic we can get into in the present book. In this book, we will be focusing most of our attention on biblical Judaism as a key to understanding "mere" Christianity while simultaneously being sensitive to Tolkien's Catholicism. Also, yes, I believe there is a connection between recovering the earliest version of Christianity and "mere" Christianity, for it is a version of the faith unencumbered by today's legion of denominations. We must always keep in mind that the most authentic interpretation of Scripture will be one from the perspective of the ancient Israelite authors, who were much more attuned to the supernatural elements of Scripture than many modern Christians are. As I will make clear later in the book, many modern Christians have ignored and skipped over many strange, difficult texts.[51] Of course, completely evading a denominational perspective will be impossible, and along the way, I do try to touch on some specifically Catholic perspectives to honor Tolkien.

Christianity's most revolutionary and challenging idea is that God has become king through Jesus and returned to the throne of King David to rule "on earth as it is in heaven" (Matt 6:10). This is also one of Christianity's most Jewish ideas. Unfortunately, this theological and political dimension of the Christian worldview has often been domesticated or criticized for its inability to fit within our predominantly secular society. By "revolutionary," I mean that it is an idea that we do not find in any other tradition. By "challenging," I mean that it subverts and undermines many ideas we have about God, human beings, and reality. There are two reasons why many moderns have forgotten (or ignored) this revolutionary and challenging idea. The first is political and the second is more theological and philosophical. First, all this talk of "king" and "kingdom" sounds very un-American. After all, we fought a war against a monarchy. Understandably, then, many modern Americans either dislike or simply do not understand the idea of God as king. The second reason is related to the first: During the Enlightenment, many European thinkers revived the Epicurean worldview, which understands reality divided into two mutually exclusive dimensions. This two-story cosmos (heaven is completely separate from earth) view led many to believe that God should mind his own business "up" in heaven while men tend to their business down here on earth. Furthermore, many began to believe (again) that God does not—and should not—get involved in history. No miracles, no incarnation, no interventions of any kind. There is no overlapping of heaven and earth as in the Jewish view of things. It is also tragic that many modern Christians are uncomfortable with some of the stranger biblical texts such as Gen 1:26–27 and Deut 32:8–9. When reading Scriptures such as these, it is common for the modern Christian to practice *eisegesis* (imposing assumptions on the text) instead of *exegesis* (leading out the original meaning of the text). Genesis 1:26–27, for example, switches between singular and plural with respect to God, and many modern Christians simply argue that God was speaking to the other members of the Trinity instead of his heavenly family, the divine council.[52] For the present book, it is vital that we understand the notion of the kingship of God from a Jewish perspective. We cannot do that unless we first understand that just as human beings are God's earthly family, God also has a heavenly family. Also helpful is a proper understanding of what it means to be made in God's image. And to understand that (and Jesus's frequent references to the "kingdom of God" and the "kingdom of heaven"), we need to understand God's original plan to make all the earth like the garden of Eden and the role God's two families have in that.

Today, much popular Christianity resembles "Platonism for the masses" instead of the deeply Jewish religion that it is.[53] According to Arthur Herman, for the early church "Plato was crucial. His works provided a framework for making Christianity intellectually respectable, while Christianity in turn gave Plato's philosophy a shining new relevance."[54] The Hellenization of Judaism began as early as the fourth century BC with Alexander the Great's conquest of Jerusalem in 332 BC. Philosophers such as Philo of Alexandria and the apostle John tried to harmonize Greek philosophy and Jewish theology in different ways. Whereas John pointed out that non-Christian worldviews contained fragments of the total truth that resides in Jesus Christ, he never indicated that all worldviews were equally valid. Nor did he indicate—like Philo had—that Judaism and Greek philosophy were completely compatible. John's use of the Greek term *logos* in his Gospel illustrates the difference. For the Stoics, the *logos* was "the impersonal, harmonious and divine structure of the cosmos as a whole," whereas for John, the *logos* is really the God of Israel who became a human being named Jesus of Nazareth.[55] John argued that the Stoics, who venerated the impersonal *logos* as the divine mind which pervades the cosmos, were, in reality, unconsciously worshiping the personal God of Israel who became incarnate in man. John did not argue that Greek and Jewish thought were both totally true, but he did argue that Greek thought contained *some* understanding of the total truth. John did not try to syncretize Stoicism and Christianity; instead, he argued that Christianity provides the "total picture, which both unifies and transcends these fragmentary and imperfect insights."[56] What John did is known as "subversion," where one tells one story in terms of another story. This is an extremely important insight for the present book, for *The Lord of the Rings* is an example of subversive literature. That is, it takes elements from non-Christian myths and retells them in terms of the Christian myth.

In the eighteenth century, Europeans in England, France, and the nascent United States would resuscitate the Greek belief in a split cosmos, insisting that God lives in the "upstairs" spiritual world while humans live "downstairs." Human beings run the world, God sits back and does not get involved. This modern belief fails to understand the deeply supernatural worldview of the ancient Jewish authors who saw heaven and earth as integrally related to one another. According to N. T. Wright,

> God was pushed upstairs like a dysfunctional and embarrassing elderly relative. People who still felt affection for him were welcome to go and visit him, in private prayer and Sunday worship. People who still believed he mattered would hope to be with him forever after their death. *But he had nothing to say about how to run the downstairs world.* Jesus's prayer that God's kingdom would come "on earth as it is in heaven" was either forgotten or reinterpreted ... private piety in the present, heaven in the future: that was Christianity. That was the good news. It had nothing much to do with what people usually call the real world.[57]

Why did the Europeans during the Enlightenment resurrect these ancient Greek ideas? Despite the efforts of the Reformers of the sixteenth century just prior to the Enlightenment, the issue was primarily that "people were constantly being told that the point of the whole game was to go to heaven, and the problem was an angry God who didn't seem to want you to get there."[58] This is not the good news about the God of Israel becoming king on earth as in heaven, which Jesus came proclaiming. This is the good news: things are going to be run differently in the world from now on because *God has returned as king to set things right*. If we want to understand this good news which is inherent in *The Lord of the Rings*, then we will need to first familiarize ourselves with the Jewish way of looking at reality. "The nature of Hebrew," writes Marvin Wilson, "is to paint verbal pictures with broad strokes of the brush."[59] As a corollary of this, Hebraic thought is characterized by metaphor and paradox. That is exactly why Jesus—and subsequently Tolkien—preferred to speak in parables. Tolkien knew Hebrew and was most likely attracted to this way of thinking because it was imaginative, concrete, and colorful. Moreover, as a Christian, Tolkien well understood that Jesus, the very heart of Christianity, is himself a paradox. The Bible is filled with allegory, parable, and proverb, all of which are examples of metaphorical speech. More profoundly, Jesus, who is called the *Logos*—the "Word"—of God in John's Gospel, is himself *a parable*. In a parable, one does not encounter the divine face to face, because God is hidden. Instead, parables are a way of "*likening* aspects of reality to what it is *not* for the sake of showing more deeply what it *is*."[60] It seems that Tolkien's understanding of myth flowed from his deeply Jewish understanding of the Christian worldview. If we do not have the same understanding, we shall run the risk of "*myth*understanding" *The Lord of the Rings*.[61]

Among the many contributing factors that led to the parting of ways between Jews and Christians—and our distancing from historic, orthodox Christianity—were Israel's two catastrophic wars with Rome (AD 66-74 and AD 132-135). Before the mid-second century, the early church was mainly made up of Jews. In fact, there were several diverse Jesus-followers in the early church: Hebraists, Hellenists, and gentile converts. There were traditional Jews who kept ties with the temple but followed Jesus Christ like James, the brother of Jesus, diaspora Greek-speaking Jews like Stephen and Paul, and gentile converts such as Cornelius (see Acts 10:36-48 for the latter). Although they disagreed on some things, all of them were bound by a love of and devotion to the Lordship of Jesus Christ. Unfortunately, this arrangement did not last long, mostly due to the first war with Rome that ended with the total destruction of Jerusalem and the temple in AD 70. The war with Rome forced many of the Hebraist Christians to choose between the church and the Pharisees, who were the only remaining non-Christian Jewish sect after AD 70. The destruction of the traditional incarnational symbol—the temple—also created tension among God's people. By AD 165 (if not much earlier), the Church of Jesus Christ was almost entirely comprised of gentile converts to Christian Judaism who felt that *they* were the new Israel. And while this is true on one level—Jesus intended to rejuvenate Israel's call to be a light to the nations—it is dangerous on another. For example, the early Christian apologist Justin Martyr, in his *Dialogue with Trypho, A Jew*, stated that the Jewish scriptures were "not yours but ours."[62] This possessiveness bordered on triumphalism and proved corrosive to future relations between Jews and Christians in the Middle Ages. Gentile converts believed this *in spite of* Paul's prophetic warning in Romans 11:18 where he reminded them that they had been "grafted in" by faith and that they "do not support the root, but the root supports you." He also urged them not to become arrogant and forget this. Unfortunately, that is exactly what happened. This brief history lesson also helps us understand how we have forgotten the Jewish roots of Christianity. If we are ignorant of the context in which Christianity was born, we will also be ignorant of the Christian worldview, and if we are ignorant of the Christian worldview, we will be blind to the story it is telling about reality.

By the fourth century, the church had completely disassociated itself from its Jewish roots. Two more developments during this century further contributed to this disassociation. First, because of early church fathers like Origen, Platonism became a significant influence on Christian thought, especially the notion of the split-level cosmos we discussed above. Second, under the influence of the early church historians Lactantius and Eusebius, the notion of the unification of "church and state" made an impact on both Christian leadership and thought. Along with many others, these two influences led to the creation of a de-Judaized Christianity which one is tempted to believe Jesus would neither recognize nor endorse. These two influences in particular also led to the development of monarchic despotism of the Middle Ages which Enlightenment thinkers would later rebel against in the eighteenth century. It began with Eusebius's reasoning that God had elected Constantine to rule the world in his name. "One empire under one absolute God, with one absolute ruler as His image on earth," writes Arthur Herman.[63] But this is not the Jewish vision of kingship that we are seeking to recover. The Old Testament has hundreds of scriptures which tell us that it is God *through* David's descendant who is the world's one true king. According to Wright, when the Bible speaks about God as king, "we notice a triple theme.... First, Israel's God is celebrated as king especially in Jerusalem, in his home in the Temple....Second, when Israel's God is enthroned as 'king,' the nations are brought under his rule....Third, when God is king, the result is proper justice, real equity, the removal of all corruption and oppression."[64] If we want to really understand this central theme of the Bible—that God is creation's rightful king—we must attend to several important passages from Genesis, Isaiah, and Ezekiel in the Old Testament.

If we read the Bible from the perspective of the ancient Israelite authors, we discover that it was not just Adam and Eve who rebelled against God's sovereignty in Eden. Together, Genesis 3, Genesis 6:1-4, Ezek 28:12-17, and Isa 14:9-15 reveal that there were two divine rebellions against Yahweh from within his divine council. This notion that God has a "posse" may come as a shock to many readers, but it is not the same as polytheism. For anyone wanting to know more on this subject, I highly recommend Michael Heiser's excellent book, *The Unseen Realm*, and Psalm 82, which can introduce you to the idea. Basically, the divine council is made up of divine, non-human beings who are part of God's unseen, heavenly family. According to Gen 1:26–27, they were with God in the beginning and witnessed God's sole creation of the cosmos and humanity. God does not need a council or humans, but it seems that he *prefers* to rule through both heavenly and earthly representatives. In the beginning, God intended his heavenly and earthly families to live together with him in Eden, which was located somewhere in the east on earth. Eden is described both as a lush garden and a high mountain throughout Scripture, but it was only a small part of earth. God's command to humanity in Gen 1:28 was to go out and make the rest of the earth like Eden, but as we learn in Gen 3, that ended up not happening. The serpent and Adam and Eve were not the only beings to rebel against God. Genesis 6:1–4 indicates that another member of God's heavenly council not only rebelled against God, but corrupted other *elohim* (a Hebrew word meaning "God" or "gods" which is plural in form, but can be either singular or plural in meaning) and tempted them to rebel against God as well. Apparently, some of these rebellious *elohim* also descended to earth at Mount Hermon in northern Israel and copulated with members of humanity.

The result of these rebellions and the Tower of Babel episode leads to God disinheriting the nations of the world and appointing lesser elohim to those nations, as Deut. 32:8–9 tells us. According to Heiser, "God decreed, in the wake of Babel, that the other nations he had forsaken would have other gods besides himself to worship."[65] Indeed, this passage from Deuteronomy is directly related to God's decision to disperse the nations and confuse speech in the Tower of Babel story (Gen 11:1–9). Genesis 6:1–4 tells us that human beings and these fallen *elohim* copulated, which was a violation of the role and function of both the *elohim* and the people who participated. Their offspring, according to Heiser, were called the Nephilim, a word which can be translated either as "fallen ones" or "giants." Dead Sea Scroll literature such as 1 Enoch also explains how the fallen *elohim* shared forbidden divine insights with humanity, which resulted in widespread corruption, which in turn led to the great flood and the Tower of Babel, which in turn led to God's desire to start fresh by calling one man, Abraham, out of one of those disinherited nations to form the nation of Israel. The Tower of Babel story, for example, is a moment in Scripture that reveals humanity's refusal to work with God on reestablishing Eden on earth on God's terms. What all these texts tell us is that neither God's divine family nor his earthly family wanted to serve as his imagers (representatives of his rule) anymore, hence the call of Abraham. The various texts we just surveyed show that God's families wanted to rule on their own terms and therefore *did not want God to be the rightful king of heaven and earth.*[66] The rest of the Bible tells the story of how God would eventually come as the "agent for his own mission" to bring Eden back to earth, reclaim the disinherited nations, and judge the dark powers behind the thrones of those nations.[67]

In conclusion, Eusebius and Lactantius's understanding of Christianity—especially the notion of God's kingship—was more Platonic than Jewish. Although Tolkien may have been aware of all this, he was quite critical of what he thought was the "Protestant fascination with the early, primitive church."[68] The good news that Christianity proclaims is that God has become king on earth as in heaven. We see this same monarchic theme emerge throughout Tolkien's mythology but especially in *The Lord of the Rings*. Tolkien himself seems to confirm this saying that *The Lord of the Rings* is about "God and his sole right to divine honor."[69] One of the most controversial issues that attends the topic of Christianity is its claim to be the only true religion. As part of our attempt to reconstruct a historic, orthodox Christianity, we will now need to pay special attention to this controversial issue.

THE ONLY TRUE RELIGION?

Two years after his walk with Tolkien and Dyson, Lewis wrote *The Pilgrim's Regress*, an allegorical and semi-autobiographical story of Lewis's journey from Christianity to atheism to theism and back to Christianity. Lewis's allegory especially addresses the contentious issue of Christianity's claim to be the one true religion and what implications that claim has for all other worldviews. The story follows the journey of an everyman pilgrim named John who is searching for the "island" of his desire while wrestling with two powers quarrelling in his soul: "The Rules" and "The Pictures." For our present purposes, what interests us about *The Pilgrim's Regress* are Lewis's comments about "the Shepherd People" who were given "The Rules" and "the Pagans" who were given "Pictures."

John eventually comes to hear an intriguing story from a hermit named "History." The hermit tells him that the Landlord has communicated with his tenants in two major ways: to the Shepherd People, who could read, he gave rules; to those who could not—the Pagans—the Landlord spoke in pictures. Unfortunately, because the Pagans could not read, they often made up seemingly arbitrary stories about the pictures they received. And though the Shepherd People were given clear rules, they could not discern the messenger through the messages. This is very clearly an allegory of non-Christian cultures and their attempt to make sense of the "images" God placed in their minds which in turn allows them to tell stories that reach out to God. Their stories were imperfect and only caught glimpses of the total picture, but non-Christians were created with the ability to know the true

God just like everyone else. What is the biblical explanation for non-Christian cultures' inability to know God through special revelation? Just earlier I pointed out the importance of Deut 32:8–9 and God's disinheritance of the fallen *elohim* and the nations that were corrupted by them. Could it be that it was because of God's actions at the Tower of Babel and his subsequent disinheritance of the nations that the gentile nations were not be able to know God more intimately? This seems a reasonable explanation based on the evidence we have compiled thus far. Let us also note, however, that the people of Israel (the "Shepherd People"), too, were in need of saving, and that despite God's decision to reveal himself more specifically to the nation of Israel, they still only knew him partially ("The Rules") as well. S. Steve Park summarizes: "So History points out the necessity of a convergence of the pictures and the rules 'by a third thing.'"[70] This allegory should be fairly transparent: the "third thing" is the Incarnation—Jesus Christ—who is the convergence of *the Rules and the Pictures*. God's ultimate desire is to reunite his two estranged families, reconcile them to himself, and make all the earth like Eden. The call of Abraham and the formation of Israel was God's first step in re-gathering all the nations.

Recall that Tolkien had explained to Lewis that the similarities between Christianity and other myths ought to be there if Jesus is the total truth. This insight became so important to Lewis later in life that he went on to write, "Christians and Pagans had much more in common with each other than either has with a post-Christian."[71] This is one of the most fascinating features of Christianity that many modern Christians fail to properly understand, especially when defending the faith or evangelizing. Paradoxically, these are often the same Christians who adore Tolkien's and Lewis's books! A closer look at Tolkien's—and Lewis's—books, however, shows that non-Christian mythologies play a significant role in understanding the Christian worldview. Unfortunately, many Tolkien scholars have erroneously argued that the *presence* of non-Christian myths is the reason why Tolkien's books should not be labeled as Christian stories.[72] Nothing could be further from the truth; the presence of elements from non-Christian mythologies further gestures toward the presence of Christ in Middle-earth. In this section, we will take a brief but detailed look at what it means to say that Christianity is the only completely true religion (rather than the only religion which contains truth) and explore the role which elements of non-Christian mythologies that are in The Lord of the Rings play in presenting it as a Christian story.

Remembering what we have discussed about Deut 32:8–9 and the various rebellions against God will help us better explain this view. It was the corrupt influence which the fallen *elohim* had on humanity as well as the spiritual legacy of Adam and Eve's rebellion against God and its noetic effects that are responsible for the incompleteness of the gentiles' myths. Although Israel is a mediator whose job is to help God gather the scattered nations, it, too, in the end needs saving. Ultimately, God himself chose to come to fill in the gaps in all the stories and show how everything was meant to fit together. Hence the need for a "third thing," the incarnation of God. The incarnation is the unity of God's two families and heaven and earth in one person. Earlier in the Introduction, we explored the interconnectedness of myth, meaning, truth, and reality. Recall that we learned that meaningfulness is the antecedent of truth, and that truth is *about* reality. According to Tolkien and Lewis, all human questing for truth and meaning is a search for God who ultimately disclosed himself *personally* in history. Before we examine the role that pre-Christian myths play as *praeparatio evangelica* (Latin for "preparation of the gospel"), we need to make sure that we fully grasp Jesus's words in John 14:6: "I am the way and the truth and the life; no one comes to the Father except through me."

Many people have pointed out that the word "only" is not to be found in John 14:6. The fact is, "only" does not have to be there once we understand the philosophy behind what Jesus said. In fact, the phrase "exclusive truth claim" is redundant; *all* truth claims are exclusive in nature. Many of my students often tell me the blind men and the elephant story to reinforce this point. One blind man feels the elephant's leg and says he has stumbled upon a tree trunk, another thinks the animal's trunk is a snake and so on. The moral of the story is that no one can see the whole truth (elephant); we all only see part of the whole truth. But how can the teller of this story claim that we can only see *part* unless he sees the *whole*? The logical conclusion to this is that we do have access to the whole truth as we assume it in everything we think, say, and do. But does this mean we are stuck with only subjective perceptions or radical skepticism? Can we really know objective truth? Indeed, we can, and 100-percent knowledge of the truth is not necessary in order to claim that we know it. Then there is the matter of revelation: what if the truth were revealed to us? That is precisely what Christians believe. God, who is truth, created the world within which truth about his character is discoverable.

According to McGrath, Tolkien and Lewis both articulated an argument for *mythos spermatikos*—an "embedded narrative"—in their imaginative writings. According to this notion, there is a "narrative embedded within the deeper structures of the created order, which enables, shapes, and molds the construction and narration of human stories."[73] We learned about this earlier in the Introduction when we discussed types. According to this ancient view, there are scattered images (types) of the great Archetype (Jesus Christ) in every myth that contains truth about reality. The biblical myth, then, plays the role of the grand narrative that weaves all the true types found in non-Christian myths into the true myth and completes them. Tolkien seemed to have this concept in mind when he wrote, "We make in our measure and in our derivative mode, because we are made: and not only made, but made in the image and likeness of a Maker."[74] This "embedded narrative," Tolkien and Lewis seemed to believe, is fully disclosed in the Bible. The Bible tells the story about a creator God who created us in his image which gave us the innate ability to discover the truth about him by embedding certain truths about himself in the created order which we could then weave into stories about him. The Bible, in other words, contains a story that is the archetype and template for all the other stories humanity has told. It also tells us why we have this narrative impulse to begin with. This means that if Jesus is *the truth* and not just *a truth*, then it necessarily follows that Jesus could be known, at least in part, anywhere, by anyone, and at any time, since all people were created with a intuitive knowledge of this "embedded narrative."

Indeed, this is exactly the teaching we find in Rom 1:19–20 where Paul says, "Since what may be known about God is plain to them, because God has made it plain to them. For since the creation of the world God's invisible qualities—his eternal power and divine nature—have been clearly seen, being understood from what has been made, so that people are without excuse." The corollary of this is that any worldview that narrates truth contains a fragment of Christ in it. According to Markos in his book *From Achilles to Christ*, Christians should be claiming that Christianity is the only *completely* true religion rather than claiming it is the only true religion. According to Markos, by saying "that Christianity is the only complete truth, we leave open the possibility that other philosophies, religions, and cultures have hit on certain aspects of the truth."[75] One interesting question that has been raised is, "How can we know that even Christianity is true?" What way do we have of getting outside Christianity to test its truthfulness? Many Christians forget that it is Jesus Christ, and not the Bible, that is our ultimate objective standard of truth. In John 5:39 Jesus tells us exactly that when he says that "these are the very Scriptures that testify about me." In other words, even the Bible does not have the monopoly on truth. Jesus is the the great Archetype, the person to which all types and true stories point.

Christians believe truth is ultimately a *person*, not a book. It is Jesus, the complete truth, who confirms that all myths—including the one in the Bible that foretold his coming into the world—testify about him. As we have said before, Christianity is the only completely true religion, not the only religion to contain truth. On the Christian view of things, if Jesus is not who he claimed to be, and Christianity is false, then it would necessarily follow that all worldviews are iterations of this lie. It is important to understand that if Christianity is not really the grand narrative it claims to be, then another narrative must be. In an essay entitled "Religion and Dogma," Lewis summarizes all this saying, "If my religion is erroneous the occurrences of similar motifs in pagan stories are . . . instances of the same . . . error. But if my religion is true, then these stories may well be a *praeparatio evangelica*, a divine hinting in poetic and ritual form at the same central truth which was later focused and historicized in the Incarnation."[76] Now that we have a clear understanding of what Christianity means when it claims to be the true religion, it's time to explore the role that non-Christian myths, especially those preceding Jesus, have in supporting this claim.

By claiming to be the objective truth in person, Jesus was making the most controversial claim in human history. Luc Ferry, a prominent skeptical French scholar, writes about Jesus's revolutionary claim in his best-selling book *A Brief History of Thought*. Ferry reminds us that in John 1, Jesus is identified as the *logos*. Ferry explains that *logos* was centrally important in Stoicism. For the Stoics, the *logos* was the "impersonal, harmonious and divine structure of the *cosmos* as a whole."[77] For the Stoics, the *logos* was ultimate reality. According to Ferry, Greek and Roman Stoics were horrified that Christians claimed that this divine principle incarnated itself in one human being. "For Greek thought in general," Ferry writes, "and for Stoicism in particular, the idea that the *Logos* could designate anything other than the rational order of the universe was unthinkable."[78] To claim that this otherwise abstract principle became a concrete reality and "happened" in human history was, to quote Ferry, "insanity" to most of Jesus's contemporaries. This is an excellent example of how a non-Christian worldview which preceded Christianity by three centuries supports Jesus's claim to be the complete truth.

Another fine example of non-Christian mythology as *praeparatio evangelica* comes from Acts 17:16–34. In this story, Paul had travelled to Athens to preach the gospel to various elders of the city and philosophers (including some Stoics!). Standing on the rock of Ares before his audience Paul said, "People of Athens! I see that in every way you are very religious. For as I walked around and looked carefully at your objects of worship, I even found an altar with this inscription: TO AN UNKNOWN GOD. So you are ignorant of the very thing you worship—and this is what I am going to proclaim to you" (vv. 22–23). Here Paul is arguing that all people have intuitive knowledge of the truth and therefore God in Jesus Christ even though they do not realize it. Paul uses something in Greek mythology—the statue dedicated to the unknown god—to make a case for the Christian myth. What Paul did in identifying the statue of the unknown god with Jesus is called *subversion*. Subversion is telling one myth in terms of another myth. It is not the same as syncretism, which is absorbing one myth into another myth. So far we have looked at two examples of non-Christian mythology as *praeparatio evangelica*. Many more examples could be given, but there is not enough space here to discuss them. It is extremely important that we recognize the special place that Israel's story has in preparing the way for the revelation of Jesus, for according to N. T. Wright, "Israel's story is . . . the microcosm and beating heart of the world's story, but also its ultimate saving energy. What God does for Israel is what God is doing in relation to the whole world . . . grasp that, and you have a pathway into the heart of the New Testament."[79] Might imaginative literature such as *The Lord of the Rings* also function as a kind of praeparatio evangelica?

Christians are accustomed to believing that Jesus's parables function as prooftexts for his divine identity, salvific vocation, and/or for Christian doctrines. According to Sallie McFague, "the point of Jesus' parables is not mere illumination, aesthetic insight, or secret wisdom," but to challenge us.[80] Moreover, the parable *is* the message. The form of the parable is the very goal God wants to achieve: the reunification of heaven and earth and his two families. Jesus's parables not only challenge the way Israel was accustomed to telling its story, but they challenge all the stories human beings tell about reality. By doing so, they are supposed to make us slightly uncomfortable. The parables are the "good news" in "nugget" story-form.[81] What is the news and why is it good? Our English word "gospel" comes from the Old English words *god* and *spell*, meaning "good story," but the New Testament was written in Greek, not Old English. Good stories, like good spells, enchant us. The original Greek *euangelion* can mean "good story," as well as "good news" and "good tidings." According to Wright, the good news is the story of how God became King.[82] Although the biblical narrative has many themes, this is the main theme that emerges most in both the Bible and *The Lord of the Rings*. The passage which alerted me to the presence of this shared theme is found toward the end of *The Return of the King*, when an eagle soaring over Minas Tirith announces, "Sing and be glad, all ye children of the West, for your King shall come again, and he shall dwell among you all the days of your life."[83] This is the gospel in a nutshell—and it is at the heart of Middle-earth. Here and later in chapter 3, we will be looking at *The Lord of the Rings* as a kind of "parabolic novel," and therefore as a proclamation of the gospel. But first, we need to understand what a parable is and what it is not. We will also need to compare parables and allegories since Tolkien often made it very clear he disliked allegory.[84] We will also look at why parables are the best literary form for containing and communicating the Christian myth and then explore why Tolkien chose this type of narrative.

Parables provide a much needed anamnesis (Greek for "recollection") that we are part of a grand narrative. Parables wake people up to a reality that is breaking in on them, that an incursion of the transcendent is breaking into their daily lives. By imitating Jesus's art of the parable, Tolkien created a story that reminds us that we are part of God's story. Tolkien's understanding of parable is not, however, consonant with how most Christians today understand parables. As we will see shortly, Tolkien's description of fairy story is quite similar to biblical scholars' description of Jesus's parables. According to Murray, "we can find in Tolkien's writings not only many passages bearing on the nature and power of this art in which Jesus excelled, but also wonderful examples of the art itself, though Tolkien never claimed the term 'parable' for any of his own stories."[85] In the next section, we will explore the Semitic context of the parable, what a parable is, and why Jesus spoke in parables.

SPEAKING IN PARABLES

Philosophically speaking, *mythos* and *logos* are both metaphysical and epistemological terms. Both terms refer to *what* is true, real, and possible, and *how* we know what is true, real, and possible. Together, these terms form the backbone of every worldview. Indeed, the very word "mythology" illustrates this. We have learned that all true stories reflect the total truth of Jesus Christ in varying degrees. The truthfulness of a mythology depends on how closely it corresponds and aligns with reality. Some myths tilt more to the *mythos* end of the spectrum whereas others, while still remaining myths (stories), tilt more to the *logos* end of the spectrum. Now, while *logos* is dependent on *mythos*, a myth that is too out of touch with the physical, rational world of *logos* is not true to reality. The opposite is also true, of course. According to Lewis, "in the enjoyment of a great myth we come nearest to experiencing as a concrete what can otherwise be understood only as an abstraction."[86] A great myth is one which balances *mythos* and *logos*, the abstract and concrete, and the metaphysical and physical. Indeed, "Tolkien's mythology is quite literally a *mythology*, a unity, that is, of the sub-creative and mythical imagination (*mythos*) on the one hand and of philosophical rationality and rigor (*logos*) on the other."[87] Such a myth has the potential to satisfy both our imaginative *and* rational faculties. One could appropriately describe such a myth as *incarnational*, for it is a type of story where *mythos* comes down from "the heaven of legend and imagination" to the level of *logos*, the "earth of history," as Lewis put it.[88] And this is exactly what a parable is and what parable does. Parables are a type of *mythos* which *re-mythologizes* reality.

Although our English word "parable" comes from the Greek words *para* and *ballein*, meaning "to cast or throw alongside," parables are more representative of Jewish rather than Greek thought. That is not to say that parables do not exist outside Jewish literature, because they do. Indeed, the first-century BC Greek thinker Theon classified *parbole* as a type of *mythos*, as we are doing here.[89] Many scholars have written about Tolkien's proclivity for ambivalence when it came to talking about *The Lord of the Rings*. This is especially true when it came to the issue of allegory, which we will be addressing shortly. Yet it is Tolkien's paradoxical comments about *The Lord of the Rings* that provides one of the greatest hints that *The Lord of the Rings* is a parable modeled on the paradigmatic parables of Jesus himself. These comments reveal a deep affinity for and immersion in Jewish thought that permeates Christianity. According to Marvin R. Wilson, the Jewish "way of thinking created a propensity for paradox, antinomy, or apparent contradiction."[90] Professor Clyde Kilby even coined a term about Tolkien's paradoxical nature, calling it his proclivity for "contrasistency."[91] But Tolkien's seeming back-and-forth about *The Lord of the Rings* was not because he was confused about the meaning of allegory or parable, or because he couldn't make up his mind, but because of the *nature* of parable itself. Tolkien's consistent contradictory stance toward what type of story *The Lord of the Rings* was may be the ultimate clue to what type of story it is.

According to Jane Chance, Tolkien's "contrasistency" was mainly due to his "perception of some underlying idea or relationship that his listener did not grasp, but often failing to be fully communicated."[92] This tension does indeed emerge from a close reading of Tolkien's letters. Although this topic is a bit technical, if we do not familiarize ourselves with it, we will ultimately fail to see how Tolkien used imaginative literature to proclaim the Gospel. Tolkien well understood that "the Hebrew mind was willing to accept the truths taught on both sides of the paradox," and that "it recognized that mystery and apparent contradiction are often signs of the divine."[93] That is exactly why Tolkien wrote to his Jesuit friend Robert Murray, "I have purposely kept all allusions to the highest matters down to mere hints, perceptible only by the most attentive, or kept them under unexplained symbolic forms."[94] With this in mind, perhaps we can finally understand why so many Tolkien scholars and fans have said that *The Lord of the Rings* both does and does not appear to be a Christian story. It is more than just a well-written story. Once more, it seems the very form of the story itself is trying to communicate something about its ultimate meaning. For example, an unbelieving man once wrote to Tolkien and said, "You create a world in which some sort of faith seems to be everywhere without a visible source, like light from an invisible lamp."[95] Here, then, is a wonderful example of the "art of the parable" which Tolkien's friend Murray spoke about. Parables break down intellectual barriers and appeal to the heart.

A cursory reading of the Bible reveals that God loves poetry. Indeed, it seems to be his preferred way of communicating with us. Metaphor is at the heart of poetry. And as McFague has said so eloquently, "a metaphor does not have a message, it *is* a message."[96] This is precisely why Jesus spoke in parables. Jesus spoke in parables because that was the only way of saying what needed to be said. Indeed, "the only legitimate way of speaking of the incursion of the divine into history, or so it appears to this tradition, is metaphorically," because "metaphor is proper to the subject-matter because God remains hidden."[97] Metaphors are also a kind of indirect language. If there really is a transcendent creator-God who created beings in his image, and this God wants to communicate that he has come to live among us, then what better way of communicating this is there than parable, "for what is more indirect—a more complete union of the realistic and the strange—than a human life as the abode of the divine?"[98] From our perspective, God is the ultimate metaphor, the ultimate parable. This is why metaphorical language seems to be God's preferred means of communication; it is perfectly suited to his—and our—mythical nature. That is also why "Christian theology should maintain an equal ultimacy of both word *and* image because at the core of our faith is this equal ultimacy in the incarnation: Word made flesh."[99] Recall that the word for "Word" in Greek is *logos*, where as Godawa's reference to "flesh" here is to "image," i.e., *mythos*. Moreover, *logos* is synonymous with philosophical and propositional language. Myths are *imaginative* stories filled with pictures, symbols, and images which contain propositional truth claims about reality. They are a fusion of "word" and "image." Therefore, a Christian story will be *incarnational* by being a unity of "word" and "flesh/image." In summary, "images are concrete expressions of abstract ideas, the existential embodiment of the rational word. Images, whether they are stories, pictures or music, are incarnations of ideas—words made flesh."[100]

It could be argued that the Jews developed a special kind of parabolic communication as a primary means of talking about God because God chose to speak in parables first. God says in Psalm 78:2, "I will open my mouth with a parable; I will utter hidden things, things from of old." Indirect communication is hardwired into us from a very early age, and scholars across many different disciplines have argued for a very long time that people across the world cannot communicate effectively without it. Although the parable is a deeply Semitic literary form, it is a type of story that other cultures, including the Greeks, have made use of. The Greek word *parabole*—which we see in the Greek New Testament—is the closest equivalent to the Hebrew word for parable, which is *mashal*. *Mashal* has a wide range of meanings: "proverb," "riddle," "anecdote," "allegory," "profound utterance," and "parable" are all possible meanings. All these examples of metaphorical speech share the central meaning of "resemblance," "likeness," "shadow," and, strangest of all, "rule or reign."[101] According to Brad Young, Hebrew *mashalim* are stories with God as king at their center. Moreover, Klyne Snodgrass has argued that parables are monarchic stories, or stories about the kingship of God. In ancient Semitic civilizations such as Israel, the earthly king was considered the "shadow" or "image" of God. *Mashalim*, then, are a type of narrative which relies on the power of metaphor to illustrate a resemblance between the word-picture and the reality. "The shadow is an inexact representation of the substance," but that is because that is the only way we can know the reality at all.[102] Parables are inseparable "from their content—there is no way of getting at the 'essence' of Christianity apart from them." Parables are metaphorical narratives that show us that "metaphor is *the* way of human knowing. It is not simply a way of embellishing something we can know in some other way. There is no other way."[103]

Curiously, this definition of *mashal* also reflects the Judeo-Christian belief that man was created in God's image (Gen 1:26–27) and likeness as well as Tolkien's idea of man as "sub-creator."[104] Recall that Tolkien once said that "we make . . . because we are made . . . in the image and likeness of a Maker." We speak in parables (stories) because we were made by a God who is himself a parable. When it came time to reveal himself to us, God did so in a way that was consistent with both his nature and our own. The incarnation—Jesus Christ himself—is the parable of God. The incarnation is the "curious wedding of realism and strangeness," which, it also happens, is a great definition of parable.[105]

In her book *Speaking in Parables*, Sallie McFague explicitly states that *The Lord of the Rings* is a "parabolic novel."[106] What does this mean? First, it means that Tolkien's mythological world (Middle-earth) is entirely credible all on its own, just as, say, any of Jesus's parable-worlds are. They may indeed be strange or even challenging worlds, but credible all the same. In other words, these stories possess a life of their own. This means that readers do not *have* to look outside the world of the story to assign meaning. In other words, the stories themselves have intrinsic meaning apart from anything they might suggest.[107] As McFague puts it, the "meaning is largely unassigned."[108] Tolkien himself says as much in one of his letters to Murray where he says that he left any inherent religious (Christian) symbolism "unexplained."[109] To say *The Lord of the Rings* is a "parabolic novel" also means that it has a unique way of illuminating reality which is quite different from other types of myth. As we will continue to learn, the juxtaposition of strangeness and familiarity in parables is one of the characteristics which make them such realistic stories. Indeed, Kreeft has said of *The Lord of the Rings* that, : "The fundamental reason for the popularity of *The Lord of the Rings* is that people sense that it is *real*."[110] He goes on to say that Fangorn Forest, for example, feels more real than our forests. How is that?? Because Tolkien shows us how reality *ought* to be, not what it is. We instinctively grasp and understand this, and so we are attracted to stories like Tolkien's. In his essay "On Fairy Stories," Tolkien argued that we all eventually become too familiar with the familiar, so much so that we cannot see reality clearly. He called the ability of myth to restore a proper vision of reality "Recovery."[111] That is why myths—especially the fairy story/parable—actually drive us more deeply *into* reality rather than away from it, as we often hear people say. "For the Christian," writes McFague, "the story of Jesus is *the* story par excellence. For his story not only is the human struggle of moving toward belief but in some way that story is the unification of the mundane and the transcendent."[112] Parables unite the mundane and transcendent, recover true reality, and restore our ability to see it clearly.

Now that we understand the Jewish origins of parable and what basically a parable is, we need to delve a little deeper and look at why Jesus spoke in parables. We will then look at why Tolkien chose the parable as his preferred literary form and whether parables are different from allegories and how. Was this something Tolkien consciously chose? Did he intend to write a Christian story? Can his story be called Christian considering how much Tolkien drew inspiration from Anglo-Saxon and Norse mythologies? Before we begin to answer these questions, we need to establish the theological basis for why Tolkien would naturally have looked to Jesus's parables as a model for his own.

PARABLES ARE INCARNATIONAL STORIES

Christians believe that Jesus is the preexistent Son of God, the Second Person of the Trinity, who is also God. Jesus has been since the very beginning. The "incarnation" is the special *historical moment* wherein God became a human being named Jesus of Nazareth. Godawa describes the incarnation as "the enfleshment of proposition."[113] We learned earlier that Christians believe Jesus is the *Logos*, a word which Stoic philosophers understood to be the name for their ultimate reality. Yet the Stoics regarded the *Logos* as an impersonal force or universal principle—*not* a human being. Jesus is the "enfleshment" of *every* truth-claim that every worldview has ever made. If the incarnation is true, then the implications of this are staggering. If

Christianity is totally true, then there are consequences for everyone, regardless of what they as individuals do or do not believe. This is why toward the end of his essay "On Fairy Stories," Tolkien wrote, "There is no tale ever told that men would rather find was true, and none which so many skeptical men have accepted as true on its own merits . . . to reject it leads either to sadness or to wrath."[114] Tolkien is saying that though the claims of Christianity seem preposterous and many would *like* it to be true, many have concluded that it just seems too unreasonable. It is too outlandish, some say; virgin births do not happen, and people do not come back from the dead. It would be nice to believe this, many tell themselves, but these things just do not happen. And yet, Tolkien is saying that there is no worldview which so many skeptical people *have* accepted as true, despite the challenging propositions of Christianity. The Christian myth has changed the hearts and minds of the most fervent skeptics (St. Paul and C. S. Lewis both come to mind). If it really is true and we have rejected it, we will lose everything; if it is not true (though it appears very likely that it is) and we have believed it, then we have nothing to lose because Christianity, when practiced appropriately, at the very least helps a person live well.

Despite his firm conviction that Christ is the total truth, Tolkien was often—but not always—reticent about identifying *The Lord of the Rings* as a Christian story. He had good reason to be cautious, as there is much that can be easily misunderstood in claiming this. Yet it is God's apparent absence which paradoxically reveals his presence in Middle-earth. Recall the story of the unbelieving man who wrote Tolkien about *The Lord of the Rings*, saying that "faith is everywhere" but without a visible source, like "light from an invisible lamp." *The Lord of the Rings* is not preachy; it does not read like a sermon. Nevertheless, many have felt that God is the story's main character.[115] According to Timothy Keller, Tolkien believed that "we have intuitions of the plotline of the Bible, namely, that the world was made to be a paradise but it has been lost."[116] Tolkien believed that every person has an imprint of the knowledge of God within them. He believed that we all live within a story-shaped vision of reality that is based on the plotline of the Bible, even if some of us have suppressed it.[117] We have already discussed the biblical explanation for this earlier in the Introduction. For Tolkien, the Christian story was the only story that could make sense of all other stories we live within. In his essay "On Fairy Stories," Tolkien speaks of the fairy story's ability to give us "glimpses" of "Joy . . . beyond the walls of the world."[118] In his autobiography *Surprised by Joy*, Lewis tells us that as an atheist, he frequently encountered and experienced something he called "Joy." Both men were speaking of the same "Joy," but what exactly is it? According to Lewis, "Joy" is the experience of "an unsatisfied desire which is itself more desirable than any other satisfaction." Lewis tells us that "Joy" is utterly distinct from happiness and pleasure except for one characteristic that they have in common: "Anyone who has experienced it will want it again."[119] For Tolkien, if a story gives one an experience of "Joy," then it is a type of story which functions like "evangelium," or the "good news."[120] According to McFague, "within the gospels are many small gospels—the parables, anecdotes, healings, teachings of Jesus—which in nugget form also image the good news."[121] Fairy stories function similarly to parables by affording us glimpses of "Joy beyond the walls of the world."

Lewis tells us that he experienced Joy as early as six years old and continued to over the course of his lifetime, even during his years as an atheist. Lewis was frequently pierced by a longing for something—or someone—through the myths he enjoyed. According to John Piper, "both romanticism and rationalism—longing and logic—led him [Lewis] out of this world to find the meaning and validity of this world."[122] Although it is very peculiar, the only way we can really know anything about reality is by speaking about what reality is not. A good myth is a marriage of direct and indirect speech. Piper summarizes: "If the key to the deepest meaning of this world lies outside this world, then the world will probably be illumined most deeply not simply by describing the world as what it is, but by likening the world to what it is not."[123] Every human being has this dialectic of romanticism and rationalism within them, but one side may be dormant; a good myth awakens both.

During his years as an atheist, Lewis struggled to find the source of the longing in this world, so he logically concluded that since nothing in this world satisfied his longing for "Joy," the object of his longing must exist beyond the world of nature and reason. One of the ways in which he discovered this was by following his modern worldview's assumptions to their logical conclusions. After becoming a Christian he wrote, "If minds are wholly dependent on brains, and brains on biochemistry, and biochemistry (in the long run) on the meaningless flux of atoms, I cannot understand how the thought of those minds should have any more significance than the sound of the wind in the trees."[124] If everything is matter, then how can conversations about matter—or ethics or aesthetics for that matter—amount to anything more than one lump of matter speaking to another lump of matter? Lewis discovered that one cannot use reason to justify rationalism and so began to think beyond it. Lewis was experiencing a "dialectic" of romanticism (*mythos*) and rationalism (*logos*) that was converging "on one goal": Jesus Christ.[125] God—who is the union of *mythos* and *logos*—planted both within all human hearts when he created us in his image. We feel "mythopathically" because God is "mythopoeic."[126] Jesus spoke in parables because the incarnation itself is a parable. The best possible way God could communicate this awesome truth was to find a way to say it in a way that is consonant with human nature. By containing the "dialectic" of romanticism and rationalism within them, parables appeal to both our imaginations and intellects.

The unbelieving man who wrote Tolkien about the pervasive presence of "light from an invisible lamp" in his fairy story seems to have been experiencing this dialectic himself. He could not seem to reconcile his unbelief with the fact that he admired a story that simultaneously did and did not feel religious. Yet anyone who "loves this story [*The Lord of the Rings*] . . . must unconsciously love the Christian story, not because *The Lord of the Rings* is an allegory of Christianity but because its author's mind and philosophy are one with that of the Author of the Christian story."[127] If we can accept that fragments of Christ can be found in every true worldview, can we not also accept the hints and suggestions of Christ found in Tolkien's imaginative world? Jesus himself used imaginative stories to help people come to belief. Both Jesus and Tolkien told stories that had "the power to reach into contexts where [the gospel] is not overtly acknowledged." Indeed, "any such story will resemble the gospel story and be properly classified as parable."[128] Recall that one of the things that held Lewis back from becoming a Christian again was that he believed becoming a Christian meant concluding that no other worldview had any truth in it. Tolkien showed Lewis that God made himself known to all people, and that wherever one discovers truth, Christ is there also. Indeed, Tolkien argued that the similarities *ought* to be there if Christianity is the totally true myth.

In his book *The Faun's Bookshelf*, Charlie Starr explains how language itself is a nod toward the incarnation as the central theme of reality. He writes that in the beginning, "when abstract thought was not divorced from concrete action, there was the 'Great Tongue,'" our true native language where "all words contained both literal and abstract meanings."[129] Once upon a time, we had a much easier time grasping this concept of "total truth," but since the fall of Adam and Eve, Christians believe that sin has distorted our ability to see the truth. Once upon a time, we spoke and thought incarnationally because we lived in an incarnational world. After Adam and Eve's exile, however, a rift appeared in reality and therefore in human thought and speech. According to McFague, "the history of language . . . is one of gradual distancing from this unity; the single meanings of language split into contrasted pairs . . . and it is the poet's burden and glory to attempt to return to this unity."[130] The incarnation was the beginning of the end of the alienation of myth from fact, or poetic (non-literal) truth from literal truth. Incarnational stories like *The Lord of the Rings* can help us see truth and reality clearly again. Indeed, Tolkien's parable can also help us see and understand how Jesus's parables do this. In a sense, it is as if we need a parable to help us understand parables properly again.

The incarnation was also the beginning of the end of man's alienation from God. It marks the historical moment when the "contrasted pairs" of heaven and earth, abstract and concrete, *mythos* and *logos*, and romanticism and rationalism began to reunite. Yet the story of reality is not yet fully told. Scholars have said that the Christian story is one of "already but not yet." We will be exploring this concept of what biblical scholars call "inaugurated eschatology" later in the book. Tolkien believed that it was the duty of a "sub-creator"—a storyteller—to return language and thought back to its mythical roots by participating in imaginative storytelling. In the beginning, when man lived with God, man was truly *mythological*; we were *whole*. Indeed, according to Starr, the human predicament is that "man is not a myth, and that is a serious, deeply spiritual problem."[131] As a Christian, Tolkien believed that the fall of man exiled us from the presence of God, who is "Perfect Myth and Perfect Fact."[132] *Mythos* and *logos* are perfectly unified in God's character and used to be in ours. We can understand the incarnation both as the beginning of our return from exile and the disappearance of the separation between *mythos* and *logos*. Jesus Christ came to "bind up the broken-hearted" and to "proclaim freedom for the captives and release from darkness for the prisoners."[133]

As compelling as all this might be, it is a well-known fact among Tolkien scholars that he did not like allegory. Allegory is a very slippery, polyvalent literary term which Tolkien used in various ways in his letters. For example, in the Foreword to the second edition of *The Lord of the Rings*, Tolkien stated that he "dislike[s] allegory in all of its manifestations."[134] And yet, in a letter written after the novel's publication in 1956, Tolkien stated, "Of course my story is not an allegory of Atomic power, but of *Power* (exerted for Domination)."[135] Literary classifications can be a tricky business because literary forms can overlap and blur together, but it seems clear from Tolkien's ambivalent usage of allegory that he was referring to two distinctly different types of allegory. As for the comment "in all of its manifestations," that could easily be understood as Tolkien claiming to dislike only one specific type of allegory. As difficult as it is to keep track of the various ways he used the term, the alternative explanation that Tolkien was confused by the meaning of allegory is unconvincing, especially because of his academic background. It is our job to properly interpret what Tolkien meant. Why didn't Tolkien ever mention parable in his letters or essays? It appears to me that it would have been a violation of his belief that communication about the good news should be suggestive, allusive, and implicit, rather than preachy. Parables are indirect communication, and one of the most powerful qualities parables possess is their suggestiveness. It is not a kind of purposefully deceitful ambiguity, but one suited for such a subject as God's kingdom arriving on earth; such a reality cannot be communicated without resorting to metaphor, which is a kind of speech that says one thing in terms that are suggestive of another, whereas strict allegory "says one thing and means another."[136]

Below I have provided a "Book Overview" for my readers to see what our "road into Jerusalem" from Middle-earth looks like. It is highly recommended that you read through this overview carefully before reading the main part of the book.

BOOK OVERVIEW

Before delving into an overview of the main arguments of the book, I want to be clear that I am not presenting a comprehensive literary analysis of any of Tolkien's books or the Bible. Nothing can replace reading either the Bible or Tolkien's books. Instead, this book will present readers with a thematic analysis of Tolkien's books which focus on the way *The Lord of the Rings* in particular—as a parabolic novel—commends the good news in the same way that Jesus's parables do. My thematic analysis is restricted to the king/kingdom thread that runs through both the Bible and Tolkien's books, which means I will be specifically focusing on Thorin and Aragorn more than any of the other characters in Tolkien's mythology. Now I would like to say a word about the approach to these subjects that I will be taking. Most Christians are most likely familiar with the notion of searching the Old Testament to discover prophecies of Jesus that are then fulfilled in the New Testament. In fact, most popular study Bibles usually have tables and graphs in various Old Testament books showing all the prophecies which Jesus fulfilled. This way of interpreting the Scriptures, however, has problems, as it does not treat the Old Testament as a text with its own inherent meanings. Furthermore, Jesus made a habit of alluding to, not appropriating, Old Testament Scripture to make a point about what God was doing in and through him. The connection between the New and Old Testaments is best seen when we look *backwards* at the Old Testament from the vantage point of Jesus and the Gospels. According to Richard B. Hays, this "act of retrospective recognition" is the best way we can make sense of how the gospel fulfills the story of Israel and humanity.[137]

Why have I adopted this retrospective approach to interpreting Tolkien's books? There are two reasons. The first and most logical reason is because Tolkien himself believed that "part of the attraction of *The Lord of the Rings* is . . . due to the glimpses of a large history in the background."[138] Furthermore, Tolkien only realized how thoroughly Christian *The Lord of the Rings* was "in the revision."[139] These comments seem to indicate that Tolkien only truly saw the interconnectivity of his mythology by looking back from the point of view of a finished *Lord of the Rings*. Although one cannot know for sure, it does seem highly likely that this understanding of his mythology was influenced by his Christian worldview. Tolkien wanted *The Lord of the Rings* and *The Silmarillion* to be published together, but the latter was eventually published posthumously. "The large history in the background" which Tolkien was referring to is obviously a reference to the events described in *The Silmarillion* and *The Hobbit*. The quote above is from a letter Tolkien wrote in 1963, eight years after the publication of the final book (*The Return of the King*) of *The Lord of the Rings*. Not only does this seem like Tolkien was reflecting on the appeal of his massively successful novel, it also comes across as the author's meditation on how to read and appreciate it fully. To fully understand *The Lord of the Rings*, one must understand its larger backstory; so, too, with the Bible. For our purposes, Tolkien's comment is one justification for adopting a retrospective approach in this book. *The Lord of the Rings* is more beautiful and makes more sense when one knows and looks back at Middle-earth's very ancient story.

The second justification for taking this retrospective approach is that it is consonant with orthodox biblical hermeneutics. This retrospective hermeneutic (method of interpretation) is a "figural interpretation" of the Bible. In other words, it is a *typological* method of interpretation. According to Hays, a hermeneutic that relies on "figural interpretation of the Bible creates deep theological coherence within the biblical narrative."[140] How? Hays argues that the correspondence between the Gospels and the Old Testament "can be discerned only after the second event has occurred and imparted a new pattern of significance to the first."[141] Recall that we discussed the concepts of types, antitypes, and archetypes early in the Introduction. Hays is essentially saying that Jesus and the authors of the Gospels read the Old Testament as one "massive typological system—one giant type" which can be understood best as a pre-figuration of Jesus and the gospel only *after* we have knowledge of the antitype.[142] Jesus's comment in John 5:46, "Moses wrote about me," and him telling the disciples on the Emmaus road that there were "things about himself" in "*all* the Scriptures" in Luke 24:27 are examples of this kind of hermeneutic. According to Heiser, "only someone who knew the outcome of the puzzle, who knew how all the elements of the messianic mosaic would come together, could make sense of the pieces."[143] The greatest justification for this way of interpreting Scripture is given by

Jesus himself, and unless we look at all the Scriptures *backwards* from his resurrected perspective, we will not be able to understand the story properly.

The relationship between the types and the antitype (which in this case is also the great Archetype!) is only discernible once there is knowledge of the latter. There is also the very important additional benefit of maintaining the integrity of Old Testament Scripture when using this hermeneutic. According to Erich Auerbach, "figural interpretation establishes a connection between two events or persons in such a way that the first signifies not only itself but also the second, while the second involves or fulfills the first."[144] As I said above, one of the strengths of this hermeneutic is that it maintains the integrity and original meaning of the Hebrew Scriptures without reducing them to mere prooftexts. According to McDermott, if we start our analysis with the Old Testament and imagine that the Old Testament authors were "predicting what would happen to or through the Messiah," this way of interpretation "misunderstands what is going on in these [Old Testament] texts."[145] "Just as Jesus was wrapped in humble swaddling cloths in the manger, so too is he wrapped in the swaddling cloths of the Law, the Prophets, and the Writings."[146] Hays argues that in order to truly understand the Gospels and the parables, we must read Scripture *backwards* "to unwind the swaddling cloths and to disclose the Christ who lies there."[147]

As with the Bible, so, too, with Tolkien's books. If we want to truly understand how Tolkien's parabolic novel communicates the Christian worldview, then we must also read Tolkien's books backwards from the perspective of the return of King Aragorn. According to Christopher Scarf, who has already recognized the necessity of reading Tolkien's books this way, "the relation of the Gospels in 'looking back' to the Old Testament is parallel to the necessity of 'looking back' at the long history of the Numenorean Kings in Tolkien's story."[148] I believe that the necessity of "looking back" in *The Lord of the Rings* on Middle-earth's ancient past is suggestive of its parabolic, and therefore Christian, character. All this tells us that Tolkien had an incredible familiarity with the Scriptures—especially Jesus's parables, a fact which Robert Murray SJ, one of Tolkien's close friends, has already persuasively argued.[149] According to a "figural reading of the Bible need not presume that the Old Testament authors—or the characters they narrate—were conscious of predicting or anticipating Christ. Rather, the discernment of a figural correspondence is necessarily retrospective rather than prospective."[150] Tolkien's conscious or unconscious structuring of his novel that lends itself to this retrospective, figural reading creates a resemblance between it and Jesus's parables. The alternative to this retrospective hermeneutic would be searching Tolkien's prequels and the Old Testament for prooftexts that predict the coming of the crucified and risen messiah both in and out of Middle-earth. Perhaps one of the reasons why some Tolkien scholars have been unable to understand how *The Lord of the Rings* communicates the Christian worldview without becoming an allegory is because they did not recognize that the "necessity of looking back" is a clue to its parabolic identity. In looking back from *The Lord of the Rings* at the history of Arda, we do not see an allegory of the gospel (itself a subversive retelling of the biblical narrative), but a parabolic announcement of it. In this book, I am not arguing that *The Lord of the Rings* is a parable *about* Jesus's parables—and therefore Christianity—but a parable about what Jesus's parables are about. The implication here is that Jesus's parables, Christianity, and by extension, *The Lord of the Rings*—are about much, much more than what we call "Christian stuff."

In the mid and late 1950s, Tolkien wrote two important tales which provide valuable insight into how he understood the interconnectedness of his mythology. The first tale, which is called "The Debate of Finrod and Andreth," was written around 1959 after the publication of the last part of *The Lord of the Rings*. The text is a dialogue between the elven king Finrod and a wise-woman named Andreth and takes place during the First Age of Middle-earth. One much shortened edition of the second tale, which is called "The Quest of Erebor," made it into the appendices of *The Return of the King* and was written sometime between 1953 and 1955. The longer and fuller version of this story can be found in the *Unfinished Tales* today. Both these stories will feature prominently in the present book for several important reasons, but I mention them here first because they are two excellent examples of "looking back," albeit in different ways. Arguably, "The Debate" was Tolkien, as author, producing a text that is very much a retrospective meditation on the entire mythology, and allowed him to see that it was pervaded by the theme of the incarnation. Interestingly, "The Quest of Erebor" narrates an in-story act of retrospection done by members of the Fellowship who are meditating on how events successfully led to the return of the king, despite all odds. As we have seen, incarnation and the return of the king go hand in glove.

Chapter 1, which is entitled "*The Lord of the Rings* as Parable," sets forth the thesis that *The Lord of the Rings* is a "parabolic novel," as McFague has argued.

Chapter 2, which is entitled "Parables Are Good News Stories," explores what it means to understand Christianity as "good news" and the role parables play in understanding Christianity as such. This is where we will also explore how parables play a role in helping us understand the incarnation.

Chapter 3, which is entitled "*The Lord of the Rings* Is Good News," brings together the insights from the previous two chapters and explores how, in being a story about the return of the king, *The Lord of the Rings* is a story about how *God became king*. The rest of this chapter is devoted to exploring how the image of Aragorn is instrumental to our understanding of Tolkien's novel as a parabolic proclamation of good news. This is also the chapter in which we begin our retrospective journey through Tolkien's mythology, starting at the furthest point in it—*The New Shadow*, Tolkien's abandoned sequel to *The Lord of the Rings*. From that point, we wind the story backwards and conclude the chapter with Aragorn's birth, childhood, and early career as a ranger.

Chapter 4, which is entitled "The King Beneath the Mountain," is all about Thorin Oakenshield and the dwarves of the House of Durin from *The Hobbit*. We will also look at how Thorin and his story prefigures Aragorn in a way that resembles the way King David prefigures Jesus Christ in the Bible.

Finally, chapter 5, which is entitled "Estel," is a chapter about *The Silmarillion* and "The Debate of Finrod and Andreth." We will explore Tolkien's cosmogony (the "Ainulindale"), or creation myth, the problem of evil, the creation of the children of Iluvatar (elves, dwarves, and men), and Thorin's and Aragorn's ancestries. Finally, we will examine "The Debate of Finrod and Andreth," which Tolkien scholar Bradley J. Birzer has called the central text in the entire mythology. According to Birzer, this debate is a mythical version of incarnational theology.[151] Moreover, I believe this text contains evidence that the way Tolkien communicated truth through *The Lord of the Rings* was deeply influenced both by Jesus's art of the parable and retrospective hermeneutic. The title of the chapter is the Sindarin (Elvish) word "Estel," which is also significant, for it simultaneously refers to the name that Gilraen, Aragorn's mother, gave to her son, and a prophecy that one day Iluvatar would enter his creation as an author does his book. By the end of this book, I hope that readers will see that *The Lord of the Rings* is a parabolic novel, that it is a story about the return of the king, and that that is good news. I hope to show that Tolkien's approach to commending the gospel is similar to Jesus's art of the parable and that it deserves to stand as a parable of the kingdom. I believe this approach honors Tolkien's desire—if his letters are any indication—to tell a Christian story in the way Jesus did.

1

The Lord of the Rings as Parable

ALLEGORY, PARABLE, AND FAIRY STORY

The word "allegory" comes from the Greek word *allegoria* which means "to speak of another." "In this sense," according to Pearce, "every word we use is an allegory."[152] Every word is a symbol that signifies, or points to, something other. This is also very close to the definition of "metaphor" from the Greek *metapherein*, meaning "to carry over." As John Dominic Crossan explains, "metaphors invite us to recognize the human necessity of 'seeing as,' the dangerous and vertiginous necessity to create the ground we stand on."[153] This means that there is technically no such thing as purely "literal" language. The Greek words *allegoria* and *metapherein* both mean to "speak of something as another," or to see something *as*, but as we will learn later, there are slight differences between allegorical speech and metaphorical speech.[154] Astoundingly then, all language is intrinsically and inescapably allegorical/metaphorical. Allegories may or may not contain metaphorical language, but they will always contain allegorical language. This means that all discursive language (*logos*) relies on allegorical/metaphorical language (*mythos*), for there is no such thing as purely literal language. Yet there is a difference between allegorical *composition* and allegorical *interpretation*. Whereas the former is in the hands of the author, the latter is in the hands of the audience. The challenge with any type of allegory is discovering to what extent the author "intends us to trace allegorical correspondence."[155] Importantly, allegorical interpretation ought to be understood "as a result of Platonism with its distinction between the transcendental world of ideas and the earthly reality of shades."[156] In fact, it may be that Tolkien disliked the "conscious and intentional" allegory precisely because it is antithetical to Jesus's art of the parable. Lewis seems to agree with Kreglinger, for he wrote of allegory as a "composition (whether pictorial or literary) in which immaterial realities are represented by feigned physical objects e.g. a pictured Cupid allegorically represents erotic love." Allegories separate while parables bring together.[157] Might it be possible that there is a spectrum of allegories? As we explore Tolkien's correspondence, it will become abundantly clear that Tolkien was aware of a spectrum of allegories.

To some degree, allegory is inevitable both in composition and in interpretation. With regards to composition, one key issue is how well allegory is woven into a narrative. Another is the worldview of the author writing the story, for it is the author's philosophical views which will determine, in part, how allegorical the story will be. How so? Although Platonism and Christianity have much in common, two areas where they differ greatly is in metaphysics and eschatology. According to J. Richard Middleton, "central to the way the New Testament conceives of the final destiny of the world is Jesus's proclamation in Matthew 19:28 of a 'regeneration' that is coming."[158] Despite its ubiquitousness in popular Christianity today, a disembodied heaven is not our final destiny. According to biblical cosmology, "heaven" refers to the transcendent aspect of reality. Moreover, the Bible consistently speaks of heaven and earth coming together one day in the future of human history. Our ultimate destiny is to live in a *new heaven and a new earth*, rather than our souls "going to heaven" when we die.[159] As it is with eschatology, so it is with metaphysics. Orthodox, historical Christianity affirms a holistic metaphysical view of reality and history and does not view heaven as completely independent of the physical universe. It was Plato and his successors who taught—in the *Phaedo* and *Timaeus* especially—that after we die, we will go to a disembodied, separate reality.[160] If an author tells a story from the Platonic rather than Judeo-Christian point of view, the narrative becomes "an earthly story with heavenly meanings" rather than a holistic, comprehensive story that sees heaven and earth overlapping and interlocking—and one day, coming completely together.[161] In the former type of allegory, allegory is on the surface of the narrative; it is explicit and usually quite apparent. In the latter type of allegory, it is latent, implicit, and generally more difficult to detect. This is just one example of how an author's worldview might influence the composition of a very allegorical story.

Regardless of which type of allegory one has in front of them, one thing is certain: neither allegorical composition nor allegorical interpretation can be completely avoided. As Lewis once wrote of the Christian tradition, while we are free to try and "restate our belief in a form free from metaphor and symbol . . . the reason we don't is that we can't."[162] As we said at the beginning of the chapter, allegory is woven into our very speech. The question for an author is not "Can I avoid allegory?" but "Can I avoid writing the kind of allegory that is translucent, explicit, and direct?" The question for the audience is how to interpret a story—for no story is self-interpreting—without turning it into the a type of story the author did not write. The reader's interpretation of the story is also worldview-dependent. In the Foreword to the second edition of *The Lord of the Rings* Tolkien stated, "I cordially dislike allegory in all of its manifestations."[163] But Tolkien could not have meant he disliked *all* forms of allegory for two reasons. First, he explicitly identifies *The Lord of the Rings* as an allegory, and second, he expressed his dislike for only *one particular* kind of allegory. Tolkien only disliked one type of allegory, which he referred to as "the conscious and intentional Allegory."[164] This kind of allegory is the "this-equals-that" story that Lewis referred to above. In a "conscious and intentional" allegory, "the whole story and also each of its component parts 'speak' of something 'other' . . . and must be decoded."[165] This kind of allegory has a "correct answer" without which it loses its meaning. In this kind of allegory, the story is ultimately irrelevant; it is mere artifice. According to Murray, the function of this kind of allegory "is powered not so much by the symbolic potency latent in things or in human life as by a plan or message which the author conceals under artificially constructed symbols, with clues to lead the reader to discover what is the intended solution in the actual world."[166] This does not mean, of course, that other kinds of allegories do not have what Tolkien called "applicability"— because they do—it just means that *this* kind of allegory "spoils the joy of working it out for oneself."[167]

Some allegories are more "translucent" than others to the reality they are speaking about.[168] A great example of this kind of allegory would be the "conscious and intentional" allegory which Tolkien disliked. The degree of an allegory's transparency, however, is dependent upon the author's intentions, skills, and, perhaps most importantly of all, one's worldview. In other words, literature is a crucible for worldview. According to Peter Kreeft, "literature not only incarnates a philosophy; it also tests it by verifying it or falsifying it." This insight explains why readers think Middle-earth feels so real: Tolkien's story tests his Christian worldview, and it is not found to be lacking.[169] According to Murray, "the functioning of allegory is powered . . . by a plan or message which the author conceals under artificially constructed symbols."[170] If the author has such a plan thought out in advance of writing the story, then it will not be difficult to discover it. For example, Tolkien believed that the Arthurian legend's fatal error was that it "explicitly contains the Christian religion."[171]

Another example of a story which "explicitly contains the Christian religion" might be Lewis's *The Lion, The Witch, and The Wardrobe* (1950) wherein the Pevensie children are referred to as the "Sons and Daughters of Eve." This author does not think that Lewis was always this explicitly allegorical, but it does illustrate the point we wish to make here. Indeed, Tolkien also strongly objected to the presence of Father Christmas in Lewis's first book, and it is no secret that Tolkien disliked the Narnia books.[172] Lastly, according to Ralph C. Wood, "unlike his friend C. S. Lewis, Tolkien refused to set forth any overt defense of the Gospel," since he felt it would be a violation—as we will see shortly—of the art of the parable.[173] Moreover, for Tolkien, "Lewis's work constitutes a restatement of Christian themes in allegorical form, reinforcing what believers already affirm. Tolkien sought, by contrast, to recast the entirety of human history by way of a massive mythological construction . . . thereby deepening and expanding our experience of the Christian metanarrative."[174] Tolkien wanted to show us that Christianity is much more than what we think it is. How could he have done that by showing us that it is exactly what we think it is via conscious allegory? We learned earlier in the Introduction that one of the ways Tolkien expands our understanding of the Christian worldview is by showing us—through *The Lord of the Rings*—that non-Christian worldviews and myths contain truth as well.

While Tolkien arguably may have succeeded more than Lewis in incarnating the Christian worldview within Middle-earth, it seems that we simply cannot avoid all allegorical language. The Christian worldview may be woven into the unique and complex history of Middle-earth such that we can hardly detect its subterranean presence, but parallels and resemblances to the story of Israel abound. The resemblances, allusions, and parallels to the story of Israel almost always have to do with the *plot structure* of the biblical narrative rather than with *specific content*. Another way to say this is to say that if we view the history of Middle-earth and the history of Israel as *stories*—myths, metanarratives—then we will notice that both histories have the same following themes, albeit in different manifestations: creation, downfall, redemption, and final restoration. By sharing the same mythology/metanarrative—that is, "narrated worldview"—these stories strongly resemble each other. Interestingly, a case can be made that every worldview has a mythology that follows this same four-part structure, which can just as easily be secularized into the following themes: Beginning (creation), conflict (fall), conflict resolution (redemption), and ending (restoration).[175] That being said, the story of the history of Middle-earth and the story of Israel are emphatically *not* the same story and often do not parallel each other explicitly, though as we will see, there are more than a few moments where they come very close.

How did Tolkien seemingly write and not write a Christian novel? First, he understood how to subsume the Christian worldview and mythology into Middle-earth without compromising his imaginative vision of reality.[176] Although Tolkien didn't feel obligated to make his story "fit" with the Christian worldview, he "actually intended it to be consonant with Christian thought and belief."[177] Second, and perhaps most importantly, Tolkien seemed to be strongly influenced by Jesus and the art of the parable. Like the Bible and Jesus's parables, *The Lord of the Rings* is "primarily literature, not philosophy . . . concrete, not abstract; narrative, not explanation."[178] If *The Lord of the Rings* is a parable, how are parables and allegories—especially the "conscious and intentional" type—related, if at all?

In a letter to Joanna de Bortadano in 1956 Tolkien wrote, "Of course my story is not an allegory of Atomic power, but of *Power* (exerted for Domination)."[179] After reading so many books about whether or not Tolkien's books (any or all of them) are allegories, it was a huge relief to discover that Tolkien himself said this. One gets the sense in many of his other letters that he hints at this but does not wish to explicitly say it since most people's understanding of allegory is of the conscious type Tolkien disliked. For good reason, it seems Tolkien feared identifying *The Lord of the Rings* as an allegory since doing so would imply certain things about his story to certain people. But this author is convinced that it was *reductionism* that Tolkien feared more than allegory. He did not want his imaginative world to be reduced to a mere sermon or parable. Tolkien resisted, it seems, identifying *The Lord of the Rings* as a parable for this same reason. Since most people—incorrectly—assume parables are just earthly stories with heavenly meanings or moral tales or—worse—mere proof narratives for the divinity of Jesus, had Tolkien called his book a parable, people would have drawn the wrong conclusion. In his book *A Hobbit's Journey*, Matthew Dickerson writes that "Tolkien doesn't argue that one should not suggest meanings in his work but rather that the *particular* meanings suggested by *certain* readers were the *wrong* meanings."[180] From this we can see that Tolkien was chiefly concerned with his readers coming to the right conclusions about the meaning of his story more than anything else. This book was written with the hope of helping people come to the right conclusion about Tolkien, allegory, parable, Christianity, and Middle-earth. If we take the time to properly understand these things, we will avoid coming to fallacious conclusions and walk away with an even greater appreciation of Tolkien's mythology.

So, in review: Yes, *The Lord of the Rings* is an allegory, but no, it is not the "conscious and intentional" type. In the same letter where he expresses his dislike for conscious allegory, Tolkien contrasts this type of allegory with his passion for "myth (not allegory!) and for fairy-story."[181] Since Tolkien referred to *The Lord of the Rings* as both a fairy story and as an allegory in his letters, we can conclude that fairy story is a type of allegory.[182] While we could stop there, we shouldn't, because there is evidence to suggest that Tolkien understood fairy stories as being quite similar to Christ's *parables*. That the title of Robert Murray's sermon at the Tolkien Centenary in 1992 is "Tolkien and the Art of the Parable" speaks volumes. Catholic scholar Joseph Pearce, who has written many great books about Tolkien, seems to have also sensed a connection between allegories, fairy stories, and parables. Murray believes that Tolkien sensed a connection between fairy story and parable because Tolkien may have been "self-conscious" of the "unbaptized roots of Faërie." As we will see, there's significant evidence in Tolkien's essay "On Fairy Stories" to suggest that he understood fairy stories and parables as two ways of saying the same thing. Furthermore, Murray argues that allegory is one "species within the genus parable."[183] Pearce, on the other hand, sees fairy story and parable as two species of the genus allegory, but does not make the connection—as Murray does—between fairy story and parable. Since we know that *mashalim* can technically include allegories *and* parables, it really comes down to choosing a "genus" of either parables *or* allegories with the excluded narrative becoming one species of the chosen genus. In this book, instead of arguing that fairy story and parable are two separate types of allegory, we will, like Murray, see them as one. Lastly, we will see Tolkien's fairy story/parable as a type of allegory which *The Lord of the Rings* is as distinct from the "conscious and intentional" allegory which he disliked (and which *The Lord of the Rings* is not).

Based on his own letters and writings, it seems that Tolkien operated from the assumption of a genus of allegories, with the fairy story/parable being preferred over and against the "conscious and intentional" allegory which he disliked. I have thus far tried to show in this book that getting around the issue of allegory is not only impossible but also unnecessary. We do not need to save either Jesus or Tolkien from allegory in general, but from a specific type of allegory. One could even conclude—as Klyne Snodgrass and other scholars have done—that allegory is not even a type of story but an "interpretive practice" (allegoresis) of turning into allegory what was "*not* intended to be allegory."[184] There a problem with this view, too, however. According to Tolkien, "any attempt to explain the purport of myth or fairytale must use allegorical language."[185] If allegoresis is also impossible to avoid, then what can one do? To resolve this paradox, Snodgrass advises that we inhabit the story-world of the parable and focus on the narrative. It is only by focusing on the story that we can eventually discern what the author may be trying to communicate. Finally, we must exercise caution about coming to certain conclusions, as Dickerson pointed out above. Thankfully, we are very lucky to have enough comments from Tolkien about the meaning of his mythology that our interpretive task is not overly difficult. Ultimately, Snodgrass argues—as we are in this book—that it is impossible to separate parables and allegories into two distinct literary forms, for according to him, though "the claim is made that allegory says something other than what it means by placing pictures in front of reality . . . *parable does the same thing*. Both are framed on the reality they seek to portray."[186]

It seems wise to follow Tolkien's lead in settling on a classification of allegories, though even if we assumed Murray's genus of parables instead, the result would practically be the same. For example, according to Murray, "allegory is woven into the fabric of the parable, but with a delicacy which does not spoil the joy of working it out for oneself."[187] What does Murray mean here? First, totally removing allegorical elements from a work is quite nearly impossible, though Murray says clearly here that allegory can be woven delicately into a narrative. Second, Murray is saying that the allegorical elements are hidden so well within Tolkien's narrative that one can hardly detect its presence. What exactly does that mean? According to Kreglinger, "allegory avoids confusion and opposition," and the allegorical elements of a story are "clear, direct, and without tension."[188] By contrast, metaphor "works on the basis of an unconventional usage of words" and is "opaque and complex."[189] It is important to maintain the distinction between allegory as a genre and a mode. As a genre, allegory is consciously planned by the author who is so eager to make their points that the story has no real heart. This is quite obviously the type of allegory Tolkien disliked and did not write. Allegory as a mode is when allegorical elements are part of a story, but do not comprise the narrative. In a well-told story, an author will masterfully alternate between metaphorical and allegorical modes, between opaque and complex speech on the one hand, and transparent, direct, and simplistic speech on the other. Jesus's parables do exactly that; they alternate between revealing and concealing his identity.[190] According to Murray, that is also exactly what Tolkien has done in his stories.

For the purposes of this book, a "genus" or even "spectrum" of allegories with the explicitly allegorical allegory lie on one end and the fairy story/parable on the other. Jesus's and Tolkien's parables/fairy stories contain a mixture of allegorical and metaphorical elements, but they are not consciously planned allegories. Since they do contain some allegorical elements, there will be some overlap between the consciously planned, strict allegory, on the one hand, and the fairy story/parable on the other.

Based on his correspondence, it seems Tolkien would agree, for in a letter to his publisher Sir Stanley Unwin, Tolkien wrote, "Of course, Allegory and Story converge, meeting somewhere in Truth."[191] Since we know that Tolkien referred to *The Lord of the Rings* as an allegory and a fairy story, we know that in referring to "Allegory" in this letter, he is referring to the conscious allegory which he disliked, not necessarily allegory as a mode. The reference to "Story" here is to fairy story. So, while the fairy story/parable is technically a type of allegory, it is on the opposite end from the strict and conscious allegory.

Keeping in mind that Snodgrass is working from a classification of parables instead of allegories, he concludes that "parables have varying levels of opacity; i.e. the ease with which one sees their lens-like character varies from parable to parable. Some are diaphanous and the hearer/reader knows easily a given story is a lens. . . . Other parables are surreptitious."[192] This book proposes that the conscious allegory is more transparent to its reality, like a window, than the fairy/story parable whose narrative is "thick, like a painting" and is to be looked *at* rather than *through*.[193] In conclusion, Murray reminds us that Tolkien recognized that even "in the greatest stories and allegorical narratives, the qualities of both modes of sub-creation"—conscious allegory and fairy story/parable—"may overlap and mingle," though "the two start out from opposite ends."[194] The difference is not quite as difficult to spot as one might initially think. A sort of "key" exists which can help us identify whether we are reading one or the other type of allegory. In his review of *The Lord of the Rings* Lewis wrote, "What shows we are reading myth, not allegory, is that there are no pointers to a specifically theological, or political, or psychological application. A myth points, for each reader, to the realm he lives in most. It is a master key; use it on what door you like."[195]

Lewis makes a profound point here: A truly great myth should have universal applicability (it can unlock all doors). Such a myth reminds "you of something you can't quite place," because it contains the "whole quality of life as we actually experience it."[196] According to Kreeft, that is also another reason why *The Lord of the Rings* is not a (conscious) allegory. It is not a conscious allegory because "I don't find myself saying, of anything in it, 'That reminds me of this or that,' but I constantly find myself saying, of this or that, 'That reminds me of something in *The Lord of the Rings*.'"[197] This myth does not remind us of something specifically topical or particular; instead, things in reality remind us of something in this story. The myth—or "narrated worldview"—which is incarnate in *The Lord of the Rings* is not just a story about something, but the story of everything.

In his essay "On Fairy Stories," Tolkien wrote the "Gospels contain a fairy story or a story of a larger kind which embraces all the essence of fairy-stories."[198] Here Tolkien is implying that the Christian fairy story—or myth—is the totally true story of reality as it gathers up all the fragments of truth found in all other stories of reality. One can also look at Tolkien's poem "Mythopoeia"—which he wrote after the Addison's Walk discussion with Lewis in 1931—for further evidence of this insight. Toward the end of this poem, after establishing the dignity and nobility of the vocation of man as "sub-creator," Tolkien says that myth-makers "loyally bring / to mint in image blurred of distant king, / or in fantastic banners weave the sheen / heraldic emblems of a lord unseen."[199] This is a very important insight, for Tolkien is giving us a poetic rendition of the *mythos spermatikos* argument we discussed earlier. The idea that humans can bring to "mint in image blurred" or "weave the sheen heraldic emblems of a lord unseen" implies that even though one may not have direct revelation of Jesus Christ, the very fact that we have a narrative impulse and that our narratives take on a certain plot shape suggests that we do know the "lord unseen."

In conclusion, the realm each of us lives in most refers to the worldview and mythology (metanarrative) each of us lives in every day. Lewis is saying that a good myth is inclusive and can be enjoyed by everyone because it contains something for everyone. When Lewis says that this kind of myth contains the "whole quality of life as we actually experience it" and that it reminds us of "something you can't quite place," he means that it is a story about *all of reality*, not just a part of it. It is a story that anyone can feel a part of. The conclusion should be clear: by "myth" Tolkien and Lewis were referring to the Christian myth. Only the Christian myth has the power to reach into other contexts where it is not explicitly known and build a bridge to the "realm" which that person lives most in. [200]

Parables seem designed to conceal in order to reveal. That is why Jesus placed great emphasis on *hearing*: "Pay attention to what you hear; the measure you give will be the measure you get, and still more will be given to you. For to those who have, more will be given; and from those who have nothing, even what they have will be taken away."[201] What are we supposed to be hearing that we have not been hearing? That God, not just a descendant of King David, has become king on earth as in heaven. What Jesus seems to be saying is that *this* truth—the incarnation—has been present in Scripture all along and that people were not seeing it. It is clear that this is what Jesus meant, for in John 5:39 he said, "You study the Scriptures diligently because you think that in them you have eternal life. These are the very Scriptures that testify about me."[202]

FAIRY STORIES ARE PARABLES

In this section, I want to present evidence for the resemblance between Tolkien's fairy story and New Testament parables. Does it really matter what type of story *The Lord of the Rings* is? To Tolkien it does, for he said that according to his own "scale of significance" his Catholic faith was the most important influence on the writing of the book.[203] As we already know, he also said that he "deliberately" wrote a story "out of certain religious ideas" and that *The Lord of the Rings* is a "fundamentally" Catholic and religious work. What kind of story is a Christian story? Parables, but as we have hopefully learned by now, these are not the tidy "earthly stories with heavenly meaning" narratives many have believed them to be. Christians worship and love a God whom they believe is the greatest storyteller. The God who revealed himself in Jesus Christ is the source of all the myths man has told throughout the centuries. He is the author of the story of reality and he loves people and the world so much that he wrote himself into it. He did this to once again recruit us in helping bring heaven and earth together as he originally intended in the beginning. To communicate this powerful and incredible truth, Jesus came speaking in parables because he knew that humans, respond best to story.

As a Christian, Tolkien believed that whenever we tell stories, we are reflecting the nature of God. There is one letter in which Tolkien seems to make an explicit connection between fairy story and parable. In the letter, Tolkien expresses that he wrote *The Lord of the Rings* for "the elucidation of truth, and the encouragement of good morals in the real world, *by the ancient device of exemplifying them in unfamiliar embodiments*, that may tend to 'bring them home.'"[204] The description here of the "ancient device" resonates with the biblical scholar's understanding of a New Testament parable, for according to McFague, "parables are stories . . . that set the familiar in an unfamiliar context."[205] It would be quite difficult to deny the similarity of description between these two passages. Be that as it may, Tolkien preferred to speak of *The Lord of the Rings* as a fairy story, and since we have already presented evidence that fairy stories are parables, it is time to look a little more closely at what a fairy story is. After we have done that, we will examine the similarities and differences between the fairy story and parable on the one hand, and conscious allegory on the other.

Tolkien once admitted that it was impossible to avoid incarnating something of an author's own worldview in one's work.[206] Immediately after saying this, he says that this is *not* the same as allegory. He says all this to explain how fairy story has a very unique and powerful way of reflecting and communicating truth that is quite distinct from other types of allegory. But the most revealing comment in this entire letter is this one: "There is no 'embodiment' of the Creator anywhere in this story or mythology."[207] Above, we learned that parables are "linguistic incarnations," or incarnational myths. But here it sounds like Tolkien is flatly telling us that there is absolutely no incarnation in Middle-earth. To resolve this problem, I suggest we look to Jesus's parables, for that is *how* he communicated the reality of the incarnation. Parables play a central role in signaling that God has become human: the parable *is* the message. If we now apply this insight to Tolkien's comment that there is no "embodiment" of God anywhere in his story, we should now have a new understanding of what he meant. The same could be said of Jesus's parables: there is no "embodiment" of God anywhere in the stories. The issue many Tolkien scholars have overlooked is *how* the incarnation is communicated. I believe this oversight is directly related to another: overlooking the parables. According to Holly Ordway, "the Incarnation has implications both for *what* we say in our apologetics and *how* we say it."[208]

In her recent book *Short Stories by Jesus*, Jewish New Testament scholar Amy-Jill Levine explains that "down through the centuries, starting with the Gospel writers themselves, the parables have been allegorized, moralized, Christologized, and otherwise tamed into either platitudes such as 'God loves us' or 'Be nice' or, worse, assurance that all is right with the world as long as we believe in Jesus."[209] In short, the parables of Jesus have been tamed and domesticated. Audiences have turned the parables of Jesus into stories that are about God becoming human, but that misses the point. These brilliant—and sometimes extremely short—stories have had all the mystery sucked out of them. Levine explains that "mystery is here not indicative of something arcane or in need of a special key to unlock a singular meaning. What makes the parables mysterious, or difficult, is that they challenge us to investigate the hidden aspects of our own values, our own lives. They bring to the surface unasked questions, and they reveal answers we have always known, but refuse to acknowledge."[210] Perhaps the biggest mystery we overlook is the very form of the parable itself. Sadly, *The Lord of the Rings*, which Tolkien called a "fundamentally religious and Catholic work," has suffered the same fate.[211]

This is because we have not only failed to understand how parables—and fairy stories—work, but also because we have misunderstood what Christianity is. Joseph Pearce is correct in pointing out that "those who are blind to theology will continue to be blind to that which is most beautiful in *The Lord of the Rings*."[212] In the letter quoted above, though initial appearances may be against us, Tolkien is *not* denying the presence of the incarnation in Middle-earth. Instead, he is denying the presence of an *allegorical representation* of the incarnation in Middle-earth. Of course, there is no explicit embodiment of Jesus Christ in *The Lord of the Rings*; that would betray a misunderstanding of *how* the incarnation is best communicated. Parables are a kind of indirect communication, "attempting to bring about new insight by framing the ordinary in an extraordinary context."[213] Although it's not entirely clear that Lewis had Jesus's parables in mind when he said this, his description of *The Chronicles of Narnia* books as "supposals" is quite helpful here: "If Aslan represented the immaterial Deity in the same way in which Giant Despair represents Despair, he would be an allegorical figure. In reality however he is an invention giving an imaginary answer to the question, 'What might Christ become like if there really were a world like Narnia and He chose to be incarnate and die and rise again in *that* world as He actually has done in ours?'"[214] Parables—like "supposals"—invite the audience to *suppose* what reality would be like if God really did become human. They invite us to consider what the implications of living in a reality where that is the truth would be like.

That all being said, it does need to be pointed out that there is no one single Christ figure in Middle-earth as there is with Aslan in Narnia. Tolkien followed the author of *Beowulf* in this regard by dividing up the offices of Christ—prophet, king, high priest—between different characters in the story. With that disclaimer aside, what Lewis is saying is that "supposals" and parables show us our reality from a different point of view. Like Jesus's own parables, Lewis and Tolkien's stories are trying to steal up on our rational objections to the Christian worldview and show us that it is not quite so unbelievable. It is quite common for someone to harden their heart and mind when they hear the same story being told again and again in the same way. That is why Tolkien said that fairy stories, when told properly, have the power to help us regain a true vision of reality. In a way, it is as if we need a parable to help us hear the parables of Jesus anew. My experience is that few people truly experience the parables as the mythical, transformative narratives that they are because we think we already know what they are about.

So, what are the features of fairy stories/parables that set them apart from "conscious and intentional" allegories? What makes them such compelling narratives? For starters, they are suggestive, not explicit, about their meaning (we will explore exactly *how* this works later). We maintain that while it is impossible to avoid allegorical language completely, it is possible to use it judiciously. The kings, servants, shepherds, fathers, widows, judges, and others who inhabit Jesus's parables are types that are *suggestive* of Jesus and the gospel. I argue that since many of these types also inhabit Middle-earth, that is why many scholars and readers of *The Lord of the Rings* have felt the presence of Christ and the gospel there. The presence of Jesus and the gospel is below the surface of the narrative, appealing to the subconscious, which is why it is so effective. Bradley J. Birzer has argued that "Tolkien made it quite clear in his letters that the king was Iluvatar's representative on Earth. If Manwe was Iluvatar's regent of the whole earth, Aragorn was Iluvatar's regent of Middle-earth, the steward of men, hobbits, Dwarves, and Elves."[215] It seems that Tolkien understood that the image of a king is one of the most powerful and effective types that points to Jesus, the great Archetype. There is nothing explicitly Christian about the image of a king, and yet for those familiar with the Bible, it is impossible not to be reminded of David and Jesus, among others. By using biblical types, Tolkien was able to hint toward Jesus and the gospels without being heavy-handed. Indeed, Lewis may have had Tolkien in mind when he wrote, "Work whose Christianity is latent may do quite as much good and may reach some whom the more obvious religious work would scare away."[216] Another feature that makes Jesus's parables and Tolkien's novel so unique and effective is their juxtaposition of the familiar alongside the unfamiliar. As a "parabolic novel," *The Lord of the Rings*, presents "a way of believing and living that initially seems ordinary, yet is so dislocated and rent from its usual context that, if the parable 'works,' the spectators becomes participants, not because they want to necessarily or simply have 'gotten the point' but because they have, for the moment 'lost control.'"[217] In Jesus's parables, for example, the story of Israel is not told in the conventional way but reconfigured around a new incarnational symbol—Jesus himself rather than Torah and temple alone. This new context for understanding the incarnation—an idea all Jews already grasped—was mysterious, unexpected, and challenging. Similarly, as we will learn, the prophecies contained in *The Silmarillion*, *The Hobbit*, and writings such as "The Debate of Finrod and Andreth" are fulfilled in a way that did not meet most people's expectations in Middle-earth. God's plan to reveal himself in human form had to be kept down to mere hints throughout history, because if he had disclosed his plan, "they would not have crucified the Lord of glory."[218]

We need to attend especially to this second feature of fairy stories/parables, because it will continue to be important throughout our analysis. Parables, as I hinted above, present familiar material in unfamiliar contexts, and simultaneosuly conceal and reveal their message.[219] It seems that this is something Tolkien understood, for he wrote, "Faërie cannot be caught in a net of words; for it is one of its qualities to be indescribable, though not imperceptible."[220] An effective fairy story/parable should not communicate truth explicitly. In his famous essay "Beowulf: The Monster and the Critics," Tolkien wrote of storytelling that "it is at its best when it is presented by a poet who feels rather than makes explicit what his theme portends; who presents it as incarnate in the world of history and geography."[221]

Nevertheless, there should be occasional glimpses in the story of the picture of reality which frames the narrative. Peter Kreeft has argued that this is yet another reason *The Lord of the Rings* isn't the kind of allegory Tolkien disliked: "If *The Lord of the Rings* were an allegory, the philosophy would be on the surface, like rocks. Instead, it is more like the molten core of the earth: central but hidden."[222]

Yet another remarkable characteristic of fairy stories and parables is what Tolkien called the "inner consistency of reality."[223] Recall that in the Introduction we argued that *The Lord of the Rings* feels real precisely because of the presence of the Christian myth in the story. Tolkien sincerely believed that God, not himself, was the true author of the story, and since God, who is the Author of the story of reality, is telling the story, that is why it feels real.[224] I have also been gradually making the case that fairy stories are analogous to New Testament parables. The first person to notice this correlation was Father Robert Murray, a friend of Tolkien's who also reviewed some portions of *The Lord of the Rings*. In 1992, Murray gave a sermon at the Tolkien Centenary entitled "Tolkien and the Art of the Parable" where he said that one of the most convincing pieces of evidence that connects fairy story with parable is Tolkien's concept of *eucatastrophe*. "Many of the parables represent persons coming to a moment of decision, the outcome of which has all-important consequences," wrote Murray. "Undoubtedly Jesus intended, by picturing vivid examples, to confront people with a challenge to realize the reality of God in a new way, and to change their values and way of life."[225] Tolkien defined eucatasrophe as a "sudden joyous 'turn'" in the narrative, a "miraculous grace."[226] Eucatastrophe "denies (in the face of much evidence, if you will) universal final defeat and in so far is evangelium, giving a fleeting glimpse of Joy, Joy beyond the walls of the world, poignant as grief."[227] The word "eucatastrophe" is a compound Greek word which literally means "good down-turn."[228] It refers to the ability that only God has to bring good out of evil. According to Pearce, "Gandalf's resurrection, like the resurrection of Christ, is indeed a sudden and miraculous grace, offering a tantalizing glimpse of the joy of the good news (*evangelium*) beyond the walls of the world."[229] For Tolkien, eucatastrophe was the heart of the fairy story and its central function and gave the reader a glimpse of the gospel. In summary, perhaps the most persuasive evidence for the resemblance between fairy story and parable is the presence of eucatastrophe in both art forms.

Tolkien concludes his essay "On Fairy Stories" with this powerful declaration: "The Gospels contain a fairy story, or a story of a larger kind which embraces all the essence of fairy-stories."[230] I believe the "story of a larger kind" that Tolkien was referring to was a person: Jesus Christ, God's parable.

God's parable came speaking in parables because there is no other way of saying what needed to be said: "sometimes fairy stories may say best what's to be said."[231] If we wish to truly understand the Christian worldview—and Tolkien's novel—then we need to keep our focus on the story itself. The story must always be our priority, not abstracting meaning from the story, though this is easier said than done. At the beginning of the Introduction, we learned that Tolkien taught Lewis the importance of embracing the mythic heart of Christianity, and that this insight was the decisive factor in Lewis's conversion. In his essay "Myth Became Fact," Lewis reminds us of the importance of this: "To be truly Christian we must both assent to the historical fact and also receive the myth (fact though it has become) with the same imaginative embrace which we accord to all myths. The one is hardly more necessary than the other."[232] Though Lewis was describing the incarnation here, he also—whether he knew it or not—gave us a perfect definition of parable as well. Elsewhere, in *Reflections on the Psalms*, it seems that Lewis is aware of the connection between the incarnation and parables, for he wrote, "Poetry too is a little incarnation, giving body to what had been before invisible and inaudible."[233] Both Jesus's and Tolkien's parables point to the reality of the incarnation by being incarnational stories. Through them, we are meant to find "some glimpse of that theme which we believe to be the very plot of the whole cosmic story—the theme of incarnation, death, and rebirth."[234] Over the course of the rest of the book, we will constantly return to this connection between fairy story and parable on the one hand and the incarnation on the other because it shows us how important both storytelling and the imagination are to God and our walk with him.

This leads us to the final characteristic of the fairy story/parable, which is its function as *praeparatio evangelica*, Latin for "preparation for the gospel." Tolkien scholar Matthew Dickerson says his main reason for concluding that *The Lord of the Rings*—and indeed Tolkien's entire mythology—is not a fully Christian story is because of the absence of a real incarnation in Middle-earth. According to him, "there would be no real way to present the actual Incarnation in Middle-earth without it becoming allegory."[235] As we have learned, in one sense, this is true, since no writer can totally avoid allegory. Dickerson's conclusion is that while Tolkien's mythology is "certainly not un-Christian nor in any way pagan, neither is it fully Christian; rather, it is a Christian understanding of a pre-Christian time."[236] There is a much better way to say what Dickerson is trying to say, however. Instead of concluding that Tolkien's mythology is ambiguously Christian, or that it is "a Christian understanding of a pre-Christian time," we should conclude that it is a *parable*. Now, Dickerson would be right if Tolkien's goal was to write a crude allegory, but we know this was not the case. Jesus's own parables can—and should—be understood as a sacramental preparation of the gospel, which is that God has become king and inaugurated his heavenly kingdom here on earth. This is not a piece of news that is easily or quickly processed, and it is too much for any human to bear because the incarnation is the most real thing that ever existed. Now, if Tolkien used Jesus's parables as his guide as we have been arguing, then it is entirely possible that the incarnation, which itself can only be understood as a parable to our finite minds, could be communicated without turning it into the kind of allegory Tolkien disliked. The only way to accomplish this while avoiding the type of allegory Tolkien disliked would be to imitate Jesus's art of the parable, which I submit he did. According to Philip Ryken, "we should expect to find Christ present in many places" in Middle-earth, though not in the "conscious and intentional" allegorical sense.[237] Ryken also adds that Tolkien did not consciously choose to put Christ into his mythology, which squares with what Tolkien himself said.[238] Again, this does not mean that Jesus is not present in Middle-earth, it draws attention to *how* he is present in Middle-earth: parabolically. What neither Ryken nor Dickerson point out, however, is that Tolkien wrote in this way because this was consistent with the way Jesus told his parables. Jesus did not come trumpeting his incarnate identity; he came speaking in parables. The reason for this is because this was the "only legitimate way of speaking of the incursion of the divine into history."[239] As a Christian, Tolkien ultimately wanted his story to point his readers to Jesus, the great Archetype. To do this most effectively, he wisely imitated Jesus's art of the parable. Had Tolkien written more explicitly and allegorically as a Christian, Tolkien would have violated his witness.

Although *praeparatio evangelica* typically refers to pagan, pre-Christian myths, we should also consider the parables of Jesus since Jesus spoke in parables to prepare people's hearts and minds for the reality of the incarnation and for the final destiny of the blessed, who will live eternally in the presence of God in the kingdom of heaven. Like Jesus's parables, *The Lord of the Rings* simultaneously functions as a herald of the incarnation while also somehow being, or at least participating in, the incarnation. Many Christians believe that some of the parables function as predictions of the second coming, while in fact they are stories about the *first* coming.[240] According to Wright, "the parable(s) of the king/master giving his servants tasks and then returning to assess their performance" teach that Jesus "was coming to Jerusalem for the last time, so YHWH was at last doing what he had promised, returning to Zion to judge and to save."[241] The parables are not just stories about what *will* happen, they are stories about what *is* happening. The parables help us prepare for this reality by communicating it to us in a way that we can process.

Before moving on to the next topic, I want to ask again, does it really matter what type of story *The Lord of the Rings* is? I hope you can see why the answer must now be an emphatic *yes*. Today, Christians have an embarrassment of riches when it comes to apologetics that honor *logos* but not *mythos*, though there are a few.[242] Can a fantasy story like *The Lord of the Rings* really change how we understand Christianity and reality? Tolkien once wrote, "The Primary World, Reality, of elves and men is the same, if differently valued and perceived."[243] What is he saying? Fantasy literature assumes the realm of *mythos* exists as part of the "Primary World," whereas many modern people do not. Tolkien is saying that we need to be more like the elves, who perceive and value this neglected aspect of reality. Reality is truly *mythological*, and we are missing it. We are disenchanted, and we are poorer human beings because of it. Fantasy literature does not take us away from reality but re-mythologizes it. It is vital that we recover our mythic sight, for myth fills us with wonder and restores significance to the familiar. Myth also broadens our vision of reality, which we so desperately need today. Tolkien advised that "we need, in any case, to clean our windows; so that the things seen clearly may be freed from the drab blur of triteness or familiarity—from possessiveness."[244] How can we make these insights part of our lives? Jesus's answer was, "Truly I tell you, unless you change and become like little children, you will never enter the kingdom of heaven."[245] By this Jesus meant that *adults* must possess "humility and innocence . . . not necessarily . . . an uncritical wonder, nor indeed an uncritical tenderness."[246] Children naturally understand how to suspend disbelief; this does not make them naïve and uncritical, it makes them wise. They seem to sense that life is a big narrative and they are a part of it. They role-play and act out their favorite stories and so reality opens more for them than it does for adults. "As long as the story lingers in our mind, the real things are more themselves," wrote Lewis in his review of *The Lord of the Rings*.[247] It is time that we adults "put away childish things," most of all "the fear of childishness and the desire to be very grown up."[248]

THE "FATAL" FLAW

In 1951, Tolkien wrote a letter where he tried to persuade Milton Waldman to agree to publish both *The Silmarillion* and *The Lord of the Rings*. This letter contains illuminating information pertaining to Tolkien's views on myth, fairy story, allegory, and his books. This is the same letter where Tolkien wrote about his passion for myth and fairy story, but not the "conscious and intentional Allegory." A little further into the letter, Tolkien explains what he believed to be the "fatal" flaw one must avoid when writing a fairy story: the inclusion of "moral and religious truth" in "explicit" forms as they are known in the "real" world.[249] Tolkien follows this comment with what may appear to be an unimportant point: "(I am speaking, of course, of our present situation, not of ancient pagan, pre-Christian days.)"[250] Tolkien meant that on this side of the Cross, Christian storytellers who desire to be effective in the art of the parable should not include "moral and religious truth" in "explicit" forms as they are known to us in reality.

Most Tolkien scholars believe that the atmosphere of Middle-earth resembles pre-Christian times. This means that Middle-earth has more in common with fifth-century BC Athens or Confucian China. Some scholars lean heavily on this point to argue that *The Lord of the Rings* is not a Christian myth, or not a *fully* Christian myth, as we heard from Dickerson earlier. *The Lord of the Rings*, says Dickerson, presents us with a "Christian understanding of a pre-Christian time."[251] In saying this, Dickerson has put his finger on what a parable is and how it works on us but he neither identifies *The Lord of the Rings* as a parable nor explores the connection between fairy story and parable. On the Christian view of things, there is no such thing as a "pre-Christian" time. History is God's story and he is its Author. As Kreeft has argued, "there are Christ figures everywhere in literature and life. This should not surprise us. For Christ was not an emergency afterthought or a freak from outer space, but the central point of the whole human story from the beginning in the Mind of its Author."[252]

All myths converge in and are completed by the incarnation because our myth-making capabilities as "sub-creators" come from being made in God's image. As Lewis once wrote, the difference between the Christian myth and non-Christian myths is not the difference between truth and falsehood, but the "difference between a real event on the one hand and dim dreams or premonitions of that same event on the other."[253] So, what does it mean that Tolkien has given us a story with a "Christian understanding of a pre-Christian time"? Even though there is technically no such thing as a "pre-Christian" time, this phrase does not have to refer to historical time prior to the incarnation. Instead, I argue that this refers to the suggestive, allusive art of the parable.

Tolkien wrote in a way that was suggestive of Christ, using images and themes to allude to him without alerting the reader of his presence explicitly. Since there is technically no such thing as a "pre-Christian" time, the phrase "pre-Christian" could simply refer to any time in which Christ's presence is not made explicitly known. When Tolkien wrote "The Third Age was not a Christian world," perhaps he was not describing a literal historical period but describing the unfamiliar context Jesus usually employed in his parables.[254] The unfamiliar context helps achieve alienation between the audience and their immediate context so that the reality the storyteller is trying to show is discernible. Many authors have convincingly made the case that Middle-earth does resemble a literal pre-Christian time, but this argument is usually coupled with the argument that there is no incarnation in Middle-earth.

Earlier in the book we discussed Lewis's "Shepherd People" and their "Rules" and "the Pagans" and their "Pictures" from *The Pilgrim's Regress*. In Jesus, God chose to communicate in a way that would make use of both. Since the reality God was trying to communicate was unfamiliar to both the "Shepherd People" *and* "the Pagans," a "third thing" was required to reach them all: *a parable*. A parable is the convergence of "Rule" and "Picture" *mythos* and *logos*, and, ultimately, God and man. The incarnation in Middle earth consists in the delivery of the story as parable. According to Klyne Snodgrass, "while a few parables . . . may have christological references, *most are not directly about Jesus*."[255] It should be clear by now that Tolkien's reference to the "fatal" flaw of a story seems to have been ingrained in him via his familiarity with Jesus' art of the parable. Like Jesus's parables, Tolkien's parabolic novel is not directly about Jesus because this would prove fatal to the integrity of the story. Once again, if the story itself is our top priority, then we will be best placed to understand what the author is trying to say. According to McFague, that is why "any attempt to paraphrase a metaphor immediately reveals one of the primary characteristics of a good poetic metaphor: its inseparability from 'what is being said.'"[256] Parables simply cannot be stated non-parabolically.

Like Jesus, Tolkien wanted to show "moral and religious truth" through the "ancient device of exemplifying them in unfamiliar embodiments," which is to say through a parable.[257] He wanted to show that Christianity could make sense in any context, to show that it was the story that makes sense of all other stories just as Jesus did. As we will explore in the final section, Tolkien accomplished this primarily by including familiar images left in "unexplained symbolic forms."[258] By including images with unassigned meanings, the reader is given the challenge of finding meaning and applicability. Jesus spoke in parables so that "they may be ever seeing but never perceiving, and ever hearing but never understanding."[259] The parables of Jesus force us not only to make a decision about what the stories mean but also to discover who the author is. The parables ask, "Who do you say that I am?"[260] Parables are supposed to challenge us like this. According to Amy-Jill Levine, "when we seek universal morals from a genre that is designed to surprise, challenge, shake up, or indict, and look for a single meaning in a form that opens to multiple interpretations, we are necessarily limiting the parables and, so, ourselves."[261] It is the inclusion of "moral and religious truth" in explicit forms as they are known in the real world that is the "fatal" flaw which a "sub-creator" must avoid; this is the "art of the parable."

UNDERSTANDING AND INTERPRETING FAIRY STORIES/PARABLES

In a letter to a reader of *The Lord of the Rings* dated March 3, 1955, Tolkien wrote that "it remains an unfailing delight to me to find my own belief justified: that the 'fairy-story' is really an adult genre, and one for which a starving audience exists."[262] Jesus's dictum to "change and be like little children" clearly had a profound influence of Tolkien. But he also did not take that to mean that fairy stories were only for children, for that was not Jesus's point. Tolkien knew that a truly mythological way of looking at reality was essential for the redemption of our fallen human nature and salvation. According to Middleton, the Bible's definition of salvation is twofold: "It is God's *deliverance* of those in a situation of need from that which impedes their well-being, resulting in their *restoration* to wholeness." Moreover, salvation is a *comprehensive* reality which affects body *and* soul, not just our souls.[263] Salvation does not take us *out* of the world, but recreates us to be of service *for* the world. Tolkien believed that the modern myth imprisoned us in a world of empiricism and materialism and that fairy stories were the key to setting us free. Fairy stories are crucial to restoring our understanding of the holistic, comprehensive biblical vision of salvation. Fairy stories/parables do not encourage an escape *from* the world, but encourage an escape *to* the world as it really is.

Tolkien wrote that when modern skeptics use the word "escape in this way . . . [they] have chosen the wrong word, and, what is more, they are confusing, not always by sincere error, the Escape of the Prisoner with the Flight of the Deserter."[264] The modern mythmakers do not want us to escape the prison of materialism and rationalism because according to them, to think that anything is truly real beyond this physical reality (the prison) is an act of treason. According to the modern view, Christians are "Deserters" because they abandon such so-called rationality. While fairy stories provide us with an "escape" from this prison, they do not do so by whisking us away to another world. Instead of the world of four walls and a roof, myths show us that the world has no roof: : "The world outside has not become less real because the prisoner cannot see it."[265] *Mythos* is not only the world outside four walls, it is the only means we have of reliably knowing what's *within* four walls (*logos*). After all, how can we know that we live in a prison—or in a purely physical universe of space, time, matter, and natural laws—unless we are seeing from a perspective that is outside the universe? One can only know one lives in a purely physical universe if one has seen from a point of view that is *metaphysical*.

The question of meaning inevitably arises in our mind as we read any story. No story is self-interpreting, and we want to know more than just what the story means for the characters in their world—we also want to know if we can apply something we learned to our own lives. There is no such thing as pure entertainment; there is always a vision of reality behind the art form. The very moment we ask the question of meaning, however, Lewis explains that we recognize we are stuck on the horns of a "tragic dilemma" of which "myth is the partial solution": "Either to taste and not to know or to know and not to taste."[266] When we go looking for the meaning of a story, we are only knowing and not tasting. By contemplating the meaning of the story, we become cut off from the experience of being part of the world in the story. And yet as we have seen, we cannot avoid doing this. Yet Lewis says, "*It is only while receiving the myth as a story that you experience the principle concretely*."[267] If, on the other hand, we try to "know by experience," we become so "caught up in the real that we can't think about it clearly."[268] Starr summarizes, "When we take a meaning out of a myth, we turn it into an abstract statement, an idea. When we leave the meaning in the myth and not try to turn it into propositional language statements, the meaning remains."[269] This does not mean that we should not interpret, but it does mean that our interpretations will be secondary to the experience of the story itself. The meaning of a myth is not independent of its form: "The meaning is not in a separate realm, something that can be pointed to; the totality of all the processes of life and thought in the parable *is* its meaning."[270]

That is why Lewis said, "In the enjoyment of a great myth we come nearest to experiencing as a concrete what can otherwise be understood only as abstraction."[271] There are, in other words, some truths that can only be understood through story. A great myth-maker, or "sub-creator," recognizes this and puts all his effort into constructing a credible and realistic story-world. God, who is the author of reality, does this supremely through the incarnation, but with one exception: in the incarnation, "Legend and History have met and fused."[272] It is not only myth, but "a myth which is also a fact."[273] Jesus is God's parable. We speak in parables because God speaks in parables. Is there any way to resolve "our tragic dilemma"? As created beings endowed with the ability to think, "we are cut off from what we think about; as tasting, touching, willing, loving, hating, we do not clearly understand. The more lucidly we think, the more we are cut off: the more deeply we enter into reality, the less we can think."²⁷⁴ Although we sense that we used to be able to think abstractly and concretely simultaneously, we no longer can. The solution to this, Tolkien and Lewis are hinting at in their essays "On Fairy Stories" and "Myth Became Fact," *is the incarnation.* God alone can—and did—overcome the split between myth and fact. God's coming into the world was the beginning of the resolution of our "tragic dilemma."

McFague explains that the reason God can do this is because he alone lives in that unified, holistic reality of myth and fact. She argues that "biblical language . . . is not of the subjective-objective variety but speaks to us deeply, as does poetry, precisely because it overcomes the split, or better yet does not recognize it. It is metaphorical language, language which in this image and in that unites the concrete and the abstract, the sensuous and the mental, the particular and the general, the subjective and the objective."²⁷⁵ The incarnation is the historical moment that initiates our return from exile. When God became human in Jesus Christ, he began the process of resolving our "tragic dilemma" by bringing "the kingdom of heaven" to earth. By accepting Jesus, we are given a place in this "new creation" that God inaugurated in and through Jesus. The Bible tells us that in the beginning, God intended for Adam and Eve to work together with God as his human imagers to assist him in making all creation become sacred like the garden of Eden, which the Bible tells us was God's heavenly home on earth. Sadly, Adam and Eve failed in their task, and creation is not yet like Eden, but one day, it will be.²⁷⁶ In the incarnation, subject and object, abstract and concrete, *mythos* and *logos*, and heaven and earth have come together, as they were originally intended in the beginning. In short, the incarnation was the beginning of the end of the estrangement caused by God's non-human and human families. One way we can understand Jesus's advent is as God's decision to give humanity another chance of access to Eden—to creation as it should have been in the beginning. Although we are still fallen beings awaiting final redemption, followers of Jesus have this renewed access to heaven on earth *now*. In his review of *The Lord of the Rings*, Lewis, recognizing the presence of the Christian myth in *The Lord of the Rings*, said that "as long as the story lingers in our mind, the real things are more themselves." We all inhabit a story about reality, but Lewis is saying that *this* story restores and enhances our apprehension of reality because the Christian story is the story of reality itself. That is why Lewis spoke of being "nourished" by a "particular pattern of events."²⁷⁷ We all desire to live in a story that makes sense of how we experience reality and to be "nourished" by it.

How can we interpret fairy story and parable without spoiling the story? Reductionism is an imminent danger, but it is not inevitable. As we have seen, this is so easy task. First, I suggest that the "pattern of events"—the storyline itself—must be our number one priority. In the same breath, we must attend to the literary form itself. The literary form of *The Lord of the Rings* has been quite a contentious issue for years, and there are some who would say it does not matter, but this is irresponsible. Sadly, most people will pick up Tolkien's novel and read it for entertainment, not realizing how much went into creating the mythology, or the painstaking efforts Tolkien took to prevent writing a crude allegory. That is partly the reason why I have written this book: the literary form mattered to Tolkien, and so it should matter to readers. Another thing we can keep in mind when seeking to understand Tolkien's novel properly is that his main goal in writing *The Lord of the Rings* was "the elucidation of truth, and the encouragement of good morals in the real world, by the ancient device of exemplifying them in unfamiliar embodiments, that may tend to 'bring them home.'"[278] Tolkien's intentions apparently were not purely recreational, but educational. Another thing to keep in mind is that if we feel we have "decoded" Tolkien's story, then we have turned it into an allegory and misunderstood it. Like Jesus's parables, *The Lord of the Rings* is ultimately meant to be mysterious, like the reality the point to. About interpreting parables, Levine says, "If the interpretation does not raise for us more questions, if it does not open us up to more conversation, if it creates a neat and tidy picture, we need to go back and read it again."[279] If the fairy story/parable has not challenged us, we have missed one of the great joys of this literary form. In a crude and conscious allegory, "the relationship between vehicle and tenor of allegorical elements is clear, direct, and without tension. The task of the vehicle is to point to the tenor, the subject matter."[280] With the fairy story/parable, the literary form *is*, in a strange and puzzling way, the subject matter. In a fairy story/parable, there is tension because we cannot completely discern and trace the exact degree of correspondence the author intends between the story and the reality they seek to portray. If *The Lord of the Rings* or Jesus's parables are not challenging and puzzling us, then we are not understanding them.

    Tolkien knew that it was difficult to focus on the story alone, for "the more 'life' a story has the more readily will it be susceptible of allegorical interpretations: while the better a deliberate allegory is made the more nearly will it be acceptable just as a story."[281] Since *The Lord of the Rings* is an example of a story which has more "life," it is obviously a story which is more susceptible to "allegorical interpretations." One way we can help keep our focus on the story is to remember that Jesus's parables and *The Lord of the Rings* are "aesthetic objects."[282] These stories are works of art that have been carefully and lovingly crafted by their authors. We did not create them and so we must we resist any postmodern temptation to assume we have total interpretive control over the text; not all interpretations are valid. Tolkien was a master of metaphor, which should be understood "as speaking about one thing in terms that are seen to be *suggestive of* another."[283] In his letters, Tolkien wrote about keeping suggestions to the most important matters—by this he meant Christian theology—almost imperceptible. This is reminiscent of Jesus's comment in Matt 13:13, which itself alludes to Isa 42:19–20: "This is why I speak to them in parables: 'Though seeing, they do not see; though hearing, they do not hear or understand.'" Jesus deliberately spoke in a suggestive, ambiguous way so that people would *not* understand. Parables conceal so that they can reveal. Of course, we cannot ultimately avoid the question of meaning since "all literature incarnates a philosophy," but it is often the literature that tells us something important about the philosophy. Literature tests worldviews, which, according to Kreeft, can be expressed by this rule: "A philosophy that cannot be translated into a good story cannot be a good philosophy."[284]

It should be noted that Tolkien only became impatient and frustrated with *certain* interpretations of his story, not all. Like Jesus, Tolkien framed his story on the biblical pattern of events of creation, fall, redemption, and restoration. Tolkien actually became "annoyed" when people did not detect the allusions to Christianity or when people did not notice any religion in it.[285] Tolkien's comment about the "eludcidation of truth" via an "ancient device" from Letter 153 should also pique our curiosity. Taken together with all the evidence we have looked at, it seems that this is the closest Tolkien ever came to explicitly mentioning parable. Interestingly, McFague describes parables in almost the same words as Tolkien described fairy stories in that letter: "A parable is an extended metaphor . . . which allows for a flash of insight . . . through a juxtaposition of the ordinary within a startling new context."[286] The juxtaposition of the ordinary within a new context or the exemplification of "truth and the encouragement of good morals" ("the ordinary") in "unfamiliar embodiments" ("new context") is not only an excellent definition of parables but of the incarnation itself.

According to Tolkien, he only realized how present his Christian worldview was in *The Lord of the Rings* "in the revision."[287] This reflection indicates that Tolkien was primarily focused on telling a good story instead of preaching. Once again, this stemmed from Tolkien's intimate understanding of Jesus's art of the parable. According to Snodgrass, Jesus's parables were seldom ever about himself; instead, they were "theocentric."[288] Instead of using direct, explicitly allegorical communication to talk about God becoming human, Jesus told stories about "God, God's kingdom, and God's expectations for humans."[289] For Jesus, then, the stories themselves were also the top priority. In a letter written shortly after the publication of *The Return of the King* in 1956, Tolkien admitted that "something of the teller's own reflections and 'values' will inevitably get worked in," but quickly followed this up with a reminder that that is *not* the same as allegory.[290] Perhaps Tolkien's sensitivity to allegory stemmed from the fact that it was a type of story which relied on the "purposed domination of the author," which Jesus never demonstrated in his parables.[291] As a Christian, Tolkien was not concerned with the story he wanted to tell, but with the story God was telling through him.

In a book such as this, there is always the danger of falling prey to the Wimsatt and Beardsley intentional fallacy whereby we the readers assume that we can absolutely know the author's intentions. We cannot. Tolkien himself warned, "The ways in which a story-germ uses the soil of experience are extremely complex."[292] But we must also clarify what this *does not* mean. This does not mean that we should *not* try to interpret authorial intent, it simply means that we should not use assume that we have the final say on what the author's intentions are. We are especially lucky that Tolkien left behind so many reflections about his writings, which certainly does help. Unfortunately, many readers have domesticated Jesus's and Tolkien's parables and not allowed them to be what they are. According to N. T. Wright and Michael Bird, "the task of reading texts faithfully should not be constructed as 'authorial intent' versus 'present meanings', but as a hermeneutical enterprise that allows an ancient text to speak to a modern audience without doing injustice to either."[293] This insight applies to *The Lord of the Rings*, as well, since the text is framed by the Christian worldview, which is very much a premodern worldview. Moreover, as a living text, *The Lord of the Rings* continues to speak to us in the present day. This brings us to yet another important piece of advice when seeking to understand the fairy story/parable: we must, to the best of our ability, set aside our own worldview assumptions while interpreting and enjoying the text. Snodgrass summarizes the importance of setting aside our worldview assumptions, explaining that "stories create worlds. By reading a story we, at least temporarily, inhabit that world. If we bring too much of ourselves into that world, we reshape it and rearrange its landscape. But if we do that, we have created a world other than what the story portrays."[294] Tolkien did warn us that entering Faërie is "perilous."[295]

In conclusion, this book's central thesis, that we can learn more about Christianity and reality from a fantasy book, does seem a bit of a stretch. Can we really learn more about Christianity and reality by entering a story filled with elves, dragons, dwarves, and magical rings? The real question is, can we know anything about reality *without* myth? We have learned that everyone has a worldview and describes reality in narrative terms. Indeed, we all live within a certain mythology. But the Christian myth is not just any story. The Christian myth of creation, fall, redemption, and restoration claims to be the *true story* of reality. This is essentially the meaning of the Greek word *euangelion*, which means "good news." If literature tests philosophy, and people love *The Lord of the Rings* as much as they seem to, should that not tell us this is worth investigating? According to McGrath, "like all narratives, the Christian story cannot be 'proved' by objective rational or scientific means. It has to be judged by its ability to make more sense of things than its present or potential rivals; by its simplicity, elegance, and comprehensiveness; and by its capacity to make sense beyond its own intended focus."[296] Are you and I living in the right story? Faërie is a "perilous land" because our perception of reality is challenged and enlarged by it, and we may not like what it shows us. Nevertheless, it is worth the risk. Millions of people have read Tolkien's books and have been tremendously moved and even haunted by them. Indeed, according to Ralph C. Wood, "one of the enduring enigmas left by the conclusion to *The Lord of the Rings* is how to deal with its surpassing sadness."[297] Wood believes that this is because it is, like the Christian story it resembles, an unfinished story of broken people in a broken world which is still plagued by the specter of death. Yet as we will see in later chapters, there is also hope and joy. The Bible tells us that the story of reality is not yet over. Christians believe we live in a fallen, sinful world, and even though Jesus won the great initial victory over sin and death on the cross, the king will one day come again to make all things new.[298] If the Christian myth is really the true myth—the story of how things really are—then this is also the reason why it is a sad story. Reality is not what it is supposed to be, and we sense that it ought to be different. Timothy Keller soberly reminds us that Christianity teaches that "there is a tragedy and a sadness to life from which no amount of celebration or rejoicing can provide a full escape. Some wounds never really heal. The festal joy that Jesus brings is always partial in this life, never full."[299] Lewis was right in saying that the "best havings are wantings."[300] Indeed, both Tolkien and Lewis would agree that Christianity is an "already and not yet" story. On the one hand, Christians believe that what God originally intended to do in the beginning for Adam and Eve—fully join heaven and earth together—God began again through Jesus Christ. On the other hand, Christians also believe that the world is still a broken place and God has not yet finished the new creation project, and that one day, Jesus will return to complete it. It is time to take a closer look at the Christian worldview as "good news," and specifically the role of parables as "good news" stories.

2

Parables Are Good News Stories

PARABLES AS "ALREADY AND NOT YET" STORIES

The thesis of this book is that *The Lord of the Rings*, a fairy story, is analogous to a New Testament parable. In the previous chapter, we made a case that Tolkien's fairy story is analogous to Jesus's parables and that contrary to what most books on this subject have argued, fairy stories/parables are a type of allegory, and thus, that *The Lord of the Rings*, is also an allegory. We may initially think that parables must be short stories like the ones we read in the Gospels, but length does not determine this literary form. Jesus's parables ought to be considered "short narrative fictions," as Kreglinger has argued.[301] We have learned that parables are narratives that contain both metaphorical and allegorical elements.[302] That is, parables contain both indirect and direct speech. A "conscious and intentional" allegory "avoids confusion and opposition," whereas in a well-told parable, which contains more metaphorical elements, the "allegorical correspondence breaks down."[303] That is, at a certain point while reading a parable—or a "parabolic novel" as McFague has called *The Lord of the Rings*—we begin to lose the ability to discover what the story is about. In other words, a well-told story is, as Lewis said, a "master key." Well-told myths, Lewis meant, had universal applicability. New Testament parables do this especially well due to the nature of the Hebraic worldview and its affection for metaphor, which incarnates them. "Metaphor works on the basis of an unconventional usage of words and cannot be replaced; the vehicle is inextricably involved in creating the meaning of the tenor [subject matter]."[304] Parables are stories that knit together the two estranged aspects of reality which were, in the beginning, intended by God to be one. Parables are holistic and comprehensive stories. The complex and opaque nature of a New Testament parable is also due to the nature of its underlying worldview. All history is God's story, and he intended us to see this *through* the story of Israel. God called Abraham so that through his descendants, all humanity would be restored to their original royal status as God's image-bearers. Yet as we saw at the end of the last chapter, the story is not yet finished. In this chapter, we will look at parables as "already and not yet" stories and as miniature proclamations of the gospel, which itself is the summing up and continuation of Israel's, and thus humanity's, story. In short, we will look at how parables are "good news" stories.

In the beginning of the biblical narrative, God created "heaven and earth" (Gen 1:1). That is, God created a holistic reality of distinct but complementary opposites (heaven and earth). Heaven is the transcendent aspect of reality whereas earth is the physical aspect where God dwells immanently alongside his creation. These are not mutually exclusive worlds, realms, or places, but two overlapping and interlocking aspects of a single reality. God then created another pair of distinct yet complementary opposites: humankind. According to Gen 1:26–27, all people were made in his image. Adam, Eve, and all humankind were appointed stewards of God's creation and were commanded to reflect this image in all that they accomplish. They were to live alongside God and contribute to the yet unfinished creation project that God had begun in Gen 1:1, but then something went wrong. The story of Adam, Eve, and the Serpent in Gen 3 tells us that humans wanted to establish order independent of God, who was the true center of wisdom and order. This distruption (sin; that is, worshiping something other than God as God) halted the creation from coming to fruition. This is what Paul refers to later in Romans 8:20 where he says, "The creation was subjected to frustration."

According to the biblical story, history is progressing to a moment when there will be a "new heaven and a new earth" (see Isa 65:17 and Rev 21:1). That is, God's sole purpose throughout history has been to bring about his original intentions from Gen 1 before we introduced disorder in Gen 3. God called Abraham and the nation that would be born from his descendants—Israel—to be a "light to the nations" (Isa 49:6), to restore *all* humankind (not just Israel) to its rightful dignified status as God's image-bearers. Along the way, Israel, God's chosen representative in this quest, lost its way and itself needed saving. God had to do something which would not only redeem Israel but, through Israel, humanity. The solution, of course, is the incarnation. In Jesus we can see Adam, Abraham, Moses, and David as they were *meant* to be. God's intention in Jesus was to restore Israel to its rightful role as leading representative of humanity so that through Israel, all people could experience restoration. Before we can proceed, we need to attend to the word "salvation," because there is a great deal of confusion about it today.

This term has been badly misunderstood, so let us begin with what it is *not*. Salvation is *not* "dying and going to heaven" or the redemption of someone's disembodied soul apart from their body. Middleton and Wright, among many others, are two active biblical scholars today who have completely revitalized the church's understanding of eschatology. So, what *is* salvation? According to J. Richard Middleton, salvation is "God's deliverance of those in a situation of need from that which impedes their well-being, resulting in a restoration to wholeness."[305] Salvation is holistic and comprehensive, as much concerned with spiritual matters as it is with physical issues. Salvation is a restoration to humanity's original royal state. This is where the gospel—the "good news"—comes into play. At the heart of the gospel is the challenging yet deeply comforting notion of the "already and not yet." Salvation is a gift of grace bestowed on us by faith in Jesus now and later. That is why we must resist allegorizing the parables, for when we do, we reduce them to "earthly stories with heavenly meanings," as Wright has commented.[306] For the very same reason, we must decidedly *not* allegorize *The Lord of the Rings*. By allegorizing the parables, we turn them into otherworldly stories, not the beautiful, holistic stories that they are.

The gospel story has two parts. First, Jesus proclaims in the Gospels that heaven and earth are coming back together in him as king, as God intended in the beginning (see Gen 1:1; Matt 6:10; Mark 1:15; Luke 17:21; and John 10:30). As we learned earlier in the book, God's original vision was that his two families would rule together with him to make all the earth Edenic. This provocative announcement radically challenged the prevailing incarnational symbols of Second Temple Judaism, which were the Torah and the temple. The point of God becoming king through Jesus was to faithfully represent Adam and Eve's original calling to be divine image-bearing creatures and to show what the Torah and temple's, and therefore Israel's, true role was *meant* to be. Unfortunately, by the first century, these incarnational symbols were not functioning the way God originally intended them to function. From the beginning, God's plan was to elevate human beings, make them members of his divine council, and commission them to make all the earth—not just the temple—like Eden.[307] Second, the gospel looks *forward* to the future, final consummation of heaven and earth which began with Jesus's first advent. The work God began doing in King Jesus would take time to complete because we were to be part of that work. This was clearly part of Tolkien's theology, for he wrote, "The Christian has still to work, with mind as well as body, to suffer, hope, and die; but he may now perceive that all his bents and faculties have a purpose, which can be redeemed."[308] The missional project which began with Adam and Eve and then continued with the Patriarchs, Moses, David, and so many other Israelites had now been set back on track by a decisive move by God himself, but it would take time and real change for the church—the renewed Israel—and the rest of humanity to adjust to its renewed vocation. God's goal, which we have been called to work cooperatively with him toward completing, has always been the same: a new heaven and a new earth (i.e., a renewed, restored reality). Thus, the gospel story is a story of "already and not yet."[309] It is now time to tie these insights back into our main topic of parables.

JESUS'S PARABLES AND *THE LORD OF THE RINGS* ARE "CHALLENGE PARABLES"

Although we have discovered that there is quite a bit of disagreement about terminology among scholars, it is reasonable to conclude that the terms "parable" and "allegory" are not mutually exclusive literary forms. That is, we have made the case that one can speak of either a classification of parables or allegories, but not parables *versus* allegories. We have shown how it is practically impossible (and pointless) to separate them into mutually exclusive literary categories. If we operate within a genus of parables, allegory is a type of parable; if we operate within a category of allegories, parable is a type of allegory. Within either classification, however, it is necessary to distinguish between a type of narrative in which the tension between indirect and direct speech is maintained versus a type of narrative in which this tension is absent. Alternatively, it is necessary to distinguish between a type of story which is holistic and comprehensive versus a type of story which is reductive and transparent. We have shown that Tolkien seems to have operated within a genus of allegory and that his description of the fairy story closely resembles the scholarly consensus of what a New Testament parable is. Tolkien also spoke of fairy story as a type of allegory and said that the Gospels contain, and the gospel itself is, the greatest of all fairy stories. Thus, the fairy story is also a type of allegory. If the fairy story resembles the scholarly consensus of what a parable is, and both are understood as a type of allegory, then *The Lord of the Rings* is also a type of allegory. We labored long to show why this is not a terrible fact and that there is nothing lost in labeling *The Lord of the Rings* as such so long as we are clear by what is meant.

Nevertheless, we have made the case that it may be helpful to refer to *The Lord of the Rings* as a "parabolic novel," or simply as a parable. Saying that *The Lord of the Rings* is a parable, which is the same as a fairy story, which is also a type of allegory is exhausting. If we continue to maintain, as many scholars do, that *The Lord of the Rings* is a fairy story only, then we will miss its intimate connection with Jesus's parables. This book has tried to simplify things as much as possible by saying that on the spectrum of allegories, parable and fairy story are on one end and the conscious allegory is on the other. No classification is perfect or comprehensive, of course. Earlier in the book I mentioned that parables can be found in other cultures and that they are not strictly the property of the Christian tradition. This is certainly true, as Tolkien's research on fairy stories should demonstrate. In his essay "On Fairy Stories," Tolkien discusses many other cultures in which we find evidence of the fairy story and, thus, the parable. Ultimately, it is not the name of the literary form that matters but how the literary form communicates truth, which itself has to do with the underlying worldview. Nevertheless, Jesus's parables are unique, not only because of the identity of the author, but also because of the worldview of the author. We should also keep in mind that Jesus's parables are not uniform; that is, they come in different shapes and sizes. Some are short and some are long, some are more metaphorical, some are more allegorical. "What is important for Tolkien is how reality is reflected in the story," says Kreglinger. Tolkien accomplishes this not by deliberately seeking to be mimetic but by expressing universal truths "in the particular."[310] Like crude and conscious allegory, parables are stories about something else, but unlike crude and conscious allegory, "the degree to which elements in the parable refer to elements of the reality depicted varies greatly."[311] Jesus's parables, unlike crude and conscious allegories, seem to contain both metaphorical and allegorical elements, and most importantly, "at a certain point in the narrative, the allegorical correspondence breaks down."[312]

Although there is not universal agreement on which of Jesus's parables those are, most scholars agree that the parables of the prodgial son (Luke 15:11–32), the good Samaritan (Luke 10:25–37), the wicked tenants (Mark 12:1–12), the wedding banquet (Matt 22:1–14), the widow and the judge (Luke 18:1–8), the rich man and Lazarus (Luke 16:19–31), and the laborers in the vineyard (Matt 20:1–16) are among those that fit our description. Unfortunately, some of these parables have been domesticated by being reduced to "earthly stories with heavenly meanings." That is, they have been misread and turned into crude allegories. John Dominic Crossan has labeled the parables described above as "Challenge Parables."[313] The "challenge parable" fits the description we gave in the previous paragraph because "it challenges us to think, to discuss, to argue, and to decide about meaning as present application."[314] That is, the allegorical correspondence in Jesus's parables breaks down and presents us with a shocking twist that challenges what we thought the story was about. Challenge parables are multivalent, amibiguous, and suggestive; one does not simply decode a challenge parable.[315] Challenge parables are like this because they are ultimately stories about God, even when they do not appear to be. According to Kreglinger, "Avoiding overt 'God-talk' is an important strategy that Jesus employs. By luring the reader into thinking the parable is just about everyday life, the defense mechanisms of Jesus' religious audience are down, and they are tricked into an understanding of God that is at least surprising, but often shocking and seemingly unacceptable."[316]

According to Crossan, "the *format* reassures you that all is culturally normal, but the *content* resolutely subverts that traditional normalcy."[317] At first, challenge parables begin in familiar territory, but then the allegorical correspondences—familiar elements—break down and the elements of the story become more ambiguous, suggestive, and even shocking or offensive. According to Kreglinger, this is because of a shift from allegorical speech to metaphorical speech. Metaphorical speech is present when a "word is taken out of its familiar context/ordinary usage and placed into a new and/or unexpected context."[318] When this shift takes place, the parable begins to *challenge*. The parable begins to say, *this* is what heaven and earth coming together *really* looks like, *this* is what it really means for God to be king. It is just as Tolkien says in "On Fairy Stories": "In Faërian drama you are in a dream that some other mind is weaving, and the knowledge of that alarming fact may slip from your grasp."[319] We think we are in familiar territory, but we are not. Thus, the familiarity of the parables is a kind of a trap designed to lure us into participation in the narrative.

Challenge parables also elicit what Crossan has called "the dark interval," the "pause between hearing and understanding or reading and interpreting . . . the holding moment between parable and interpretation or challenge and response."[320] An excellent example of a parable which elicits the "dark interval" can be found in Jesus's riddle about the messiah from Matt 22:41–46. "Whose son is the messiah?" Jesus asks, quoting the well-known messianic Ps 110:1. Is the messiah David's son or Lord? Or both? Crossan also makes an extremely important point about how long it took for Jesus to tell his parables, reminding us that while our reading of the good Samaritan parable may take less than a minute, we should give Jesus an hour, accounting for interruptions from his audience in the form of questions, objections, comments, and disagreements. That is why length does not determine whether a story is parabolic or not. Indeed, Crossan also makes a good case for book-length challenge parables in the Old Testament in the form of the books of Ruth, Jonah, and Job.[321] This precdent is why it is not unreasonable to conclude that *The Lord of the Rings* is a parabolic novel.

Although Crossan believes that it is better to work within a typology of parables with allegory being a type of parable, we have decided to follow Tolkien's line of thought in this book and do things the other way around. Other scholars like Klyne Snodgrass have followed Crossan's suit, whereas the Catholic Tolkien scholars Robert Murray SJ and Joseph Pearce have followed Tolkien's line of thinking. With parables, says Kreglinger, "the point is not to define allegory over and against metaphor but to show how they are different from one another [and] in what way they might work together."[322] One strength of defining allegorical speech as working at a "substitionary level" and metaphorical speech as "instrinsically suggestive in nature, refusing to be substituted" is clarity in discussing the difference between one allegory and another.[323] In place of the term "metaphorical," Tolkien spoke of *The Lord of the Rings* as more "mythical" than allegorical, though it seems he meant the same thing by "mythical" as Kreglinger means by "metaphorical."[324] Although it may have seemed superfluous to introduce Crossan's "challenge parable," identifying Jesus's parables as challenge parables helps us to recognize them for the unique literary forms that they are. This digression is also giving us more time and evidence to explore the analogous relationship of fairy story and (challenge) parable.

In conclusion, I would like to present three features which illuminate this relationship further. First, in a fairy story/parable, God is the main character, though he is never explicitly named. In a letter written in July 1956 Tolkien alluded to this when he said that "the Other Power . . . took over: the Writer of the Story (by which I do not mean myself), 'that one ever-present Person who is never absent and never named.'"[325] In the Epilogue of "On Fairy Stories," Tolkien writes that "the peculiar quality of the 'joy' in successful Fantasy can thus be explained as a sudden glimpse of the underlying reality or truth."[326] As a Christian, Tolkien believed that truth is the person of Jesus Christ. In giving a "sudden glimpse of the underlying reality or truth," the fairy story gives us a glimpse of the gospel. Thus, God is both the main character and main subject of the fairy story. Similarly, "even though the parables of Jesus are about God and his dealings with humanity or the Kingdom of God, God is never overtly mentioned as the subject matter."[327] Second, some familiarity in a fairy story/parable is necessary as a lure for participation. Kreglinger writes, "The parables of Jesus are usually taken from every day life, using familiar images, and depicting realistic situations of first-century Palestine, at least initially."[328] In the same vein, Tolkien argued that "Faërie contains many things besides elves and fays, and besides dwarfs, witches, trolls, giants, or dragons: it holds the seas, the sun, the moon, the sky; and the earth, and all things that are in it: tree and bird, water and stone, wine and bread, and ourselves, mortal men, when we are enchanted."[329] Like (challenge) parables, fairy stories contain images and settings taken from familiar aspects of reality. According to Gregory Bassham, "by juxtaposing the enchanted with the familiar, the magical with the mundane, fantasy provides vivid contrasts that help us see the world with fresh eyes."[330]

This leads us to the third and final characteristic of the (challenge) parable/fairy story. At first, the familiarity of Middle-earth and Jesus's parabolic microworlds functions as an invitation to decode the story, but then there is a sudden turn or twist—a *eucatastrophe*, we might argue. This is especially clear in the way that both Jesus and Tolkien talk about the kings in their stories. Speaking of God as king was one of the most common but powerful ways of talking about God in Jewish culture. However, neither Tolkien's kings (i.e., Thorin and Aragorn) nor Jesus's kings (i.e., Matt 18:23–27; 20:1–15; and Luke 12:37) live up to popular expectations. The kings of Middle-earth and in Jesus's parables do not look, speak, or act according to convention. For example, in *The Hobbit*, Gandalf tells Thorin, "You are not making a very splendid figure as King under the Moutain."[331] Thorin has not lived up to the songs sung and prophecies told about his return to Erebor. Similarly, in *The Lord of the Rings*, when the hobbits first meet Strider (Aragorn), he subverts their expectations about how a king should look and feel. Frodo confesses that though Aragorn has frightened him several times during the evening, he has never done so in the way the Enemy would, for he believes that servants of the Enemy would "seem fairer and feel fouler." At this, Aragorn laughs, saying, "I see, I look foul and feel fair. Is that it? *All that is gold does not glitter, not all those who wander are lost.*"[332] According to Kreglinger, "by bringing into interaction the surprising idea of an 'unkingly' king with the idea of God, the parable shifts into metaphorical mode and the surprise is doubled."[333] In conclusion, says Crossan, "challenge parables submit their destinies to their audiences. Jesus can hope and intend, to be sure, but ultimately he cedes control to his hearers."[334] Our final tasks in this chapter are to explore what it means to say Christianity is "good news" and how that relates to these three features of the (challenge) parable/fairy story.

CHRISTIANITY AS GOOD NEWS

Tolkien's parabolic novel—*The Lord of the Rings*—is a parable about what Jesus's parables are about. We have seen that this means that the stories are ultimately about everything, giving us a "glimpse of the underlying reality."

We have also seen that this means that the parables are about God and his kingdom of "already and not yet." Now we must take a closer look at how this makes Jesus's and Tolkien's parables "good news," for that is what the word "gospel" means. Tolkien's comment that *The Lord of the Rings* is not "'about' anything but itself" does not mean that he was saying the story isn't about anything, or that it was devoid of meaning.[335] On the contrary, he was hinting that what the story is "about" is inseparable from the form (parable/fairy story) in which it is being said. The parable *is* the message. Jesus and Tolkien spoke in parables because there was no other way of saying what needed to be said. It is also impossible for any story to avoid gesturing beyond itself (Tolkien himself admitted to this).[336] As we have learned, it is the extent to which an author intends the inevitable allegorical correspondences to be made that turns the story into a "conscious and intentional" allegory. Tolkien was also saying that his story should not be subjected to reductionism, as if it could be reduced to be about only something "religious" or "political." Christianity is a comprehensive worldview, which means that it embraces all aspects of human life. As we learned in the Introduction, this also means that Christianity—in being the only completely true worldview—contains aspects of other myths within it. The quotation above—seen alongside other quotations by Tolkien about *The Lord of the Rings* being a Christian story—only demonstrates that Tolkien was concerned that the popular cultural understanding of the Christian worldview was wrong. That might explain why Tolkien was upset to discover that some reviewers of *The Lord of the Rings* did not find any religion in it. Yet perhaps some have not discovered Christ in Middle-earth because they do not know what to look for. If we do not have a correct understanding of Christianity, we will not recognize it when we see it.

According to McFague, "within the gospels are many small gospels—the parables, anecdotes, healings, teachings of Jesus—which in nugget form also image the good news."[337] The English word "gospel" comes from the Old English words "god" and "spell," meaning "good story" or "good news." "Good news" is *evangelium* in Latin and *euangelion* in Greek, the language of the New Testament. Jesus himself used this word to describe what we now call "Christianity": "The time has come," Jesus said. "The kingdom of God has come near. Repent and believe the good news!"[338] The reason why some scholars and readers of *The Lord of the Rings* do not see it as a Christian story—or misunderstand it as an allegory of Christianity—is because they think of Christianity as good advice instead of good news. One of the biggest obstacles to grasping Christianity as good news is bad philosophy. One will not understand Christianity as good news if one has difficulty acknowledging that the nature of truth is absolute and objective.

Unfortunately, Christians often misinterpret Jesus's statement in John 14:6 to mean that Christianity is the *only* religion to contain truth. Ironically, this betrays a healthy understanding of truth as absolute and objective. To accept Christianity as the one true religion means to accept that it is the "fulfillment of all myths—the 'true myth'—toward which all other myths merely point."[339] This means that all the world's religions have the potential to contain some fragment of the total truth which is manifest completely in Jesus Christ. Religious pluralism, which we discussed at length in the Introduction, goes hand-in-hand with what Nancy Pearcey has called the "sacred/secular divide," an issue which creates further difficulty in understanding Christianity as good news.[340]

Building on the work of the Christian apologist Francis Schaeffer, Pearcey argues that since the Enlightenment and continuing into the present day, the concept of truth has been divided. Schaeffer used the example of a two-story building to illustrate this. The lower story is the realm of science and reason. Things in the lower story are public and claimed as objectively true. The upper story is the realm of *mythos*, religion, and moral and aesthetic values and is considered to be a purely subjective realm, since allegedly nothing in this realm can be proven objectively. In the upper story, things are not considered "factual" since they cannot be proven using the lower story epistemologies. This is the realm of "true for you, but not necessarily for me," or pluralism and relativism. Things in the upper story are not even considered in the realm of true and false; everything is based on feelings and preferences. The main problem with this understanding of truth is that it backfires. The person who believes in the validity of this division does not believe that the realm of values lies in the realm of objective truth. To legitimize their belief in this division, they must leap to the upper story and use the upper story's traditional understanding of truth to deny the upper story's traditional understanding of truth. Truth is objective whether we are doing politics, ethics, science, or religion. Another problem with this division is that it assumes that there is empirical, scientific evidence for the assertion, "Do not trust anything without any empirical, scientific evidence" when there is none. It assumes that the lower story's epistemologies are the only legitimate ways of knowing truth. It is this circular reasoning that has created a barrier to understanding Christianity as good news. The power of parable lies in its ability to create a bridge between these two stories and thus restore integrity to the nature of truth.

So, just what does it mean to say that Christianity is good news? According to Gregory Koukl, to say that Christianity is good news is to say that it "is the story of the way the world really is," the one true story about the way things are.[341] This is a far cry from the religious pluralist's understanding of religion which views all religious teachings as good *advice*—that is, "an option you might like to take up if you feel so inclined."[342] Unfortunately, many Christians, too, view Christianity as good advice. News is different from advice; news is an announcement of something that has happened "as a result of which the world is a different place."[343] News is an objective, factual truth claim, a claim about what reality is like. According to Wright, "one can debate the merits of a religion, moral system, or philosophy, but a news event is discussed in a different way."[344] Advice, on the other hand, is something one does "to get a desired result."[345] To say that Tolkien's parable is about what Jesus's parables are about is to say *The Lord of the Rings* is good news—not good advice.

According to Wright, "the gospel of Jesus Christ comes as news within a larger story. It points to a wonderful new future. And it introduces a new period of waiting that changes our expectations."[346] There are, then, three characteristics of good news. First, news is an announcement of something significant that has happened "because of which everything will now be different." Second, the "new and unexpected development" only makes sense within a much longer story (Israel's).[347] Lastly, news transforms the present moment (the "already") and points forward to a glorious new future (the "not yet"). How does this unfold in the Gospels and *The Lord of the Rings*? First, the announcement is that God has become king in Jesus on earth as it is in heaven. Second, this is happening "according to the Scriptures" of Israel (1 Cor 15:3-4). That is, Jesus's advent only makes sense within the much longer story of Israel, which goes back to the call of Abraham. Finally, the good news transforms the present moment in that what God promised to do one day in the future—remake heaven and earth—is *already* beginning to happen, and that one day, God will return to fully consummate this promise. These same three characteristics undergird *The Lord of the Rings*.

Tolkien's parable tells the story of the return of the one true king and his kingdom (#1) whose advent can only be understood within the much longer narrative of Arda (#2). Finally, like Jesus's, Aragorn's advent ushers in a kingdom of already and not yet. Just as in the Gospels, even after the defeat of the dark power, people still must go on living, working, and suffering. Just as in the Gospels, the advent of God's/Iluvatar's kingdom on earth does not immediately solve all the world's problems. As in the Gospels, there is also no hint whatsoever that people die and go to heaven in *The Lord of the Rings*. Instead, the story ends with signs of a future consummated kingdom and a hint of Aragorn's return.[348] Indeed nowhere is the notion of "already and not yet" made clearer than in the words of Gandalf to Aragorn about the sapling from one of the Two Trees which were once planted in Valinor: "Remember this. For if ever a fruit ripens, it should be planted, lest the line die out of the world."³⁴⁹ That a sapling of one the Two Trees that once bloomed in the Undying Land of the Valar has been found in Minas Tirith by Aragorn shows the connection between Iluvatar, the Valar, and Aragorn's reign. Furthermore, Gandalf's admonition that the lineage of the tree must be maintained from this *present moment* into the *future* "lest the line die out of the world" underscores the already/not-yet aspect of the gospel. Perhaps more importantly, Tolkien is reminding us that the Bible teaches the doctrine of *palingenesia* (Greek for "re-creation of all things"), not a doctrine of otherworldly Platonism or Gnosticism.³⁵⁰

In the final chapter of *The Return of the King*, Tolkien tells us that Frodo entitled his and Bilbo's journal—which contained the story of all their adventures—"The Downfall of the Lord of the Rings and the Return of the King."³⁵¹ The entire gospel is contained in this succinct title. The defeat of Sauron and the return of the king is the announcement; the larger story within which this announcement is made is the story of Middle-earth as told in *The Silmarillion* and *The Hobbit*; the transformation of the present moment which sits between the "even that *has* happened and the further event that *will* happen" is evident in the kingdom which Aragorn establishes at the end of the novel; and the new future which this announcement points to is referred to in "The Debate of Finrod and Andreth" and hinted at in *The Lord of the Rings* as "Arda Healed."³⁵² The themes of creation, fall, redemption, and restoration are clearly evident in Tolkien's mythology. Before we can begin our analysis of *The Lord of the Rings*, we need to tackle the final issue of what Paul meant in 1 Cor 15:4 by "according to the Scriptures," for this has to do with the larger backstory found both in the Old Testament and *The Hobbit* and *The Silmarillion*.³⁵³ If we fail to understand the way the New Testament interacts with the Old Testament, we will also fail to understand the way *The Lord of the Rings* interacts with Tolkien's various prequel writings.

"ACCORDING TO THE SCRIPTURES"

If we want to understand *The Lord of the Rings* as a good news story (a parable), then we must know what to look for first. One of the features of Tolkien's books that resembles the biblical writings is their intertextuality, that is, the way the books interact. To understand Christianity as good news, we learned above, we must understand the larger context in which this news was announced. That larger context is, of course, the story of Israel found in the Old Testament. By creating an intertextuality with his books, Tolkien has created a resemblance to the intertextuality of the biblical writings. The intertextuality in *The Lord of the Rings* with *The Silmarillion* alone gives the former a very Gospel-like feel. According to Wright, "only by knowing this backstory can we understand why the new announcement is good news."[354] Tolkien's parabolic novel is filled with allusions to Middle-earth's larger backstory that narrates a story that resembles Israel's in the Old Testament. As a parable, *The Lord of the Rings* is most effective, like Jesus's parables, when it provides us with suggestive but not explicit allusions to the larger backstory. According to Tolkien, these allusions to the history of Middle-earth further contribute to the story's deeper sense of realism. The allusions to an ancient past, Tolkien says, are like a distant island glittering on the horizon, just out of reach. The allusions create a tension by showing us the story's familiarity on the one hand and its ultimate unfathomability on the other.[355] The island on the horizon is a trap, a lure for participation. The connections between Tolkien's parabolic novel and the prequel writings can be best appreciated retrospectively. When reading *The Lord of the Rings* and the New Testament with their frequent allusions to a bigger story, we are lured into wanting to learn more. Tolkien was right to comment that "part of the appeal" of *The Lord of the Rings* is "due to the glimpses of a large history in the background." As master storytellers, Jesus and Tolkien also understood that "unless new unattaible vistas are again revealed," the story will lose its enchantment—and therefore its deep realism.[356] The already/not-yet quality of Jesus's and Tolkien's stories accounts for the stories' vastness and realism. That is also why we cannot stop reading them; there is always something to learn through another reading.

One common mistake in biblical interpretation is to search the Old Testament first for prooftexts about Jesus. Similarly, were we to begin our analysis of Tolkien's writings with "The Debate of Finrod and Andreth" or *The Silmarillion*, and plunder those texts for prooftexts about Aragorn, we would greatly impoverish our enjoyment and understanding of *The Lord of the Rings* and how it is a good news story. A prospective hermeneutic also reduces the whole story to a crude allegory by making "this-equals-that" equations. Additionally, a prospective hermeneutic threatens the intrinsic meanings of the Old Testament and Tolkien's prequel writings. A prospective reading ultimately devalues the independently valuable backstories of both the gospel and *The Lord of the Rings*. In Middle-earth, allusions to Israel's story alternate between the stories of the elves, dwarves, and Numenoreans. In other words, none of those races by themselves "represents" Israel; all of them do, and do not. For example, that all the children of Iluvatar produce great monarchies is suggestive of the House of David in the Old Testament, but one will not find any one king in Middle-earth corresponding exactly with another in the Bible. That is because we must remember that *The Silmarillion* and *The Hobbit* comprise the historical backstory of *The Lord of the Rings*. Therefore, they do not "stand" for books in the Bible, but they function in the same way that the Old Testament functions for the gospel. They must stand on their own as tales worth being told, just like the Old Testament. Viewing the Old Testament as merely a repository of prophecies for the New Testament compromises the unique intregrity of the former. Similarly, if we were to just mine Tolkien's historical books for prooftexts for what we find in *The Lord of the Rings*, we would miss out on all that is true, good, and beautiful in those writings.

The Silmarillion and *The Hobbit* tell a very similar story to that which we read in the Old Testament. These are stories about a God who created a good world that was later marred by evil, about the creation of image-bearing representatives that failed to reflect the divine image, and about God's committment to sustain and perfect his creation. Just as in the Old Testament, they are stories that explore what happens when God's stewards try to rule without him. Just as in the Old Testament, we see that even God's chosen people need redemption. In Middle-earth, Tolkien did not allegorize Israel through one of Iluvatar's children. Instead, allusions to Israel's story are scattered across all their storylines. According to Michael Drout, "this technique of taking the attributes of medieval characters and dividing them among multiple *Lord of the Rings* characters is necessary . . . in order to make a modern audience accept the characters in *Lord of the Rings*."[357] This insight is applicable to both characters and events. By dividing parallels to the story of Israel among the elves, dwarves, and Numenoreans, Tolkien made his story more credible and realistic. In this way, his story acquires the same kind of historical realism that the Old Testament has.

There may also be an additional explanation, however. Earlier in the book we heard from Tolkien that he "thought of the dwarves like the Jews."[358] If Thorin and his race resemble Israel and the House of David the most closely—as we will see in chapter 4—then it makes sense to ultimately have the messianic figure come from both inside *and* outside their story, just as Jesus does in the Bible. Perhaps we cannot quite see how this works in Middle-earth because we are reading the Bible wrong. The traditional interpretation of the word "begotten" in John 3:16 is that it means that Jesus was God's *only* "Son," but according to Heiser, this is not correct. Scholars used to believe that the Greek word *monogenes* derived from the two Greek words *monos* and *gennao*, meaning "only" and "to bear or beget," respectively, but this is no longer the case. Scholars now believe that the second word is not *gennao* but derives instead from the noun *genos*, meaning "class or kind." A new translation of the Scripture, then, would have this text say that Jesus is God's *unique* "Son," who, unlike the other members of the divine council, is one with Yahweh. The point is still that no one is like Jesus, but now we can say that this is true of beings on earth *and* in heaven.[359] So how does this relate to Aragorn and his status as messiah in Middle-earth? I think now you can see. Aragorn, as I will point out later, descends from men, elves, and even a Maia, a junior divine being—*elohim*—and member of Iluvatar's divine council. Aragorn is, like Jesus, one of a kind, and comes from outside—heaven—and inside—earth—the story. We also must recognize that the Bible affirms that both Adam and Israel were called God's son and that God had originally intended to bring Adam and Eve into the divine council.[360] Like Jesus, Aragorn is the descendant of a member of Iluvatar's divine council on one side and a descendant of the race of men on the other.[361]

If we were thinking allegorically, then we would expect that the messiah in Middle-earth would be a dwarf. Of course, Aragorn—who is a Numenorean—does not descend from Thorin's people, but he does not have to for the resemblance to work. This is not necessary to argue based on what we just discussed above. Since all Iluvatar's children resemble Israel in their own unique ways, we can still see the relationship between David and Jesus reflected in Thorin and Aragorn while at the same time seeing how Aragorn also comes from outside Thorin's story. Further support for this comes from the story of Aule's creation of the dwarves in *The Silmarillion*. Although we will examine this story more closely in chapter 5, it is worth pointing out here that the dwarves were, like Israel, adopted as God's "firstborn son."[362] Indeed, Aule, who grew impatient for the coming of Iluvatar's "children of choice" (elves and men), created the dwarves first. And even though he offers to destroy his own children, Iluvatar not only permits the dwarves to live—though they will slumber until the coming of the elves—he also promises to one day "hallow them and give them a place among the Children in the End."[363] Parallels with Rom 11:11-12 are unmistakable here: "Again I ask: Did they [Israel] stumble so as to fall beyond recovery? Not at all! Rather, because of their transgression, salvation has come to the gentiles to make Israel envious. But if their transgression means riches for the world, and their loss means riches for the gentiles, how much greater riches will their full inclusion bring!" We will not find an exact one-to-one correspondence in Middle-earth to the "gentiles" (Greek for "nations"), though there are several moments in the story where we see the relationship between the elves and the dwarves resemble the Jewish/gentile relationship.

Another example worth pointing out at this time is how Tolkien handles the tricky topic Paul addressed above in Rom 11 concerning Israel. Tolkien was very sensitive about anti-Semitism, so we know he would not have agreed with Justin Martyr's comment we saw earlier in the book about the early church's emerging replacement theology. In fact, in Rom 11:18, Paul warned the gentiles coming into the church *not* to behave as if they had an advantage over either non-Christian Jews *or* Jewish members of the church: "Do not consider yourself to be superior to those other branches. If you do, consider this: You do not support the root, but the root supports you." By Justin Martyr's time (mid-second century), however, this warning went unheeded, largely due to two Jewish revolts against Rome, increasing tension between the various sects of Judaism, and the rise of a new messiah, Simon bar Kokhba. As we will see, Tolkien offered a corrective for this real historical problem through the relationship between Gimli and Legolas, who are close companions of Aragorn. Indeed, Aragorn's return brings these two races back together, itself an indication that Aragorn resembles Jesus typologically. By including allusions to Israel's story in the stories of elves and men in addition to the dwarves, Tolkien may have had Gal 3:28 in mind where Paul says, "There is neither Jew nor gentile, neither slave nor free, nor is there male and female, for you are all one in Christ Jesus." This can be seen especially in the friendship between Aragorn, Gimli, and Legolas throughout the novel. And then there is Aragorn, whose Numenorean bloodline is a mixture of divinity, elves, and men. Aragorn is the insider-outsider of the story who is in a perfect position to heal the schisms brought about by the Enemy between the children of Iluvatar (more on this later). Aragorn's return to the throne ultimately redeems all Iluvatar's children.

Through the contrasting characters of Thorin and Aragorn, Tolkien may have wanted to show that God had not forgotten or forsaken Israel. As Iluvatar's firstborn son, the dwarves were supposed to set an example, much like Israel, but for most of their history, they turn inward and become suspicious of outsiders. Heiser's book *The Unseen Realm* examines the long history of Israel's ultimate failure to be God's chosen instrument to reunite the disinherited nations (recall Deut 32:8–9) in detail. That Israel ultimately failed does not mean they never succeeded at all, for that is simply untrue. God never abandoned them. The most sigifnicant evidence for this is that God still chose to reveal himself through Israel. For the dwarves to fulfill their proper task of being a "light to the nations" like Israel, they needed someone from *outside* their story to help them. In this way, Tolkien may have had in mind one of the most paradoxical teachings of Christianity: Jesus was not only David's son but David's Lord.[364] According to Matt 12:42, Jesus himself tells us that "something greater than Solomon is here." Wright explains that "the new event" that is the gospel—the return of the king—"hasn't come from within the story as it was," but is "*both* the fulfillment of the vocation of Israel *and* divine judgment on the mess and muddle that Israel's story had become."[365] God, who is the font of all myths, chose to enter his story—the story of Israel—because it was through this grand narrative that the whole story of reality was being told. Aragorn is, like Jesus, something totally *other*. Just as with Jesus in the Bible, Aragorn is the "third thing." Recall that earlier in the book we discussed Lewis's book *The Pilgrim's Regress*, which introduced the "Shepherds" and the "Pagans" as well as the "rules" and the "pictures." According to Lewis, since "the pictures alone are dangerous, and the rules alone are dangerous," we must focus on the "third thing which is neither the rules nor the pictures and which was brought into the country by the Landlord's Son."[366] Parables are, like the incarnation itself, a "third thing," neither the rules nor the picture, but something independent of them both. According to Lewis, "the truth is that a Shepherd is only half a man, and a Pagan is only half a man, so that neither people was well without the other, nor could either be healed until the Landlord's Son came into the country."[367]

So, Paul's comment that everything has happened "according to the Scriptures" refers to the necessity of a retrospective (typological) hermeneutic in both the Gospels and *The Lord of the Rings*. The connection between Aragorn and Thorin is only discovered by looking back at the prequel writings from the events of *The Lord of the Rings*, just as the connection between Jesus and David is only discovered by looking back at the Old Testament from the events of the New Testament. As we will see, were it not for Thorin's return to Erebor, a ten-year-old Aragorn—living in Rivendell during the events of *The Hobbit*—would most likely not have survived Smaug's subsequent destruction of northern Middle-earth. Even if he did, Aragorn's return to the throne would have been made much more difficult, if not impossible. Similarly, Israel's return from exile to Jerusalem in the sixth century BC paved the way for the advent of Jesus in the first century. Interestingly, it seems that Tolkien understood the advantages of a retrospective hermeneutic because he has one of his major characters—Gimli—adopt this position in a version of "The Quest of Erebor." This story is mainly told from the point of view of Gandalf after the defeat of Sauron, who is looking back on all the events that led to the return of the king and the downfall of Sauron. Gimli wants to know who "wove the web," which is very obviously a nod toward a divine being and his involvement in the story. Then he asks, "Did not the recovery of the Kingship under the Mountain, and the fall of Smaug, begin there [the Shire]? Not to mention the end of Barad-Dur, though both were strangely woven together. Strangely, very strangely."[368] It is only from this position in time, after Aragorn had become king, that Gimli sensed a mysterious, intimate connection between the events of *The Hobbit* and *The Lord of the Rings*. As readers, we are meant to share in Gimli's amazement at the interconnectedness of everything that has unfolded.

This example further justifies our decision to adopt a retrospective hermeneutic in our analysis of Tolkien's writings. By reading *The Silmarillion* and *The Hobbit* in light of Aragorn's return in *The Lord of the Rings*, readers will experience the good news in the same way that they experience it through Jesus's parables and the Gospels. According to Scarf, readers "become more aware of the significance of King Aragorn as they 'look back,' an action parallel to a Christian 'looking back' at the Old Testament, to understand better the full meaning of the accounts of Christ's life in the Gospels."[369] Many, if not most, Christians believe that Paul's statement "according to the Scriptures" has to do with going back to the Old Testament to search for prooftexts, but this is a misunderstanding. We risk missing the gospel as good news if we do not get this right. Here we need to remind ourselves of two things we have already discussed at length. First, God called Abraham (Israel) so that Israel could call the entire human race to return to its original vocation as priestly image-bearers. God's original intentions for creation were to fully join heaven and earth together, with God at the center. Since Adam and Eve failed, God chose one representative nation from among their descendants, to be a "light" for all the other nations. Unfortunately, despite Israel's many successes, she, too, eventually failed to fulfill her sacred vocation. This, in turn, precipitated the need for God to come and do himself in person what Israel—and the rest of the nations—could not do themselves. This is also why we find Jesus and Paul repeatedly stating that salvation comes "first to the Jews, then the gentiles" throughout the New Testament.[370]

Second, we need to understand what "looking back" entails. According to Hays, "reading Scripture figurally—reading backwards in light of the story of Jesus—is an essential means of discerning the anticipatory traces of God the Word in his self-revelation to the world."[371] For this hermeneutic to work properly, one must not search the Scriptures looking for a prediction of Jesus, but one must look backward from the point of view of the Gospels for prefigurations of it. A figural interpretation of Scripture does not assume that the authors of the Old Testament were "conscious of predicting or anticipating Christ," thus retaining the standalone intregity of the Old Testament Scriptures. Too often has Scripture been twisted to say what it does not say. Instead, writes Hays, "the discernment of a figural correspondence is necessarily retrospective," and, "because the two poles of a figure are events within 'the flowing steam' of time, the correspondence can be discerned only after the second event has occurred and imparted a new pattern of significance to the first."[372] The gospel—and the parables within which it is embodied—proclaim a new moment in an ancient story which takes it in a fresh, new direction. But this truth can only be fully grasped by looking back at Israel's ancient story, which frames and shapes the gospel. Similarly, we must approach *The Lord of the Rings* with "a Gospel-shaped hermeneutic," which "necessarily entails *reading backwards*, reinterpreting Israel's Scripture in light of the story of Jesus." Furthermore, "such a reading is necessarily a *figural reading*, a reading that grasps patterns of correspondence between temporally distinct events, so that these freshly illuminate each other."[373] To truly see how *The Lord of the Rings* is a Christian story, then, we must employ the same "Gospel-shaped hermeneutic" that we do with the Scriptures. As a result, we will discover that what makes Tolkien's parable "Christian" is in its faithful correspondence to reality, not in any correspondences between it and the Bible. Again, *The Lord of the Rings* is a parable about what Jesus's parables are about.

When we look back at the long history of Middle-earth from the perspective of *The Lord of the Rings*, we experience something very similar to when we are reading Scripture. I believe Tolkien's decision to include glimpses to the vast history of Middle-earth in *The Lord of the Rings* accomplishes at least two things. First, he has created an imaginative version of the scriptural experience. I have found my own reading of Scripture reenchanted and enhanced because Tolkien's books replicate the scriptural experience. There is a sense of wonder and awe in reading my Bible that was not there before. It is almost as if Tolkien did this to restore a proper way of interpreting Scripture. This is what he meant by "Recovery" and "Escape" in his essay "On Fairy Stories," as we learned earlier in the book. "Recovery," remember, is "regaining a clear view . . . so that the things seen clearly may be freed from the drab blur of triteness or familiarity—from possessiveness."[374] By beckoning us to look back at Middle-earth's ancient history in order to fully understand *The Lord of the Rings*, he faithfully recreates the same experience that Jesus did when he told his parables. This gives readers a sense that they themselves are part of this ancient, ongoing story. Well, as a matter of fact, we *are* part of an ancient, ongoing story. Consequently, Tolkien remythologizes our perception of reality, showing us how integral *mythos* is in understanding reality. It took me many years of reflecting on why *The Lord of the Rings* affected me so much and then many more years of research to arrive at these conclusions, but it was worth it.

Second, the frequent glimpses we are given to Middle-earth's history in *The Lord of the Rings* forces us to be more careful in how we read and interpret. It is easy to read too much into the glimpses, and I have frequently reminded myself of Tolkien's warning that to sail to that far off "unvisited island" we spoke about earlier "is to destroy the magic, unless new unattainable vistas are again revealed."[375] This warning is for both the author and the audience. For the author, Tolkien is saying that if you make your story too transparent, you will break the enchantment that the narrative has on the readers. When that happens, the story loses its ability to illuminate reality and provide us with more applicability. For readers, we must not ever think we have figured the story out or decoded it, especially since now we know how delicate and careful Tolkien was in shifting between allegorical and metaphorical modes. The Scriptures of Israel—and Tolkien's prequel books—lose their unique, literary intregrity if we assume a prospective hermeneutic and if we just view them as texts that say one thing but mean another. Jesus is clear about this in several places in the Gospels. For example, in Luke 24:27, Luke says, "And beginning with Moses and all the Prophets, he explained to them what was said in all the Scriptures concerning himself." It is important to follow this up with the observation that this is only said *after* the Resurrection. That is, "what was said in all the Scriptures concerning himself" is only apparent *after* the "temporally distinct" events of the Resurrection. Jesus is inviting us to read Scripture *backwards*.

Too many people approach the Bible expecting it to be the type of story that imparts good advice or is more like an instruction manual than the book of wisdom that it is. Similarly, many have approached Tolkien's books expecting it to conform to their preconceived notions. There is so much more to these stories than meets the eye, however. Peter Kreeft captures this perfectly in his book about the Christian worldview in *The Lord of the Rings*: "You can tell everything about your fantasies, your dreams, or your thoughts, but not about anything real. That is also why *The Lord of the Rings* bears endless rereading: it is heavy enough to bear the mind's journeys into it, like our world."[376] This is yet another characteristic that shows *The Lord of the Rings* is good news: like the gospel, *The Lord of the Rings* is "*always different from what people think it will be.*"[377] We know that Tolkien believed that God took over the writing of *The Lord of the Rings* and that Tolkien eventually had a sense that he was "recording" what was already there rather than "inventing."[378] Like Father Murray, I believe that the world of Faërie stands as "a parable of the Kingdom preached by Jesus," that *The Lord of the Rings* is a parable of the kingdom of heaven spoken through Tolkien by the Master himself.[379] Yet if we are to see this, Wright explains, we must stop insisting "on keeping our mental, emotional, and imaginative world the way it's always been," because "the good news just won't fit. We will then either reject it or distort it, cutting off the bits we can't fit in or reshaping parts to conform to the ideas we already have."[380] Tolkien's parabolic novel can prevent this distortion and can help us not only restore what we may have lost in our reading of Scripture, but enhance our understanding of Christianity as good news.

3

The Lord of the Rings Is Good News

"YOUR KING SHALL COME AGAIN"

On September 21, 3021 of the Third Age of Middle-earth, Frodo set out from the Shire for the last time. It had almost been exactly three years since Frodo left Bag End on his quest to destroy the One Ring (he left on September 23, 3018). Although Frodo and Sam have been back in the Shire since November of 3019 (Sauron was defeated on March 25 of 3019), Frodo became frequently ill between 3019 and 3021. Sam married the love of his life and started a family. Everyone around him was prospering, but things were just not the same for Frodo. One day, Frodo asks Rose, Sam's wife, if he could take her husband on one last adventure. Before they leave, as Frodo and Sam are sifting through Frodo's various possessions, they come across "The Red Book of Westmarch," a book which both Bilbo and Frodo contributed to.[381] The title page of this book had "many titles on it, crossed out one after another": "My Diary. My Unexpected Journey. There and Back Again. And What Happened After," and so on. Not long after they set out, to what will be the Grey Havens, the two hobbits encountered a few old friends: Gildor, Galadriel, Elrond, and, of course, Bilbo. Not long after, Bilbo asks Frodo if he is coming with the old hobbit, at which point Sam asks the same question of Frodo that Peter once asked of the risen Jesus: "*Domine, Quo Vadis?*"[382] This is Latin for, "Lord, where are you going?" Frodo responds that he is going to the Grey Havens to leave Middle-earth and tells Sam that he cannot join him this time—"not yet anyway."[383] "'But,' said Sam, and tears started in his eyes, 'I thought you were going to enjoy the Shire, too, for years and years, after all you have done." Frodo then explains to Sam that he cannot, for he has been too deeply wounded, and though the Shire has been saved, it has not been saved for him. And then, in words that clearly reflect the gospel, Frodo says, "It must often be so, Sam, when things are in danger: someone has to give them up, lose them, so that others may keep them."[384] According to Matt 16:25, Jesus said, "For whoever wants to save their life will lose it, but whoever loses their life for me will find it."

The conversation between Frodo and Sam is more than redolent of events from the Gospels. Reflected in Sam's question, "Where are you going, Master?" is Thomas's own: "Lord, we don't know where you are going, so how can we know the way?" And in Sam's tearful lament we can also hear the lament of the two disciples walking along the Emmaus road in Luke 24:2: "We had hoped that he [Jesus] was the Messiah, who had come to rescue Israel."

Returning to the Red Book, Bilbo had apparently been experimenting with various titles for as we saw, he had several crossed out. Where the list of titles Bilbo had penned ended, Frodo wrote:

> THE DOWNFALL
> OF THE
> LORD OF THE RINGS
> AND THE
> RETURN OF THE KING[385]

Not only is this an apt summary of the Red Book—Tolkien's conceit for his mythology—but it is also a fitting summary of the gospel of Jesus Christ. It also expresses, in succinct summary, what a *mashal*, or parable, is. Parables are, by their very nature, monarchical stories. Recall that the old root word behind the Hebrew term *mashal* refers to "shadow," and that "shadow" refers to an ancient Semitic "king," who was the "image" or "shadow" of God on earth.[386] The main meaning of the Hebrew word *mashal* and the Greek word *parabole* is "resemblance" or "comparison." That is why the word "parable is instructive . . . as highlighting the likeness between divine majesty and human royalty."[387] Parables are, then, the perfect vehicles for announcing the good news of God becoming king through Jesus (or Aragorn) on earth as it is in heaven. Parables are incarnational stories, faithfully reflecting the nature of their author. The very form of the story reveals what its content is. According to Wright, "the very form of the parable thus embodies the content it is trying to communicate: heaven appearing on earth."[388] Why did Tolkien say that he kept all "allusions to the highest matters down to mere hints, perceptible only by the most attentive"? Perhaps he understood that that this was the best way to speak authentically about Christ.[389] Jesus said something quite similar when his disciples asked why he only spoke in parables (see Matt 13 and Mark 4). Jesus said that he spoke in parables so that "they may indeed see but not perceive and may indeed hear but not understand."[390] Jesus's provocative words are meant to take us into deeper discipleship, learning to listen not only to what is being said, but also how. According to McDermott, "Jesus expected his disciples to know where the prophecies and types were in Scripture and his teachings, *and* to be able to figure out the meanings without his having to explain them."[391]

According to Godawa, "images are concrete expressions of abstract ideas, the existential embodiment of the rational word . . . words made flesh."[392] In other words, parables are miniature incarnations. The reason why parables are "one of the most powerful means of communication" is because their form *is* the content they are seeking to communicate.[393] Recall that as a corollary to this and from an ancient Semitic perspective, a parable's form reveals its monarchic content. There is, then, a connection between incarnation and monarchy. Perhaps we do not immediately connect with this point on a mental level, but according to Peter Kreeft, that may mean we are not being honest enough with ourselves: "Though we do not have kings in America, or want them, our unconscious mind both has them and wants them."[394] The old stories about returning kings resonate with an intuition we all have hidden deep in our hearts. If you are an American, it is practically part of our DNA to feel put off by this notion, since our founders fought a revolution to get *rid* of a monarchy, among other things. Wright argues that "at the heart of 'the Enlightenment' was a resolute determination that 'God'—whoever 'God' might be—should no longer be allowed to interfere, either directly or through those who claimed to be his spokesmen, in the affairs of the world."[395] But Jesus's rule is a very different kind of rule: "Jesus called them together and said, 'You know that the rulers of the gentiles lord it over them, and their high officials exercise authority over them. Not so with you. Instead, whoever wants to become great among you must be your servant, and whoever wants to be first must be your slave—just as the Son of Man did not come to be served, but to serve, and to give his life as a ransom for many.'"[396] Ironically, the very concerns many people have with theocracy in the gospel is the central shaping theme of *The Lord of the Rings*—and people love *The Lord of the Rings*! It must be pointed out, however, that many Christians throughout the church's history—and still today—miss what Jesus was talking about in Matt 20:25–28.

Also ironic is the fact that culture is flooded today with stories of superheroes. Perhaps the true, underlying reason for our love of fantasy and heroes is because something in us yearns for a true king. "When we read *The Lord of the Rings*," says Kreeft, this true king "returns to his throne in our minds. . . . Back into our consciousness from the tomb of the unconscious, where he was sleeping."[397] In Middle-earth, as in our world, the king is "Iluvatar's representative on Earth."[398] Thus within Tolkien's parable, Aragorn functions similarly to the variety of monarchical images which Jesus employs in his parables that speak of God becoming king on earth as it is in heaven. This incredible reality cannot be grasped apart from the parables. A proper understanding of parables is central, not peripheral, to an orthodox understanding of Christianity. That may have been part of what Tolkien was ultimately trying to say in writing *The Lord of the Rings*. Jesus did not speak in parables to be deliberately secretive, there was simply no other way of saying what needed to be said. The incarnation is a profound mystery which can only be grasped through myth. Jesus is present in *The Lord of the Rings* the same way he is present through his own parables. Sadly, some scholars have taken Jesus's evasion of "God-talk" to mean that he never claimed to be divine.[399]

Yet according to Brant Pitre, the fact that Jesus spoke obliquely in parables "does not mean that Jesus never taught that he was God; it just means that he did so in a strategic way, by using *riddles* and *questions* designed to *reveal* his identity to those who were open to believing and to *conceal* his identity from those who would oppose them."[400] As we will see in this chapter, that is why Tolkien paid so much attention to Aragorn's appearance throughout the novel. Jesus spoke in riddles and parables because of their suggestive nature. Pitre believes that the best explanation for why Jesus relied primarily on parables to talk about his identity was that they bought him time.[401] We see the same thing happen in Tolkien's parable; Aragorn's royal identity is revealed incrementally until the right moment. Tolkien was quite clear that the main theme of *The Lord of the Rings* is "tyranny against kingship," and "the overthrow of the last incarnation of Evil . . . and the return in majesty of the true King."[402] The argument we wish to put forward in this chapter is that *this* story—about the defeat of evil and the return of the king—is the good news which Christianity claims to be. Yet part of the issue, as we have seen thus far, is that many Christians and non-Christians do not know that this is the story they ought to be looking for in the Gospels. Jesus makes this quite clear in Luke 19:41–44 when he says, "You didn't know the moment when God was visiting you." The whole point of this and other statements like it in the Gospels is this: "Jesus is talking about God becoming king *in order to explain the things he himself is doing*. He isn't pointing away from himself to God. He is pointing to God in order to explain his own actions."[403] Unfortunately, the sad reality is that the Gospels tell the story of

God becoming king, but "the creeds are focused on Jesus being God." That is not to say that the Gospels do not "think about Jesus as divine, but that this isn't the primary thing... they presuppose it. It is the key in which they write their music, rather than the main tune itself."[404] Indeed, the main tune is "the return in majesty of the true King," as Tolkien said.

One of the clearest connections between Aragorn and Jesus can be found in what scholars have called "the messianic secret"—a theory in theology that suggests that Jesus, in Mark's Gospel especially, spoke cryptically about his identity, and that this was in keeping with Jewish (and parabolic) thought. Parables, of course, play a pivotal role in the Gospels in conveying the messianic secret. How does Tolkien reflect the messianic secret in Middle-earth? The answer is, of course, *parabolically*. That is, Tolkien speaks of one thing in terms that are *suggestive* of another. And how does he do this? Two ways. First, the messianic secret is reflected through the riddles, poems, and prophecies about Aragorn in the novel. In a way, they are there to remind us of the importance of understanding Jesus through parable. Second, Tolkien spends a great deal of time describing Strider/Aragorn's appearance throughout the story, which is further echoed, for example, in the "Riddle of Strider" from book I, chapter 10 of *The Fellowship of the Ring*. In his book *The Messiah Comes to Middle-earth*, Phil Ryken argues that there is "a messianic secret in Middle-earth."[405] Nevertheless, Ryken—like Ralph C. Wood, Matthew Dickerson, Bradley J. Birzer and others—believes that the Third and Fourth Ages of Middle-earth are still pre-incarnational. Again, this misses the point about how the incarnation is presented in Middle-earth. These scholars have mistaken key for tune, and as a result, have not been looking for the right criteria when trying to discern whether the incarnation is present in Middle-earth. Wood, for example, understands the Fourth Age as it is depicted in *The New Shadow* (Tolkien's abandoned sequel to *The Lord of the Rings*), as the first-century world Jesus was born into. Wood, like all these other scholars, sees Tolkien's parable as a forerunner of the gospel rather than a proclamation of it, and that is because, among other things, they have overlooked the role parables play in communicating the gospel.

In the Gospels, the main way Jesus reveals his identity is by *concealing* it through parables. For example, Aragorn's response to the hobbits after hearing "The Riddle of Strider" in *The Fellowship of the Ring* resembles Jesus's interpretation of Ps 110:1 in Matt 22:41–46. People were incredulous toward both kings and saw a disconnect between their appearance and who they claimed to be. In fact, the Gospel of Mark—where the "messianic secret" is seen most explicitly—seems to have been a main source of inspiration for Tolkien's authorial tone. According to Richard B. Hays, "Mark's way of drawing upon Scripture, like his narrative style more generally, is indirect and allusive."[406] Hays suggests that this is because Jesus's narrative style was indirect and allusive. Hays and others believe that Mark wrote in this way about Jesus because he was reporting on the facts. The evidence we have looked at from Tolkien's letters and essays suggests that he was quite familiar with Mark's record of Jesus's "art of the parable." Mark seems to have understood that Jesus spoke in parables because "there is a kind of truth which, when it is said, becomes untrue."[407] From what we have learned about Tolkien, this kind of thinking would have appealed to him greatly. Although Mark's historical portrait of Jesus is consistent with the other Synoptic Gospels, it is markedly different in style than John's, whose Jesus places "overt theological claims on the table."[408] As a counter-balance to Hays's statement here about John, we should hasten to point out that there are ambiguous, implicit references to Jesus's divine identity in John, too.[409] This author concurs with Hays that we should eliminate the so-called distinction between "High Christology" and "Low Christology," as it presupposes *a priori* that the Four Evangelists had mutually exclusive understandings about the God of Israel. John's tone is less parabolic than the Synoptics (indeed, there are no parables in John), but that does not mean that John is the only evangelist to think Jesus was divine. Perhaps the reason why Tolkien was attracted more to Mark and the other Synoptic authors' narrative style was the prominent place which parables have in them.

Two more echoes of the gospel in *The Lord of the Rings* are the recurring events where one sees a display of Aragorn's *parousia* and *exousia*, Greek words meaning "royal presence" and "power of authority," respectively. These were alluded to above when we referred to the attention Tolkien paid to Aragorn's appearance in the novel. One frequently encounters passages in the Gospels when Jesus shocks, astounds, surprises, or even offends his audience because of his teachings or behavior. These are usually moments when Jesus's authority is on full display. The most famous example of Jesus's *exousia* is the transfiguration, when he took Peter, James, and John up on a mountain where "he was transfigured before them" and "his face shone like the sun, and his clothes became as white as the light."[410] In the Matthew 22 passage mentioned above, verse 46 informs us that after teaching that the messiah is not only David's son, but also his Lord, "no one could say a word in reply, and from that day on no one dared to ask him any more questions." Similarly, in Mark 12:34, after a discussion about the greatest commandment, we are told, "And from then on no one dared ask him any more questions." Once more, after being questioned by the Sadducees about the resurrection, Luke 20:40 says, "And no one dared to ask him any more questions." Lastly, in Mark 2:10, Jesus proclaims to a group of scribes that "the Son of Man has authority on earth to forgive sins." In each one of these Scriptures (and many more could be cited) Jesus exudes and exerts *exousia*. If one reads *The Lord of the Rings* carefully, it will be easily apparent that there are several episodes where Aragorn also exudes *exousia*.[411]

As for examples of Jesus's *parousia*, they are ubiquitous since anywhere Jesus went, he made his royal presence felt. Perhaps the most important illustrations of Jesus's *parousia* are the parables themselves, for they are stories about God becoming king on earth as in heaven, *here and now*. Many scholars believe that the *parousia* strictly refers to Jesus's *second* coming, but this is a misunderstanding. According to Wright, some mistakenly believe that some of Jesus's parables are about the second coming rather than the first: "The stories Jesus told about a king or a master returning to see how his subjects or servants have been getting on with their tasks were never intended originally . . . as predictions of the *second* coming of Jesus."[412] Grasping this is crucial for not only understanding the gospel, but *The Lord of the Rings*, too. The eagle's proclamation of Aragorn's return (see the Introduction) is reminiscent of Jesus's *first* coming, whereas Aragorn and Gandalf's meeting on the slopes of Mount Mindolluin—right after this event—reminds us of the second. By overly focusing on the doctrine of the second coming, we may miss the first and most important advent. Indeed, this focus on the fully realized future kingdom has caused a great many Christians to neglect Jesus's teaching about the kingdom as it is manifest in the present, which is what Jesus spends more time teaching about. Unfortunately, this issue has also led some scholars to misunderstand how the gospel is reflected in Middle-earth. For example, Louis Markos, in his book *On the Shoulders of Hobbits*, argues that Aragorn's coronation in the novel contains allusions to Jesus's second, not first, advent.[413] Yet Jesus's parables are best understood when we see that they allude to *both*.

The main point of many of Jesus's parables—and the Gospels—is about his *immediate royal presence*, not his eventual return. Above all else, Jesus's parables and *The Lord of the Rings* are stories about God becoming king here and now. In chapter 2, we spoke of the importance of understanding the good news in the context of the larger story of Israel. We also spoke of the importance of grasping this retrospectively, following the model of Jesus on the road to Emmaus in Luke 24:27. In the beginning of this chapter, we explored how God becoming king / the return of the king is the shared central theme of Jesus's parables/the gospel and *The Lord of the Rings*. We also noted how this monarchic theme is related to the literary form of the parable. We are about to begin our journey through Tolkien's great parabolic novel, starting as we should with the gospel, and then, in subsequent chapters, looking back at *The Hobbit* and *The Silmarillion* to see how everything is "strangely woven together."[414] Only by proceeding in this way will we hear *The Lord of the Rings*, like Jesus's parables, as a proclamation of the good news that "your King shall come again, and he shall dwell among you all the days of your life."[415] Yet there is still one more obstacle in our way to understanding the good news as the story of the return of the true king, namely, *that* thesis. Is this really good news?

"TYRANNY AGAINST KINGSHIP"

Before we begin our analysis of Tolkien's parable and Aragorn's story, it is crucial we establish the difficulties that many modern people have in understanding God becoming king as good news. We've picked up this conversation several times in the book because it is very important. Tolkien was quite clear: *The Lord of the Rings* is a story about "God, and his sole right to divine honor," and "tyranny against kingship."[416] When we set these and other quotes like it side by side with the scholarship of N. T. Wright and several others who see things from the same perspective, it is impossible to deny the resemblance between the gospel and *The Lord of the Rings*: both are stories about the good news about the return of the king. That being said, as Wright has pointed out in his book *Simply Good News*, understanding Christianity as good news is, itself, *news* to a lot of people today.[417] Understanding Christianity thusly is also compounded by the fact that most Christians today do not look at their tradition through Jewish eyes. This is vital: if we come to Tolkien's parable with a caricature of Christianity instead of the authentic item, then we will completely misunderstand *The Lord of the Rings*. In other words, distorted gospels have led to distorted readings of *The Lord of the Rings*.

In chapter 4 of *Simply Good News*, Wright summarizes why the theme of God becoming king can be extremely challenging and off-putting:

> Jesus wasn't content to leave existing structures in place and start up a nice, quiet, unobtrusive movement somewhere else. He didn't want the rest of the world to go on with its idea of kingship while he started a sect, a separatist movement that wouldn't challenge that notion . . . what he was doing was far more radical. Not only was Jesus plugging in to the ancient scriptural promises that spoke of God coming back at last to be king of his people and the whole world. He was insisting that this kingdom of God, this new reality, the heart of his good news, was a different sort of rule based on a different sort of power. *And that it*

> was designed to challenge the present powers of the world with a new kingship that would trump theirs altogether.[418]

This message is difficult in any era. Although many try to reduce him to such, Jesus was much more than a charismatic moral teacher (though he was at least that). Not only was Jesus claiming to be a new kind of messiah to Israel, his claims also challenged the Roman emperor's sovereignty. But most people do not like those who rock the boat as much as Jesus did. We want to control people like this, keep them subdued. This, then, is why seeing God as king is challenging both then and now. Furthermore, the idea of God "reigning" over people intimately is, at first glance, unattractive, as is the idea of an objective moral law that is a logical entailment of God's reign. As we discovered earlier in the book, if we do not understand that God has a divine council," then we will misunderstand what it means to say that God is king. What is more, Jesus was breaking the number one rule most people live by in the modern West: do not talk about religion and politics together! But in Jesus's world, there was not as much of a wall between these two disciplines as there is today, so everything Jesus says is not only theological, but sociopolitical as well. Jesus did not live in a society which assented to the sacred/secular split cosmology which we described earlier. Since the good news is holistic, the sacred and secular dimensions of reality are not mutually exclusive. Then there are the topics of Jesus's death and resurrection and the issue of salvation. What Jesus did on the cross is directly related to the kingdom he announced. The topic of salvation is thorny and usually elicits many good questions from non-Christians such as: If Jesus died for our sins, why is there still evil in the world? Why doesn't God step in and help from time to time? Why would a loving God send people to hell? Wouldn't good news imply something about my/our happiness? These are all excellent questions, some of which we will address and some of which have been addressed thoroughly elsewhere. While most of these questions can be addressed logically, one of the most beautiful things about *The Lord of the Rings* is how the novel sublimates and addresses these questions mythically. In the same way, Tolkien's parable shows us that we really do want a king, even if we do not consciously acknowledge it (see Peter Kreeft's quote from earlier in the chapter). To discover why, we must let the story *interpret us* rather than us interpret the story.

Might there be other reasons why the monarchical language of the gospel could be difficult to relate to? Indeed, there are. Perhaps the biggest factor to consider here is our Western cultural heritage, especially the one we have inherited from the Enlightenment. Recall from the Introduction that much of Enlightenment rationalism was derived from Epicureanism, which stated that God—if he exists—has "retired" to an upstairs CEO penthouse while we hard-working, objective intellectuals must learn to be self-sufficient and run the company—without God—"downstairs."[419] This notion of the sacred/secular split has, as we have learned, made it very difficult to understand Christianity in its own terms. As we have also seen, the church itself has not been exempt from this type of thinking. Perhaps many find the notion of God becoming king offensive, archaic, or meaningless because they have been taught to understand Christianity through these Platonic and Hellenistic lenses. They have been shown a God who is distant and out of touch with his creation and taught that the world is hurtling toward a great cosmic destruction and so are turned off to the idea of God ruling. Another reason modern people may not find the notion of God becoming king as good news is our inherited distrust of divine monarchs and their abuse of power from the Middle Ages. As a result, in the Enlightenment, philosophers did whatever they could to keep God out of real life.[420] But this Enlightenment view of God is a reaction to a *bad news* caricature of Christianity that was, unfortunately, common in the Middle Ages and beyond. What if God is a king who is worthy of our love and devotion and who inspires us to serve him genuinely? In this book, we are arguing that this is what the transformation moments of Aragorn rouse in us when we read *The Lord of the Rings*, even if we do not realize it. There is something incredibly powerful about the nineteen-plus moments in Tolkien's parable where we are given a glimpse of the real Aragorn, not the weary ranger, Strider.

The descriptions Tolkien gives us awaken something deep within us which we were not even aware was there in the first place. According to Kreeft, "if an antireligious person loves this story, he must unconsciously love the Christian story, not because *The Lord of the Rings* is an allegory of Christianity but because its author's mind and philosophy are one with that of the Author of the Christian story."[421] Kreeft adds that if a non-Christian person loves this story, he or she must unconsciously love the Christian story. It has been my experience that people are offended at this assumption because their understanding of Christianity is a caricature rather than the real deal. According to Wright, people then and now may have "their heads and hearts full of wrong ideas" about what Christianity is and forget that "the good news is always different from what people think it will be."[422] That is why narrative can sometimes accomplish what propositional argument cannot. Sometimes, the issue that people have with Christianity, or Christian stories, is a heart, not a head, issue. Good storytellers know that an image or an event can communicate the point they wish to make more effectively than an argument.

In the rest of this chapter, we have four goals. First, we will take a close look at the many moments in *The Lord of the Rings* where Aragorn's *exousia* and *parousia* are on display. Why did Tolkien pay extraordinary attention to Aragorn's appearance, identity, and constitution? Because he wanted to show that his story was about "tyranny against kingship," just as the gospel is.[423] *The Lord of the Rings* and the Gospels are about the "kingdom of God and the kingdoms of the world," and the dramatic contrast between them.[424] The incarnation *means* God becoming king on earth as in heaven, *not* Jesus being divine (which is implied). Aragorn is frequently described as being transfigured or transformed from the weary ranger into a tall and kingly figure throughout the novel. His very presence commands authority and even amazes his enemies. These descriptions are not accidental or superfluous, but a reflection of Tolkien's Christian worldview and commitment to "deliberately write a tale, which is built on or out of certain 'religious' ideas."[425] The point of these passages is to show what it looks like when God takes charge of his creation in person. They are there to show us that when God becomes king, "hearts will be transformed."[426]

Our second goal will be to discuss how, in being a story about the return of the king, *The Lord of the Rings* is good news. That means that we will be referring to Jesus, his ministry, and his parables frequently to show how Tolkien's parable reflects the good news in the same way Jesus's parables do. Tolkien was clear in his letters that his story was about God's exclusive right to rule and about sacred kingship versus tyranny. By the end of the novel, Tolkien becomes slightly more forward about connecting this monarchic theme with the notion of good news. By the end of this chapter, readers will understand why the return of the king is good news and what that means. Our third goal is to have readers walk away from *The Lord of the Rings* with a deeper understanding of Aragorn's central role in the story. Not only will we trace his role in *The Lord of the Rings* retrospectively, we will also look at his crucial yet often overlooked role behind the scenes, such as his friendship with Gandalf, his hunt for Gollum, and his guardianship of the Shire. Readers will hopefully walk away from the chapter understanding Aragorn's character arc, transformation from ranger to king, and how his transformation resembles Jesus's in the Gospels. In short, Aragorn is perhaps the most powerful, yet not the only, type for the messiah in Middle-earth.

Lastly, by beginning with a chapter on Aragorn's life in *The Lord of the Rings*, we will be in a perfect position to look back and see how the relationship between that novel and *The Hobbit* and *The Silmarillion* resembles the relationship between the New Testament and Old Testament. Only by approaching things retrospectively can we eventually discover that the incarnation—God becoming king—has been planned since the beginning of Arda. Tolkien's novel is not a forerunner of the gospel, as Philip Ryken has argued, but is, itself, an announcement of the good news that God has become king.

Although if Ryken means by "forerunner" something like a herald proclaiming good news, then he is right on point. *The Lord of the Rings* does not conclude with the hope that one day Iluvatar will enter his creation, for he already has in Aragorn. In other words, Tolkien's parable, like Jesus's parables, announces the advent of the world's one true king and the inauguration of his kingdom and looks forward to its full consummation in the future when "everything sad" will come "untrue."[427] In short, the return of the king *means* God is present in Middle-earth. In the end, it is this author's hope that readers see how Tolkien's parable proclaims the good news by being a story about the return of the king, just as the Gospels and Jesus's parables do.

From this point through the end of the book, we will begin our retrospective journey through Tolkien's mythology, beginning with *The New Shadow*, the abandoned sequel Tolkien began writing to *The Lord of the Rings*. Above all our other goals, our primary job in this chapter is to explore the ways in which *The Lord of the Rings* is good news and that the good news is that God has become king on earth as in heaven. According to the Bible, this is good news for everybody. "In Israel's scriptures, the reason Israel's story matters is that *the creator of the world has chosen and called Israel to be the people through whom he will redeem the world . . .* the call of Abraham is the answer to the sin of Adam."[428] Once again, it is critical to understand the distinction between good news and good advice, which we discussed earlier in the book. Yet it is also important to remind ourselves that one does not have to have a Christian worldview or an understanding of the difference between news and advice to enjoy the benefits of *The Lord of the Rings*, though it certainly does help. As an analogy, we are able to enjoy a five-star meal without knowing all the cutting-edge culinary techniques that went into making it, but knowledge of them does *enhance* our enjoyment of the meal. One of the benefits of understanding *The Lord of the Rings* as good news is that, like the gospel which it resembles, it has "the power to reach into contexts where it is not overtly acknowledged and nonetheless turn hearts and lives to God."[429] Countless readers of *The Lord of the Rings* have commented on its ability to invite endless rereadings. That is because it is modeled on the parables of Jesus, which, when taken "seriously not as answers but as invitations, can continue to inform our lives, even as our lives continue to open up the parables to new readings."[430]

THE NEW SHADOW

We begin with Tolkien's unfinished sequel to *The Lord of the Rings* which "he had abandoned after a few pages" and "sat up till four a.m. reading it and thinking about it."[431] This story, along with a few scant details found in *The Lord of the Rings*, "On Fairy Stories," and *The Silmarillion* together comprise Tolkien's ideas on eschatology and specifically on how the second coming figures into his mythology. We also begin with *The New Shadow* because, in our retrospective approach, it is the most distant point in the future of Middle-earth (the Fourth Age) from which we can then look back at its entire history. The world of *The New Shadow* is a world after Iluvatar's kingdom has been established in Middle-earth through Aragorn. It is the Fourth Age of Middle-earth and Aragorn's descendants are still reigning, but there is a problem. It is, like our own world, a world sitting between the moment of the inauguration of God's kingdom and its full consummation. It is not a world still *awaiting* the incarnation of Iluvatar, as most Tolkien scholars have claimed, it is an age in which "he must reign until he has put all his enemies under his feet."[432] God has become king on earth as in heaven, evil and death have been disarmed, but there is still work to be done. This is what Christianity teaches; anything else is a caricature or worse. Contrary to what some scholars believe, most of the first Christians did *not* believe the "end of the world" was imminent.[433] The first Christians believed that they must live in light of the belief that the creation clean-up project still wasn't finished, and that Jesus would return again in the future to complete the project—not destroy it.

According to a letter written in 1964, Tolkien explains that *The New Shadow* takes place "100 years after the Downfall [of Sauron]."[434] He goes on to explain that since this is a story about human beings, we know that it will therefore be a story about one of our most lamentable qualities: our "quick satiety with good."[435] One hundred years after Sauron's defeat, children are playing at "being Orcs" while a new "Satanistic religion" and "revolutionary plots" begin cropping up.[436] Sadly, within one hundred years of the death of Jesus (c. AD 130), the once diverse but unified church of Jesus Christ began to show signs of rot and familial squabbling. For starters, the church was almost exclusively made up of gentiles. Although the Jerusalem Council (c. AD 50) had decided that gentile converts did not have to observe Jewish practices, there was remarkable tolerance, fellowship, and unity in the church until the end of the century.[437] Other factors, however, began to exert pressure on the church until it cracked: the persecution of Christians in Rome by Nero (c. AD 64), the first Jewish Revolt (AD 66–74) and destruction of the Jerusalem temple (AD 70), sporadic persecution of Christians under Emperor Trajan (c. AD 97–117), and the *second* Jewish Revolt (AD 132–135) all contributed to the breakdown of the diverse yet unified early Christian church. Other factors included disagreement over

Jesus's messianic status, the resurrection, and the nature of Jesus himself.[438] Tolkien may have had this in mind when brainstorming about *The New Shadow*. And this makes sense because if *The Lord of the Rings* resembles the gospel and the time of Jesus's ministry, then *The New Shadow* would resemble the aftermath of the return of the king. Unfortunately, we will never know much more than that because Tolkien quickly abandoned the project. What it does show us, however, is that Tolkien had given some thought to what the world was like *after* the return of the king.

As we saw above, *The New Shadow* was going to be a story about Middle-earth one hundred years after Sauron's defeat in which people were growing complacent with peace and goodness. Children began pretending to be orcs and rumors of a new evil . . . isn't this simply a description of life as it has always been? Even if we were to screen out the return of the king for a moment, isn't it true that in spite of the king's advent, wickedness, complacency, and cruelty endure? There is, then, a grain of truth in the criticism that Jesus didn't really solve any of the many perennial human issues. But this is where the good news comes in: *if* that criticism is ultimately true, and *if* heaven and earth did not begin to come together in Jesus Christ, *if* there will not be a new heaven and a new earth sometime in the future, *if* "this life is all there is, and there is no God or life beyond this material world, then it will not ultimately matter whether you are a genocidal maniac or an altruist," because "in the end what you do will make no difference whatsoever."[439] Let us hasten to add that this does not mean that secular people or non-Christians don't find life meaningful—or find their suffering meaningful—but it does mean that they may not know what it's all *for*. Of course, it is always possible to retort, "Who says all this is *for* anything or anyone?" But that response, which implies that the meaning of life is that it has no ultimate meaning, is still *a meaning*.

We can infer from Tolkien's stories what he may have thought about such Scriptures as 1 Thess 4:15–17 and Platonic interpretations of the book of Revelation which suggest that when Jesus comes again, he will destroy the world and take the faithful out of it. According to 1 Thess 4:16–17, in the end, "the Lord himself will come down from heaven, with a loud command, with the voice of the archangel and with the trumpet call of God, and the dead in Christ will rise first. After that, we who are still alive and are left will be caught up together with them in the clouds to meet the Lord in the air. And so we will be with the Lord forever." A cursory reading of this Scripture would lead anyone to conclude that popular Christian books like *Left Behind* reflect what Christians believe about the end of history, but this is not true. This is also one of the passages in the New Testament where the word *parousia* is used. Most Christians have looked at this passage through Platonic lenses and come to the erroneous conclusion that in the end, Jesus will come down on a cloud and rescue faithful Christians by taking them up into heaven with him, leaving this sinful world behind. But this verse, like all Scripture, needs to be understood within its original Jewish context, not a Greek one. What happens when we do that? According to Wright, two things. First, we discover that the word *parousia* was used to refer to the "mysterious presence of a god or divinity, particularly when the power of this god was revealed in healing."[440] For example, in his book *Jewish Antiquities*, Josephus occasionally uses this word to refer to "YHWH's coming to the rescue of Israel." Second, this word was often used to describe the visit of a Roman emperor, or other persons of high rank. In that context it refers to an emperor's "royal presence" when he visits a colony or province. Paul, the author of this passage, is also drawing on ancient Jewish stories and images from the story of Moses and Daniel.

One thinks of the famous Dan 7:13–14 passage, which speaks of the "Son of Man" coming "on the clouds of heaven," and of Moses coming down from Mount Sinai in Exod 34:29–35. These Old Testament stories communicate that we are in the presence of someone royal. As for the "in the air" portion of this passage, it is a powerful metaphor for meeting with this royal presence, as one would do in greeting a visiting royal emperor, with the implication that we then usher this royal figure into the colony he is visiting. In conclusion, there is not the "slightest suggestion of anybody flying around on a cloud. Nor is there any hint of the imminent collapse or destruction of the space-time universe."[441] When we turn to *The Lord of the Rings*, we see this unfold in the same way. In *The Return of the King*, the eagle, who acts as a herald of the king, exorts the citizens of Minas Tirith (the colony) to "sing and rejoice." A few pages later, we are given a beautiful description of Aragorn's triumphant entrance into the city filled with exuberant citizens: "A hush fell upon all as out from the host stepped the Dunedain in silver and grey; and before them came walking slow the Lord Aragorn."[442] This passage also resembles Jesus's triumphant entry into Jerusalem in the Gospels. Most importantly, it is perhaps the clearest example of the good news of God becoming king on earth as it is in heaven. Between this example from *The Return of the King* and our exploration of *The New Shadow* we can clearly see that Tolkien's eschatological view aligned with the holistic Jewish rather than the dualistic Platonic worldview. Not according to Matthew Dickerson, however: "Since that hope has not yet been fulfilled, and indeed is not even widely known among the peoples of Middle-earth, it is not surprising that the stories are so full of sorrow and sadness; Melkor's evil is still without a cure."[443] Once again, this interpretation of Tolkien's parable is the result of looking at the story through Platonic rather than Jewish lenses. The incarnation is indeed present in Middle earth, but it is communicated in a very Jewish and parabolic way. Dickerson has "mistaken key for tune," however. Yes, "the key in which the gospels are set is that of incarnational Christology," says Wright, "but the melody is that of the kingdom and of 'Christology' in the much stricter sense of 'Jesus as Messiah.'"[444] The problem has been that we have all been reading as "the main text what the gospels treat as presupposition." The Gospels *presuppose* that Jesus is divine, but that is neither their nor Jesus's main message. Instead, the entire narrative is the story of "how God became king."[445]

Dickerson's understanding of the incarnation has clear Platonic presuppositions that have long been present in the church. Indeed, Bart Ehrman's main criticism of the Gospels is that Jesus never "went around Galilee proclaiming himself to be a divine being sent from God."[446] This understanding assumes that heaven and earth are separated by a gaping chasm and that a claim to divinity would have to be explicitly otherworldly. Sadly, this Platonic assumption is at the root of many misunderstandings of the gospel today. Jesus's reliance on parable is the quintessential Jewish way of disclosing his identity. In no way are we suggesting that there is no division between God and man or heaven and earth (that would be pantheism). In Judaism and Christianity, God and man and heaven and earth overlap and interact in several ways while remaining very different from one another, which brings us back to how the parables "say" Jesus is God. Parables work through the power of *suggestion*. If we miss this in the Gospels, then we will miss it in *The Lord of the Rings*. Unfortunately, Dickerson's interpretation has become the rule in most Tolkien scholarship. Then there is the issue with Dickerson's understanding of Christian eschatology. He seems to believe that the sadness and sorrow of the parable is proof that the incarnation is a far-off event in Middle-earth, but this is not true. As we have just learned, God's first advent as king does not heal all the evil caused by Satan and human beings. As Christians, we believe that God has come in Jesus Christ, but that he has also not yet finished his great work. The great renewal of all things will be fully accomplished at Christ's second advent. We have seen that Tolkien himself understood this, writing that the "Christian has still to work . . . to suffer, hope, and die."[447] Thus, to assume that Christ is not incarnate in Middle-earth due to the enduring presence of evil misunderstands a core Christian teaching. According to Keller, "there is a tragedy and sadness to life from which no amount of celebration or rejoicing can provide a full escape . . . the festal joy that Jesus brings is always partial in this life, never full."[448] This biblical insight can help us understand the real reason why so many have commented on the pervasive sadness in *The Lord of the Rings*.[449]

"IN SORROW WE MUST GO, BUT NOT IN DESPAIR"

These are among the final words spoken by Aragorn before he gives up his life. They can be found in "Appendix A" of *The Lord of the Rings* and once again reflect Tolkien's belief—which we read in "On Fairy Stories"—that the Christian must "suffer, hope, and die" and wait for "the last enemy" (death) to be put under Jesus's feet.[450] Jesus himself experienced real suffering and death. But of course, Christians also believe that one day they will rise because Christ is risen. But not yet. Here, at the very end of *The Lord of the Rings*, we catch a gleam of the gospel, but if we aren't careful, we will miss it. Were we to allegorize Aragorn's death, we would expect to see him rise from the dead three days after he willingly lays down his life, but this is not that kind of allegory. Significantly, Aragorn also does this in sight of his bride—a symbol of Israel and the church throughout the Bible—Arwen. We will note this now and return to it in the final chapter, but it is quite telling that Arwen cries out, "Estel! Estel!" when Aragorn lays down his life. Why is this important? As we will see, not only is Estel—which is Sindarin for "hope"—one of Aragorn's many names, it is also the name which Andreth uses to describe a belief that one day, Iluvatar will enter his creation personally. In other words, it is the name which the denizens of Middle-earth use to refer to the belief in their equivalent of the incarnation. Incredibly, Andreth refers to this belief as the "Old Hope" already in the First Age! This reference comes from a text called "The Debate of Finrod and Andreth" that Tolkien wrote in the late 1950s after he had finished *The Lord of the Rings*, and we will return to it in the final chapter. There is one more salient detail in the story of Aragorn's death: Tolkien does not say that Aragorn *dies*, but falls asleep.[451]

Although we might be tempted to stop the analysis there since this *does not* happen, we would be foolish to do so, for though Christians believe Christ is risen, he has also "ascended" into heaven, "God's space, which in biblical cosmology *intersects* with earth, our space . . . the control room, the place from which everything is now run."[452] Yes, Christ is very much alive, but he dwells in a very different kind of space, time, and matter than we do. In a sense, then, sometimes God can feel "dead," though he is most certainly not. No, he has, as he says in John 14:2, gone away to "prepare a place" for us. Late in *The Return of the King*, Aragorn passes through the Paths of the Dead, which is clearly a parallel to Jesus's death in the Gospels. Although there is "no literal, bodily resurrection," says Philip Ryken, Aragorn passes "through death in one way or another" and then returns to life . . . they are all changed, or else revealed in some new degree of glory."[453] And there is more than a hint of the possibility of the second coming in Aragorn's final words to Arwen: "We are not bound forever to the circles of the world, and beyond them is more than memory. Farewell!"454 All of these parallels, however, are reflected in Middle-earth the way that they are hinted at in Jesus's parables. For example, Jesus's death and resurrection is hinted at in the parable of the wicked tenants in Mark 12:1–12, but neither the death nor resurrection of the messiah was something any first-century Jew anticipated.455 Another glimmer of the gospel found at the end of Tolkien's parable can be seen in the friendship of Legolas and Gimli, who sailed "over Sea" together after the death of Aragorn.456 As we pointed out earlier, the friendship of elf and dwarf symbolizes the reconciliation of Jew and gentile which Paul speaks about in Gal 3:28. As we will see in the final chapter of this book, though Iluvatar tells Aule that "often strife will arise between thine and mine, the children of my adoption and the children of my choice," that strife begins to disappear with the enduring friendship between Legolas and Gimli.457

"STRANGELY WOVEN TOGETHER"

Tolkien intimately tied together the narratives of the House of Durin and the Numenoreans to implicitly express the theme of God returning as king to the House of David. This is made quite clear in a short story entitled "The Quest of Erebor," which is told from Gandalf's point of view right after the return of the king. In it, we learn from the wizard that had it not been for the quest of Thorin Oakenshield and Bilbo Baggins, Sauron (known as "the Necromancer" in *The Hobbit*) would have unleashed Smaug the dragon upon Rivendell (and the rest of northern Middle-earth) killing a ten-year-old "Estel" (Aragorn) in the process. "Dragon-fire and savage swords in Eriador, night in Rivendell," says Gandalf.458 Aragorn's survival, we learn, was dependent on the successful reclamation of Erebor by Thorin—tragic though that event was. In an earlier version of this tale, Gimli the dwarf is speaking with Frodo and Gandalf in Minas Tirith after the fall of Sauron about how Bilbo's and Frodo's quests seemed to be fatefully connected. "No Dwarf," says Gimli, "of the House of Durin could fail to look with wonder on that land [the Shire]. Did not the recovery of the Kingship under the Mountain, and the fall of Smaug, begin there? Not to mention the end of Barad-Dur, *though both were strangely woven together. Strangely, very strangely.*"459 This is one of many providential statements which give readers the impression of what the prophet Isaiah called "the arm of YHWH."460 Just as the resurrected Jesus does with the two disciples walking on the road to Emmaus (see Luke 24:13–35), Tolkien takes us "through the writings of Moses and the prophets, explaining from all the Scriptures the things concerning himself" (Luke 24:27), but without being explicitly allegorical. The importance of these two passages cannot be overstated, for they will help us understand how the interconnectedness of the events of *The Hobbit* and *The Lord of the Rings* reflect the interconnectedness of events in the Bible.

"THE CROWNLESS AGAIN SHALL BE KING"

Tolkien pays a great deal of attention to Aragorn's appearance, perhaps more than any other character in the novel—why? On the one hand, Tolkien describes Aragorn as "lean" or "one who has labored in sleepless pain for many nights" or "pale and drawn."[461] On the other hand, he undergoes glorious metamorphoses throughout the novel, being described as "kingly" and "a king returning from exile."[462] According to Angela P. Nicholas, "Aragorn's looks . . . were affected by his need for secrecy," in order to protect him from the enemy.[463] Tolkien alternates between descriptions of his disguise and descriptions of his true regal identity throughout the novel. It is clearly not for nothing, so what is Tolkien trying to communicate besides excellent characterization? One could argue that the alternation between the concealment and revelation of Aragorn's identity is another characteristic which illustrates the novel's parabolic structure. The metamorphoses of Aragorn—the manifestations of his royal authority and presence—function similarly to the regal images in Jesus's parables, which subsequently gesture toward Jesus as king. These powerful moments in Tolkien's parable suggest that we look at Jesus in the same way we look at Aragorn: an exiled king returning to his rightful throne. Additionally, Tolkien is reminding us that this is what Jesus himself was suggesting through his parables. The descriptions of Aragorn serve as an *anamnesis*, "or a way for a people to recall encounters with transcendence that had helped to order their souls and their society."[464]

Sandra Richter's personal testimony is an excellent illustration of how *anamnesis* works. According to her, "the *first* gospel" she heard "was that of a king, exiled from his throne . . . who, although the heir of Numenor, had taken the form of a vagabond and, being found in the appearance of a Ranger, lived out his life on the margins of his own lawful inheritance, tirelessly laboring to undermine the enemy who held his citizenry captive."[465] Although she only recognized this later in retrospect, Richter's first encounter with the gospel took place outside the Gospels. Richter's experiences remind one of Lewis's famous words: "I suspect that men have sometimes derived more spiritual sustenance from myths they did not believe than from the religion they professed."[466] Furthermore, Richter's allusions to Phil 2:6–7 in her testimony are important, for she seems to imply that Tolkien may have been influenced by this passage in his characterization of Aragorn. Moreover, Richter's testimony also suggests that Tolkien may have been influenced by the Suffering Servant poems, which can be found in chapters 42, 49, 52, and 53 of the book of Isaiah. According to Nicholas, "he was pale and lean but nevertheless extremely strong and fit," and "grim and weather-beaten."[467] When the hobbits first meet Aragorn in Bree, he confesses that he hoped the hobbits would accept him as he appeared, for a "hunted man sometimes wearies of distrust and longs for friendship."[468] This is reminiscent of Isaiah's description of the Suffering Servant who is "despised and rejected by mankind, a man of suffering, and familiar with pain."[469] Like Jesus, Aragorn is frequently described as someone who does not fit people's expectations about the promised king. That is why Tolkien alternates between these humbler descriptions and the exalted moments where Aragorn appears to be transfigured in the novel: he wants to show that despite his grim appearance, Aragorn is the rightful king. Tolkien's descriptions of Aragorn and the overarching monarchic theme of his parable are responsible for showing that *The Lord of the Rings* is good news.

Richter first encountered the gospel *outside* the Gospels, which, among other things, is a testimony to the Christian worldview's ability to make sense in any context. Her story is a powerful attestation to the gospel's universal applicability and status as the master myth, which we explored earlier in the book. Just as with the regal images and characters in Jesus's parables, the descriptions of Aragorn in Tolkien's parable serve as an *anamnesis* (Greek for "recollection") of the good news which we all have innate knowledge of since we were made by its author. At the heart of many, if not most, great myths are the archetypes of king and kingdom. There is something primal and familiar about the idea of a lost paradise/kingdom and exiled king. This myth addresses a deeply hidden need or yearning in the human heart, for all of us acknowledge that there is something wrong with the humanity and the world and that it ought not to be this way. Like Richter, some of us may discover that, in hindsight, we first heard the good news in Middle-earth before we heard it in the New Testament. Others may be encountering these topics for the first time in a serious, sustained way.

Working our way back from Aragorn's death, perhaps the most powerful cluster of metamorphoses of Aragorn takes place at the end of the novel in chapter 5 of book VI of *The Return of the King*. In this chapter we witness the long-awaited marriage of Aragorn and Arwen, Aragorn and Gandalf's discovery of a sapling of one of the Two Trees of Valinor, and his coronation, among other significant moments. As we begin to unwind the parable from this point, we will gradually see how all the alternating descriptions of Aragorn's appearance have led to this conclusion. Though we will not examine every one of these (nineteen-plus) transformative moments where Aragorn's royal authority/presence is manifest, from the handful of examples we analyze it will be abundantly clear that Tolkien clearly had Jesus in mind. The marriage of Aragorn and Arwen, the discovery of the sapling, and Aragorn's coronation all echo the good news of God becoming king and heaven and earth coming back together, just as we see in the Gospels. Together, these three events communicate the already/not-yet characteristic of the gospel. Gandalf's words to Sam, "A great Shadow has departed," reinforce this.[470] He does not say *the* great Shadow has departed, or that *all* shadows, evil, and suffering have departed. It is just as Paul said in 1 Cor 15:26: "The last enemy to be destroyed is death." As we have already seen, Sauron's downfall and Aragorn's coronation do not completely eliminate evil, suffering, and death, but they are disarmed. This is still very much cause for celebration: "Then he [Gandalf] laughed, and the sound was like music, or like water in a parched land."[471] Aragorn's marriage to Arwen further reinforces the feeling of joy we get toward the end of the novel. Although there is great beauty and meaning in their marriage, it does not resolve all of Middle-earth's problems, as we have seen from our review of *The New Shadow*. Instead, we see in the marriage a foretaste of a more permanent union which is still far in the future, just as it is in Rev 21:1–3. Considering other things Tolkien wrote, the marriage of Aragorn and Arwen is not the fairy-tale ending it may appear to be. It is a glimpse of the new creation, the new heaven and new earth that was begun with Aragorn's/Jesus's coronation and will be completed when they return. Pitre has made a convincing case that the day of Jesus's crucifixion was his wedding day. This idea is borne out by a reading of the parable of the bridegroom found in Mark 2:19–20, in which Jesus draws an analogy between he and his disciples as a bridegroom and groomsmen. The "party," strangely enough, is Jesus's crucifixion; his passion and death on the cross will bring God's divine and human families back together and reconcile the disinherited nations to himself again.[472] We can see how this plays out somewhat in *The Lord of the Rings* with the tight sequence of Aragorn's journey along the Paths of the Dead, his triumph over the forces of darkness, and then his coronation and wedding to Arwen. Indeed, the wedding of Aragorn and Arwen reflects the reconciliation of God's/Iluvatar's children, as members of each race are present.

Throughout the novel, Tolkien reminds us that no joy is complete in the current age. Keller writes in his book *The Meaning of Marriage* that "marriage is so painful and yet wonderful" because "it is a reflection of the gospel, which is painful and wonderful at once."[473] There is a great battle raging around us, even though the king has returned to his throne. Though we have been wed to the bridegroom, he has left us temporarily to finish renovating the house that is the cosmos. Ancient Jews like Jesus saw the cosmos itself—heaven and earth—as a temple. It is therefore fitting that Tolkien concludes the novel with a marriage of an immortal elf and Numenorean man. It is a sign of things yet to come, the "firstfruits" of the new creation.[474] Perhaps Tolkien was suggesting that *The Lord of the Rings*, like the gospel which it reflects and proclaims, is "painful and wonderful at once." This may be the most important lesson which Tolkien's parable—and Christianity—can teach us. Yet as we have already seen, Tolkien scholars have not written about the presence of inaugurated eschatology in *The Lord of the Rings*. Instead, most interpretations are framed by a Platonic reading of the gospel even if the authors themselves are not aware of it. Even Wood, whose book *The Gospel According to Tolkien* comes closest to understanding Tolkien's theological views, unfortunately concludes that "in the world of Middle-earth, the Consummation of All Things occurs neither with the fall of Mordor nor the coronation of Aragorn, but with the coming incarnation of Iluvatar."[475]

Once more, this is the same theological misunderstanding that we discussed earlier with Dickerson's book. The gospel is an already/not-yet story which understands the incarnation *as* God becoming king in and through Jesus of Nazareth. Like Dickerson, Wood seems to believe that the incarnation is still a far-off, unfulfilled hope in Middle-earth. Moreover, his mention of the "Consummation of All Things" refers to Jesus's *second* coming and therefore the "not yet" portion of the gospel. And yet confusingly, he mentions this in the same breath as the "coming incarnation of Iluvatar," meaning that the *first* advent has not yet occurred in Middle-earth. This is conflating two separate events of the gospel story, however. What's more, on the last page of his book, Wood seems to imply that Aragorn has "already inaugurated his Kingdom by losing his own life," though he isn't entirely clear if he is referring to Jesus and Aragorn or just Jesus.[476] My reading of the text, has produced a different conclusion.. Aragorn's coronation *is* a clear indication that God—Iluvatar—has entered his creation by becoming king through Aragorn. The incarnation must be understood first and foremost as the enthronement of God as king.

According to Pitre, one of the other messianic titles Jesus is given in the Gospels is that of "the bridegroom."[477] Following the example of Jesus, Tolkien reflects the gospel by writing of Aragorn as a bridegroom toward the end of the story. Since (challenge) parables/fairy stories have their "own mode of reflecting 'truth,' different from allegory," we should not be surprised to discover that there are not one-to-one correspondences between Aragorn and Jesus.[478] Tolkien's parable reflects the truth of who Aragorn is in the same way that Jesus's parables reflect the truth of who he is. The incarnation can only be seen "as" something else. We will not find direct, explicit announcements of the messiah's divinity, because this is already something the worldview of the Four Evangelists and Tolkien presupposed. We will notice that the resemblances between Jesus and Aragorn do not conform to the same chronology, either. That is, the order of things as they happen in Aragorn's life does not equal the order of things as they happen in Jesus's. Once again, parables reveal *and* conceal; that is their mode of "reflecting truth." So, for example, in the Gospels, the day of Jesus's crucifixion is presented as his wedding day, but in *The Lord of the Rings*, Aragorn marries Arwen before he lays down his life. Even so, when Aragorn does die, he gives up his life willingly, just as Jesus did.[479] What's more, as we saw above, just before he dies, Aragorn suggests to Arwen that we are not "bound by the circles of the world." This suggests—rather than "says"—that Aragorn, like Jesus, has gone away to prepare the fully consummated kingdom in heaven for us and will one day return to reveal it. As in the Gospels, the bridegroom promises to come back for his bride. Importantly, Aragorn tells Arwen not to despair, just as Jesus tells his disciples in John 14:1, "Do not let your hearts be troubled." So, while the day of Aragorn's death is not his wedding day as it is for Jesus, Aragorn's death and hinted eventual return echo Jewish wedding customs. According to Pitre, "in ancient Jewish tradition, one of the duties of the bridegroom *was to prepare a home for his bride*, so that when the wedding was finally consummated he could take her from her own family and bring her to live with him and be a part of his family in his father's house."[480]

Immediately preceding the wedding of Aragorn and Arwen is Aragorn's discovery of "a sapling of the line of Nimloth the fair . . . that was a seedling of Galathilion, and that a fruit of Telperion of many names, Eldest of Trees."[481] This event is heavily laden with biblical allusions. One could even suggest that the tree resembles the cross that is the means by which the messiah establishes the kingdom of heaven on earth. But doesn't Aragorn walk the Paths of the Dead before his discovery of the sapling, and wouldn't that event better resemble Jesus's crucifixion? Yes and no. Yes, there is a resemblance between Aragorn's journey along the Paths of the Dead and Jesus's crucifixion and death, but there are no explicit, direct correspondences between one and the other. But no, because Aragorn does not die, per se, while walking the Paths of the Dead. And yet, yes again: Aragorn's decision to take the Paths of the Dead eventually gives him command of the dead, just like Jesus himself. Back and forth, yes and no; this is how parables work. We get a glimpse of something that sounds familiar and just as we begin to figure it out, there is a twist and the familiarity becomes ambiguity again. This parallel between the sapling and the cross is more credible than it may initially appear, however. This sapling is a descendent of Telperion, one of the Two Trees that bloomed on Valinor, home of the Valar, that was once visible in Middle-earth. Then, of course, there are the two trees from Eden that this event reminds us of, and how Rev 22:1–3 envisions a future when the Tree of Life will have leaves that bring "healing to the nations."

As we will learn later, Valinor used to be within the sight of the races of Middle-earth (heaven on earth). Yet that paradise was eventually taken from view because one of Aragorn's Numenorean ancestors tried to sail to Valinor and claim what he believed was the prerogative of his species—immortality. This act of hubris, in turn, caused Iluvatar to conceal Valinor from the races of Middle-earth. Valinor's resemblance to Eden and humanity's exile from it are poignant. The importance of the endurance of the White Tree also clearly parallels the endurance of the kingdom which both Jesus and Aragorn establish via their enthronements. As we already saw earlier in the chapter, Aragorn's coronation also causes the coming together of elves, dwarves, and men, just as Jesus's reconstitution of Israel through his twelve disciples brings together Jews and gentiles. These two events—the coronation of Aragorn and his subsequent discovery of a sapling of Nimloth the Fair—taken together clearly resemble the cross and the kingdom. Aragorn tells Gandalf that he knows that he will die one day, just as Jesus did, and that he is concerned about who will rule after he is gone. Yet both Jesus and the Bible tell us that God will rule through Israel and the church, through the power of the Holy Spirit. The discovery of the sapling—which Tolkien interestingly says is a "sign"—is the answer to Aragorn's concern. According to J. Richard Middleton, "the garden is the initial core location of God's presence on earth . . . the garden is thus the link between earth and heaven, at least at the beginning of human history," just as it is in Tolkien's mythology.[482] The sapling's providential appearance immediately after Aragorn's return and coronation is not coincidental, and Gandalf says as much: "Remember this. For if ever a fruit ripens, it should be planted, lest the line die out of the world. Here it has lain hidden on the mountain, even as the race of Elendil lay hidden in the wastes of the North. Yet the line of Nimloth is older far than your line, King Elessar."[483]

As we will discover in the final chapter, the Valar and Maiar (who together are known as the Ainur) are the mythological equivalents of God's divine council in the Bible. We will explore who these heavenly beings are and how best to understand them later. For now, the important thing is that this tree is the symbol of Aragorn's people, the Numenoreans, and they have the best of both worlds, as Numenoreans are half elf and half man. The tree is also a symbol of the Numenorean bloodline's right to rule Middle-earth and a remnant of heaven on earth. Nimloth the Fair used to bloom on the island of Numenor before it was destroyed, and that tree descended from

Telperion, which used to bloom on Valinor. The White Tree, then, is not only the symbol of the king but also of his kingdom. As we discussed earlier, it is very important that we do not separate what Christianity views as a holistic unity. According to Wright, kingdom and cross are often separated into the "kingdom of religion/faith and the kingdom of the state," but this is a mistake. Jesus's disciples "believed themselves to be living between Jesus's *accomplishment* of the reign of God and its full *implementation*," says Wright. "But the eschatology in question was not just the personal or 'spiritual' eschatology of so much Western thought . . . but the social, cultural, political, and even cosmic eschatology of Matthew, Paul, Revelation and of course—perhaps above all—the fourth gospel."[484] God's reign is comprehensive, not particular; "therefore what God has joined together, let no one separate."[485] As a Christian, Tolkien believed that "the creator God wanted the world to be ordered and ruled by his image-bearing humans," and that this world is holistic unity of heaven *and* earth.[486]

The sapling's discovery is directly related to the event which precedes it: Aragorn's coronation. Nowhere in the novel is it made clearer that this is a story about how God became king on earth as it is in heaven. "A hush fell upon all as out from the host stepped the Dunedain in silver and grey; and before them came walking slow the Lord Aragorn," Tolkien begins. After Faramir announces the return of the king, he asks the people of Minas Tirith if they will accept Aragorn as their king, to which the "host and all the people cried *yea* with one voice." Aragorn receives his crown from Faramir, but *gives it back*, just as Jesus "made himself nothing by taking the very nature of a servant."[487] Next, Tolkien tells us that Aragorn requests that Frodo and Gandalf, who Philip Ryken has argued are the other two "offices of the messiah"—High Priest and Prophet—participate in placing the crown on his head.[488] Next, Frodo takes the crown from Faramir, the steward, and then brings it to Gandalf, who places the crown on Aragorn's head and proclaims: "Now come the days of the King, and may they be blessed while the thrones of the Valar endure!" When Aragorn arose with the crown on his head Tolkien tells us that "all that beheld him gazed in silence, for it seemed to them he was revealed to them now for the first time." Behold the king, indeed![489] The coup de grace is that right before Aragorn's triumphant entry and coronation, a great eagle "bore tidings beyond hope," much like the herald in Isa 52:7 who proclaims: "Your God reigns!" In fact, the eagle says exactly that: "Sing and be glad, all ye children of the West, for your King shall come again, and he shall dwell among you all the days of your life and the Tree that was withered shall be renewed."[490] We can also see that the eagle foreshadows the discovery of the sapling of the White Tree. King and kingdom, heaven and earth, already and not yet: this is the good news.

And then there are the parallels all this has with Jesus's parables. The parables of the prodigal son and wicked tenants, for example, with their contrasting images of extravagant/dutiful sons returning to their fathers or at their fathers' behests, have clear parallels in Aragorn's life. Both sons in the parables are rejected in some way and both sons reflect characteristics of the kind of messiah Jesus claimed to be. In the prodigal son from Luke's Gospel, we could infer that the prodigal son resembles, in a way, Israel/the messiahs of the House of David squandering their father's inheritance—to be a light to the nations—and yet nevertheless deciding to repent and make a change. The parable may also shed light on the kind of "son" the messiah will be. In Israel's ancient Scriptures, the king of Israel is also God's son, implying the close relationship between the two. But this is not the kind of king/son we would expect, and that is part of the challenge of the parable. In Mark's parable, however, the son is sent by his father to hold the wicked tenants accountable. Here the messiah is characterized as a faithful and loyal son who does what his father commands, even though it costs him his life. These insights have their parallels in *The Lord of the Rings* through Aragorn's ranger-appearance/status and, later, his descent into the Paths of the Dead as part of the journey he must take to the throne. But like in the Gospels, death has no power over the king, and it is the dead who ultimately obey the king.

Indeed, Aragorn's power over disease and death and his ability to command the dead are the next topics we must discuss. In book V, chapter 8 of *The Return of the King*, immediately after the Battle of the Pelennor Fields (chapter 6), Aragorn's healing of Faramir, Eowyn, and Merry has clear parallels with the story in Mark 5:25–34 of the woman with the issue of blood. Besides the proverb with a very clear messianic allusion from the wise woman Ioreth, "The hands of the king are the hands of a healer, and so shall the rightful king be known," Tolkien tells us that while Aragorn was healing Faramir, "Aragorn's face grew grey with weariness."[491] When Jesus was on his way to heal Jairus's daughter, the hem of his robe was touched by a woman with a severe bleeding problem who pressed through a crowd of people just to make physical contact with the king. The most fascinating verse of Mark 5:25–34 is verse 30, which tells us that "Jesus realized that power had gone out from him." The healings evidently taxed both kings' constitutions. The king's healing hands are a manifestation of his *exousia*, "royal authority," over the black breath. That Aragorn's hands can mend and heal is a significant parallel to Jesus, but a parallel of even greater significance is his power to command the dead. Recalling their harrowing journey along the Paths of the Dead, Legolas tells Pippin and Merry, "At his command they fell back."[492] Throughout the novel Aragorn frequently speaks of his destiny and the heavy toll it has exacted over the years. When the Dunedain and sons of Elrond bring word to Aragorn that he ought to take this perilous journey "if thou art in haste," Aragorn replies, "But great indeed will be my haste ere I take that road."[493] Like Jesus, Aragorn trembles at the thought that his journey to the throne will take him through death itself. At this point in the story, Aragorn, Legolas, Gimli, and others are at Helm's Deep formulating a plan to come to the aid of Minas Tirith. We have seen that Aragorn is reluctant to take the Paths of the Dead, just as Jesus prayed to his Father, "If it is possible, may this cup be taken from me. Yet not as I will, but as you will."[494] As we have previously mentioned, Tolkien spends a great deal of time describing Aragorn's appearance throughout the novel. The day that Aragorn and the Grey Company decide to set out for the Paths of the Dead is a somber day. The night before, we are told that "some dark doubt or care sits on him." In the morning, emerging from what must have been a spiritual wrestling match, Merry tells us that "so startling was the change that he saw in him, as if in one night many years had fallen on his head. Grim was his face, grey-hued and weary."[495] What could have possibly happened in a single night that could cause such weariness to fall on Aragorn's shoulders? He looked into the Palantir, one of the ancient Numenorean seeing-stones of his people to reveal himself to Sauron and identify himself as the one true king of Middle-earth.

That Aragorn's revelation of his identity to Sauron and his decision to take the Paths of the Dead coincide is once again not a coincidence. Jesus, too, wrestled with the enemy and his destiny in the garden of Gethsemane immediately prior to his arrest, trial, torture, and crucifixion. These two events in *The Lord of the Rings* bring to mind two events which they resemble in the Gospels. First, it is quite interesting that Aragorn tells Gimli that he revealed himself to Sauron "in other guise than you see me here."[496] This means that Aragorn revealed his fully *transfigured, regal* self to Sauron, not the weary, "grey-hued" ranger. This resembles the transfiguration on the mountain in the Gospels where it is written that "he [Jesus] was transfigured before them," and that "his clothes became dazzling white, whiter than anyone in the world could bleach them."[497] Aragorn's decision to reveal himself to Sauron resembles both the transfiguration and Jesus's prayer in Gethsemane the night before his crucifixion. Similarly, Aragorn's struggle with the Palantir—though he is its rightful owner—takes quite a toll on him, which echoes what Luke 22:44 tells us about Jesus's prayer in Gethsemane: "And being in anguish, he prayed more earnestly, and his sweat was like drops of blood falling to the ground." The parallels between Jesus and Aragorn here are quite clear, though not identical. Both kings' trials precede their passion and/or experience with death, and both kings emerge transfigured from their respective experiences with death. Jesus rises from the dead and Aragorn emerges from the Paths of the Dead commanding an army of the dead to bring justice to Minas Tirith. According to Middleton, in the Bible, resurrection "is a reversal of the earthly situation of oppression" which fulfills "the original human dignity and status in Genesis 1:26–28 and Psalm 8:4–8, where humans are granted rule of the earth."[498] All of the moments we have surveyed thus far are examples of manifestations of Aragorn's royal authority and presence. They are also excellent examples which reinforce the thesis of this chapter, which is that *The Lord of the Rings* is the good news that God has become king on earth as in heaven. But these events in *The Return of the King* have been long in the making. In the next two and final sections of this chapter, we will follow Aragorn's journey all the way back to his departure from Rivendell and trials in the wilderness, his friendship with Gandalf, his hunt for Gollum, his role behind the scenes during the events of *The Fellowship of the Ring*, and his gradual transformation from a Dunedain ranger into the king we have seen him as in *The Return of the King*.

"A LIGHT FROM THE SHADOWS SHALL SPRING"

Since the last event we discussed was Aragorn's revelation of his true identity to Sauron through the Palantir, we will begin with Pippin's curious encounter with the seeing-stone on the road to Helm's Deep. Pippin discovered the Palantir back at Isengard after the Battle of Helm's Deep, but was quickly commanded to hand it over to Gandalf for safe keeping. After the company finished business with Saruman, they began their journey back to Helm's Deep, which is where we left off in the previous section. En route, the company stopped to camp, and a restless Pippin felt "driven by some impulse that he did not understand" to take the Palantir from a sleeping Gandalf.[499] Stealing away from the camp to a little green hill, Pippin looked into the Palantir and was confronted by the Dark Lord himself. Fortunately, Pippin was not interrogated by Sauron and so he did not reveal any sensitive information about Frodo's quest to destroy the One Ring. After this close call, Gandalf approaches Aragorn and asks him if he will guard it, though it is a perilous task, to which Aragorn replies, "Dangerous indeed, but not to all. There is one who may claim it by right . . . now my hour draws near. I will take it."[500] One of the unique features of John's Gospel are the frequent references Jesus makes to his "hour."[501] According to Brant Pitre in his book *Jesus the Bridegroom*, Jesus uses this "expression in a technical way to refer to the *time of his passion and death.*"[502] It is the same in Tolkien's parable. There are several important moments in the novel when Aragorn speaks of his "hour" or "the hour," which refers to his destiny to return to the throne of Minas Tirith.[503] As we have already seen, the path to the throne takes Aragorn through death itself. In fact, it is quite interesting that references to Aragorn's "hour" begin at the Council of Elrond, right before Anduril is reforged and the Fellowship of the Ring sets out on its quest on December 25. And though Tolkien denied that he intentionally chose this date for its Christian significance in an interview given in 1966, considering what we just learned makes this comment much harder to believe.[504] In a sense, then, the departure from Rivendell in one sense resembles the wedding at Cana, which is the first occurrence of Jesus's "hour" in the Gospel of John.[505]

There are two insights we can walk away with from the taking of the Palantir by Aragorn. First, like Jesus's, Aragorn's path to the throne is not without great sacrifice. The consistent references to Aragorn's "hour" strongly resemble those in the Gospel of John. Once again, these are hints woven into the narrative delicately that suggest that the gospel is the story of how God became king. The second insight is similar to the episodes from the Houses of Healing and Paths of the Dead: as the rightful king, Aragorn has the power and authority to heal the sick, command the dead, and resist corruption. We have also seen that Aragorn, like Jesus, chose to confront death directly and to finally lay down his life on his own terms.[506] Originally, the Palantiri belonged to the kings of Numenor and were used for communication between the realms of Numenor in exile. Sauron used the Palantir to corrupt Saruman and to abuse the original purpose of the seeing stones of Numenor. Aragorn's ability to hold the stone *and* later confront Sauron demonstrates his power to resist temptation and his mastery over evil. In fact, it is remarkable how few instances there are in the novel where Aragorn errs. There are moments where Aragorn doubts the choices he has made and laments, but this in keeping with him as a type of Christ, who was the "man of sorrows."[507]

Working backward from this event, we now come to the Battle of Helm's Deep, where one of the most profound revelations of Aragorn's regal authority and presence occurs. Although there are several similarities between Peter Jackson's movie version and the book, much is lost in the translation from page to the big screen. Perhaps the most regrettable omission is Aragorn's brave decision to walk out on the ramparts and speak directly to the Uruk-Hai, who have all but breached the fortress. In these final moments before dawn, Aragorn comes forward to warn the orcs and evil men besieging the mountain fastness that dawn will bring the death of them all. As he said this, "so great a power and royalty was revealed in Aragorn, as he stood there alone above the ruined gates before the host of his enemies, that many of the wild men paused, and looked back over their shoulders to the valley, and some looked up doubtfully at the sky."[508] At that, Aragorn leapt down into the midst of his enemies to confront them head-on. Here we even see the word "royalty" being used to communicate the authority that Aragorn's presence exudes. In this chapter of *The Two Towers*, we are witnessing the transformation of Strider the Dunedain ranger into the King of Arnor and Gondor which he eventually becomes. Once again, Tolkien emphasizes Aragorn's transfigured appearance to foreshadow what will eventually occur at the end of the story. Not only that, but this is another excellent example of how Tolkien's parable reflects the good news. Another significant theological parallel worth pointing out here is that both Jesus and Aragorn must do battle with the Enemy in order to bring about their kingdom. As Ryken has pointed out, "the warrior-king could not fully claim his rightful crown until he gained victory in battle. Only then would his kingship be acknowledged by all his subjects and secured in the presence of his foes."[509] This reminds one of what Jesus said in Mark 3:27 about Satan: "No one can enter a strong man's house without first tying him up. Then he can plunder the strong man's house." In the next part of this chapter, we will be taking a closer look at Aragorn's role in the first part of *The Lord of the Rings*, *The Fellowship of the Ring*. Of particular importance for us is chapter 2 of book II, which is the Council of Elrond, as we will use this chapter to begin looking at Aragorn's role in the story before the events of the War of the Ring. In this last section we will also see how Aragorn is introduced into the main story and how Tolkien subtly hints toward Aragorn's regal identity very early in the book. Last, but not least, we will once again turn to the appendices of the novel to look at Aragorn's birth, youth, initiation, and trials in the wilderness which lead up to the events of the novel.

"NOT ALL THOSE WHO WANDER ARE LOST"

On February 16, 3019 TA (Third Age), the Fellowship of the Ring sets out from Lothlorien on the second half of their great quest to destroy the One Ring. We last saw Aragorn at the Battle of Helm's Deep, which took place on March 3, 3019. The most significant—and tragic—event that happened between these two events was the breaking of the Fellowship itself, which took place on February 26, 3019. Boromir dies in a heroic last stand to defend Merry and Pippin from the orcs while Frodo and Sam begin their lonely quest toward Mordor.[510] Another interesting moment occurs in the chapter before the death of Boromir: Aragorn and the Fellowship pass through the Argonath, the Pillars of the Kings of Numenor. The company had been given boats to travel down the Anduin river by Galadriel and Celeborn of

Lothlorien. As Aragorn passes through the massive stone statues of his Numenorean ancestors, we are told that he is "a king returning from exile to his own land."[511] The theme of exile is something that both Tolkien's and Jesus's parables have in common. In the Gospels, Jesus is depicted as the long-lost king of the House of David, returning out of ancient exile to his native land. This is also an important theme in the story of Thorin in *The Hobbit*, as we will see in the next chapter. Indeed, this exile status which Aragorn and Thorin share is one of the central images Tolkien employs to reflect the gospel. Moreover, many of Jesus's parables, such as the parables of the prodigal son and the wicked tenants, have exile as a main theme.[512] Jesus himself refers to his own exile status in a few passages in the Gospels. In Matthew 8:20, he says, "Foxes have dens and birds have nests, but the Son of Man has no place to lay his head," and in Mark 6:4, "A prophet is not without honor except in his own town, among his relatives and in his own home."

The One Ring corrupted Boromir, who then tried to take it from Frodo, which should give us pause for a moment to consider how Tolkien understood the One Ring. According to Bradley J. Birzer, "indeed, the sole purpose of the One Ring is to re-order the world in Sauron's image, to mock, to corrupt, and to pervert Ilúvatar's creation."[513] In Christian terms, the One Ring is an idol. Idols are good or bad things that we love more than God, which we cannot live without. Idols destroy our ability to reflect God's image out into the world. Basically, anything or anyone that we love more than God will disappoint us, depress us, die on us, or otherwise eventually fail us in some way, and in so doing, destroy us. Before the breaking of the Fellowship, the company took refuge in Lothlorien because they were being pursued by orcs from Moria, which the Fellowship had just traveled through. Tragically, the journey through Moria took a heavy toll, as Gandalf lost his life defending the Fellowship from a Balrog. Balrogs are ancient demonic lieutenants who fought in the army of Melkor, the first Dark Lord, whom we shall meet in the final chapter. After Gandalf died, Aragorn took charge of the Fellowship and led them to safety in the woods of Lorien.

While in Lorien, the company meets Galadriel, a very ancient and important elf who bestows gifts upon each member of the Fellowship. Galadriel, who is Arwen's grandmother, gives Aragorn two gifts: a sheath for Anduril, Aragorn's sword, and a "clear green, set in silver brooch that was wrought in the likeness of an eagle with outspread wings." Taking the brooch and pinning it upon his breast, "those who saw him wondered; for they had not marked before how tall and kingly he stood, and it seemed to them that many years of toil had fallen from his shoulders."[514] Here again in Lorien, we can see Tolkien taking the time to describe how Aragorn's appearance is transfigured, intimating the full revelation of his greatness at his future coronation. This moment in Lorien also foreshadows Aragorn's wedding to Arwen. Recall the haunting beauty of Aragorn's coronation when "all that beheld him gazed in silence." "Tall as the sea-kings of old, he stood above all that were near; ancient of days he seemed and yet in the flower of manhood; and wisdom sat upon his brow, and strength and healing were in his hands, and a light was about him."[515] By now we have hopefully begun to notice certain recurring words which Tolkien employs to describe Aragorn's royal presence and authority. It's interesting to also note how frequently both Aragorn and Jesus are described as possessing "wisdom" and "authority." For example, after delivering the Sermon on the Mount, Matt 7:9 says, "he taught as one who had authority, and not as their teachers of the law." And in Luke 7:35, after responding to criticism about Jesus's proclivity to celebrate everywhere he went, Jesus refers to his "wisdom" by saying that "wisdom is proved right by all her children."

In this last stretch of the chapter, we will conclude by exploring Aragorn's role behind the scenes of the novel's main events and finish with a brief overview of his birth, upbringing, and trials in the wilderness, which all occur prior to the beginning of *The Fellowship of the Ring*. It's important to point out that though our Aragorn-centric survey of *The Lord of the Rings* is coming to an end, we are not finished talking about Aragorn himself. It has been the primary goal of this chapter to show how the story of the return of the king is the story of how God became king, and how *that* story is what it means to understand Christianity as good news. By being a story about the return of the king, Tolkien's parable is itself a proclamation of good news. But we have also watched the story of Aragorn unwind to this point where we first meet him in Bree as Strider the ranger and have hopefully learned how Tolkien reflected the gospel through his descriptions of the gradual transformation of Aragorn from ranger into king. Attentive readers will have probably noticed that Jesus's identity is also revealed incrementally in the Gospels. In fact, when we read the Gospels *backward*, we can see Jesus's ministry, death, and resurrection hinted at in several key moments in the story. This is also true if we extend that retrospective approach further back to the Old Testament. In fact, that is exactly what we will be doing in the next two (and final) chapters of the book for Aragorn. We will be asking, "How is Aragorn's return prefigured in *The Hobbit* and *The Silmarillion* in the same way that Jesus's is in the Old Testament?"

The next moment in our retrospective journey through Tolkien's parable is the Council of Elrond, which takes place on October 25, 3018. Exactly two months later, the Fellowship of the Ring sets out on December 25 from Rivendell. In her excellent book *The Battle for Middle-earth*, biblical scholar Fleming Rutledge points out that this departure date reflects the seriousness of the Christian task "of taking up the cross," which Jesus speaks of in Matt 16:24: "If anyone would come after me, let him deny himself and take up his cross and follow me." According to Rutledge, Tolkien's decision to have the Fellowship leave Rivendell on December 25 is quite meaningful, for it is the Feast of the Nativity. "The mission of the Fellowship is itself incarnational, that is, grounded or embodied." Tolkien seems to suggest there is a resemblance between the departure date of December 25 and the "birth of the Son of God."[516] In the terms we have set out in this book, we would say that Tolkien reflects the birth of Jesus parabolically. But what is meant by the suggestion? One possible way we might look at this is to understand it as the beginning—"birth"—of Jesus's/Aragorn's ministries. Unlike in the movies, Narsil—the Numenorean sword of his ancestors—is reforged *before* the Fellowship leaves Rivendell. Elrond gives this sword to Aragorn as he sets out on the final stage of his journey to reclaim his throne. Of course, in a parable, there is no direct symbolic correspondence, so we must be careful here. Nevertheless, this is suggestive of Rev 19:15, which says, "Coming out of his mouth is a sharp sword with which to strike down the nations." Aragorn has gone out into the world to defeat Sauron and reclaim his throne from this usurper as the rightful king of the world. Aragorn himself makes this clear at the council, saying, "A new hour comes. Isildur's Bane is found. Battle is at hand. The Sword shall be reforged. I will come to Minas Tirith."[517] It doesn't matter that Rev 19:15 describes the second *parousia* of Christ; it still applies, for Christians believe that Jesus is already reigning.

Furthermore, if we understand the Fellowship to resemble the church, and Aragorn is its eventual leader after the death of Gandalf in Moria, we could suggest that there is a resemblance to what Paul says about Christ being "the head of the body, the church" in Col 1:18 here. From this event, we move back to the actual council itself where we hear about Aragorn's role behind the scenes hunting for Gollum with Gandalf during the events of *The Fellowship of the Ring*. In fact, Aragorn and Gandalf hunt for Gollum on and off for eight years, from 3009–3017. (To put things in chronological perspective, the *Fellowship* opens in September 3001 with Bilbo's 111th birthday party.) Readers may be interested to know that Aragorn and Gandalf first met all the way back in 2956, forty-five years before Bilbo's party.[518] In a moment, we will return to that meeting and discuss Aragorn's early life, but before we do, we should discuss more specifically why Aragorn and Gandalf were searching for Gollum and a few other important moments at the Council of Elrond. Before we begin, it would be helpful to establish a timeline. Readers may recall that in the movie version of *The Fellowship of the Ring*, Galadriel, played by Cate Blanchett, who narrates the beginning minutes of the film, tells us that Gollum was once called Smeagol, and that he possessed and was himself possessed by the One Ring for five hundred years. According to "Appendix B" of *The Return of the King*, Smeagol/Gollum fled into the Misty Mountains with his newly discovered "precious" in 2470, exactly 531 years before Bilbo's birthday celebration, but he found the ring in 2463. In the ensuing seven years, Smeagol was cast out from his community and corrupted by the Ring.

To give us some perspective and to get us excited for the next chapter, Smaug the Magnificent (a dragon) invades and occupies Erebor—the Lonely Mountain—in 2770, three hundred years after Gollum retreats into the Misty Mountains (on a side note, Erebor was founded by the dwarves in 1999). During the Council of Elrond, Gandalf tells the elves, dwarves, men, and hobbits assembled there that "some here will remember that many years ago I myself dared to pass the doors of the Necromancer in Dol Guldur, and secretly explored his ways, and found thus that our fears were true: he was none other than Sauron, our Enemy of old."[519] This was the first of two harrowing journeys into Dol Guldur which Gandalf would make, and it occurred in 2063, which is also when Tolkien says the "Watchful Peace" began. Gandalf went to Dol Guldur in Mirkwood to investigate whether Sauron, "our Enemy of old," had returned, but Sauron would not return there until 2460, just around the time the One Ring would reveal itself. According to Tolkien, 2460 is also the year the Watchful Peace ended. Three years later, the same year Smeagol murdered his relative Deagol (who actually found the Ring) and took the Ring for his own, the White Council was formed. The White Council was led by Saruman the White, the chief wizard of Middle-earth and, at the time, Gandalf's superior. In this same year as the finding of the One Ring, the White Council "drove the evil out of Mirkwood."[520] This council functioned as a guardian against the rise of Sauron, but in reality, Saruman used it as a cover to search for the One Ring himself.

Indeed, Gandalf later enters Dol Guldur a second time in 2850 and finds that Sauron "is gathering all the Rings and seeking for news of the One, and of Isildur's Heir."[521] There he also finds Thrain, Thorin Oakenshield's father, in the dungeons of Sauron. In his final moments, Thrain gives Gandalf the key to Erebor, which Gandalf will later give to Thorin (more on this in the next chapter). Aragorn—"Isildur's Heir"—is born in 2931 and brought to Rivendell by his widowed mother, Gilraen, in 2933, who conceals her son's ancestry from the Enemy by naming him "Estel," which means "hope" in Sindarin. This is a very significant detail, and readers are encouraged to make a note to remember this. Why? Because this name—"Estel"—is prefigured in a conversation which takes place in the First Age of Middle-earth, found in a text known as "The Debate of Finrod and Andreth." Finrod and Andreth speak of a messiah-like figure eventually coming into the world from the race of men and refer to this prophecy as the "Old Hope [Estel]."[522] Once again, this connection can only be comprehended retrospectively, with knowledge of the figure of Aragorn/Christ firmly in mind. And this is not the only way the messiah appears in Middle-earth. As we will see in the next chapter, Thorin is, like Aragorn, an exiled king without a crown who also returns to his throne. If Israel is reflected in all Iluvatar's children, then it also logically follows that we can and should understand Thorin as a prefiguration of Aragorn/Christ, even though Thorin and Aragorn are quite different. This is no different from comparing the resemblances between David and Jesus in the Bible. The events of *The Hobbit* take place during the year 2941, when Aragorn is only ten years-old. As readers of that book know, Gandalf leaves Thorin and company before they enter Mirkwood. Why? Gandalf leaves them to convince Saruman and the White Council to attack Sauron in his fortress of Dol Guldur, which is ultimately successful. Interestingly, Saruman only agrees to this because he wants to prevent Sauron from finding the One Ring, even though Gollum will not leave the Misty Mountains to search for the "thief" who stole it from him (Bilbo) until 2944, three years after the events of *The Hobbit*.

Gandalf, having successfully driven Sauron from Dol Guldur, returns to Thorin and company just in the nick of time for the Battle of Five Armies at the conclusion of *The Hobbit*. However, in 2951 "Sauron declares himself openly and gathers power in Mordor."[523] In this very same year, Elrond reveals to Estel his "true name and ancestry, and delivers to him the shards of Narsil."[524] At twenty, Aragorn then goes out "into the wild" presumably to test himself, which does have an interesting parallel with Jesus's retreat into the wilderness after his baptism in the Gospels. One year after meeting Gandalf for the first time in 2956, Aragorn "undertakes his great journeys and errantries" under the alias "Thorongil," which means "Eagle of the Star."[525] It is very interesting to think of Aragorn—the future king—serving the fathers of two men who are not his equal. This, too, has parallels in the gospel. According to Mark 10:45, Jesus said, "For even the Son of Man did not come to be served, but to serve, and to give his life as a ransom for many." Throughout the Gospels Jesus consistently serves people who are broken and sinful rather than demanding obeisance from them as he could. It seems that both kings preferred to hide in plain sight.

Now come forward to 3001, the beginning of the novel. Tolkien tells us that after Bilbo leaves for Rivendell that same year, Gandalf also leaves to seek for news of Gollum and "calls on the help of Aragorn." We can see now that Gandalf and Aragorn have very important reasons to search for Gollum, who possessed the One Ring for over five hundred years and who desperately wants it back. But above all, Gandalf and Aragorn feared that Gollum would reveal to Sauron that the One Ring had indeed not been lost and was in the hands of a hobbit from the Shire. Sometime around 3009, Tolkien tells us that Gollum was eventually captured by Sauron, who in turn commanded the Nazgul to search the Shire for the Ring, which happens on September 23 of 3018, the very day Frodo leaves Bag End for Rivendell. Obviously, Gollum revealed this crucial information during his imprisonment in Mordor. Shortly after Gollum was released by Sauron, Aragorn captures him and brings him to Legolas's father, Thranduil, in Mirkwood. Returning now to the Council of Elrond, Aragorn and the others learn there from Legolas that Gollum eventually escaped from the elves of Mirkwood. The rest of the conversation at the council focuses on Saruman's betrayal, Gandalf's imprisonment in Orthanc, and his subsequent journeys to find Strider, Frodo, and the hobbits in the wilderness while they were en route to Rivendell.

The hobbits first meet Strider in Bree in chapter 10 of book I, where, after reading aloud a letter Gandalf had left there for the hobbits about Strider's identity, Aragorn pledged his life to protect Frodo. We could also point out here that one of the earliest moments where we get a hint of Strider's regal identity occurs as Aragorn tells the hobbits the tale of Beren and Luthien, who are his ancestors. Their love story is quite obviously paralleled by Aragorn and Arwen's in the novel, as Beren was a man and Luthien was an elf maiden. As he is telling the hobbits this story before the events which occur on Weathertop, Tolkien gives us the first significant description of Strider as the coronated Aragorn, but it is a subtle moment: "Above him was a black starry sky. Suddenly a pale light appeared over the crown of Weathertop behind him. The waxing moon was climbing slowly above the hill that overshadowed them, and the stars above the hill-top faded."[526] Weathertop used to be a watchtower of the Numenoreans, Aragorn's people, so it is significant that Tolkien says that a "pale light appeared over the *crown* of Weathertop behind him." Upon closer examination, it is obvious that Tolkien is playing with the word "crown" to suggest that the pale light on the crown of the hill formed a sort of actual crown that would later actually appear on Aragorn's head at the conclusion of the novel.

THE BIRTH AND UPBRINGING OF THE MESSIAH

We will conclude this chapter with a brief but very important section about the nativities and early years of Jesus and Aragorn, and especially how the latter resembles the former. We would also be remiss not the discuss the very important role which Gilraen—Aragorn's mother—plays early in his life and how she resembles the Blessed Virgin Mary. Tolkien was, after all, a devout Catholic.

To put it simply, Protestants and Catholics sharply disagree about the status and role of the Virgin Mary. For Protestants, she is an ordinary yet honored member of the sinful human race who conceived by the Holy Spirit and gave birth to Jesus the messiah. Protestants (and Jews) often point out that the Hebrew word *almah* and Greek word *parthenos* can be translated as "virgin" *or* "young woman." She is not the Mother of God (Greek *theotokos*), she was not conceived in her mother's womb without sin (the immaculate conception), and she is not assumed into heaven body and soul upon her death. Catholics, on the other hand, believe that Mary remained a virgin her entire life (perpetual virginity), was created without sin (immaculate conception) and remained sinless her entire life, and was taken up into heaven as the "Queen of Heaven" when she died (bodily assumption).[527] Moreover, for Catholics, Mary is the New Eve, the New Ark of the Covenant, the Queen Mother, and the New Rachel.[528] We will very briefly explore all these roles of Mary because parallels to each can be found in Gilraen, the mother of Aragorn, in "Appendix A" of *The Lord of the Rings*. We will discuss Mary and Gilraen simultaneously and then show how both women reveal more about the messiah. After all, both women were the first "disciples" of their regal sons.

Just as Jesus lost the protection of his earthly father, Joseph, (presumably) early in his life, Aragorn's father, Arathorn, "was slain by an orc-arrow that pierced his eye" when Aragorn was just two years old. Interestingly, Tolkien seems to suggest that Elrond also resembles Joseph, for it is Elrond who becomes the young man's protector from that day forward. In another sense, Elrond also bears a resemblance to God the Father, because Elrond's revelation of Aragorn's true identity reminds us of Jesus's baptism in the Gospels. Tolkien tells us that this occurred when Aragorn was twenty years old. Note how Tolkien's wording clearly echoes the wording of the Gospels where God says, for example in Mark 1:11, "You are my Son, whom I love; with you, I am well pleased." In Tolkien's account he writes, "Elrond looked at him [Aragorn] and was pleased."[529] From two years to twenty, Aragorn's identity was kept secret, and he was given the name "Estel," which means "hope." We will return to this alias in the final chapter where we will learn that during the First Age, the hope that one day Iluvatar would enter his creation (the incarnation) was called "Estel." Here again is the "messianic secret" that we have already discussed. Why the secrecy? Tolkien tells us that the Enemy was searching for an heir of Isildur so that he could eliminate him before he proved a threat. We should keep this in mind going into the next chapter where we will see that Thorin Oakenshield's return to Erebor (the Lonely Mountain) essentially prevented Sauron from killing Aragorn.

Catholics believe that Mary is the New Eve, whose son Jesus is not only seen to be the New Adam but who was also prophesied in Gen 3:15 to do battle in the future with the Serpent. There is a clear parallel here between Mary/Gilraen and Jesus/Aragorn, who both outshine their broken bloodlines and defeat a great evil. Both Gilraen and Elrond tell Aragorn that a "great doom" awaits him and that he will "walk in the wild alone." It is interesting to note here that "doom" is the Old English word for "choice." Aragorn, like Jesus, must choose either to succumb to the weakness of his bloodline, or "rise above the height of all your fathers."[530] Both men face extended trials in the wilderness and face many temptations from the Enemy. As the New Adam, Jesus must "undo the effects of the Fall of Adam and Eve."[531] Similarly, Aragorn must undo the corruption which the One Ring caused in his ancestor, Isildur. Gilraen, like Mary, is the New Eve, whose son will bring about the "new heaven and new earth" and "Arda Remade," which Rev 21:1 and "The Debate of Finrod and Andreth" both speak of. Mary and Gilraen, then, are women who herald the beginning of the new creation.[532]

In the Catholic tradition, Mary is also the New Ark of the Covenant, the place where the *shekinah* (Hebrew "glory presence") of God dwells. Historically, the ancient Israelites understood the ark of the covenant to be the throne of God on earth. In the Old Testament, this was an ornate object, vividly described in Exod 25. In the New Testament, the story of the annunciation in Luke 1:26–38 shows Mary as the New Ark. Indeed, the angel Gabriel's words in verse 35 explicitly convey this: "The Holy Spirit will come upon you and the power of the Most High will overshadow you." The annunciation is prefigured in Exod 40:35 when we are told that Moses could not enter the tabernacle because God's glory had settled/overshadowed it. Although there is no exact parallel between Mary and Gilraen as the New Ark, Gilraen is the one who brought "Estel," hope, into the world. There is, however, a clear parallel between Mary/Gilraen in their role as *gebirah*, Hebrew for "queen mother." In ancient Israel, the king's queen was not his wife, but his mother.[533] We have already learned how Arwen resembles the "bride" of Christ—Israel, the church—and now we can see that Gilraen, too, reflects another important biblical idea. Interestingly, Gilraen is prefigured by the loremaster Andreth in the same way that the queen mother in the Old Testament prefigures Mary in the New Testament. As we will learn in the final chapter, Andreth speaks of "Estel" as the hope which men have in the eventual coming of Iluvatar into Arda (even though she herself is skeptical of it). "The Debate of Finrod and Andreth" has important parallels in

Old Testament prophecies such as Mic 5:2–3 and Isa 7:10–14, both of which speak of a woman who will one day give birth to a savior.

Finally, there is the Catholic belief of seeing Mary as the New Rachel, the "sorrowful mother of all Israel."[534] Both Mary and Gilraen predict, or are told, that their sons will suffer greatly in their lives. One thinks of Simeon's prophecy to Mary that "a sword will pierce your own soul, too" from Luke 2:35 when hearing how Gilraen speaks to her son about his great destiny. According to Pitre, "Rachel is not just the mother of Joseph and Benjamin . . . she is also the *mother of all Israel*, who somehow suffers with them and weeps for them, *even after her death*."[535] There is a clear parallel to this in Gilraen's parting words to Aragorn: "I gave Hope to the Dunedain; I have kept no hope for myself."[536] Gilraen's parting words to her son resemble Mary's role as the New Rachel. What does all of this tell us? First, it tells us how important Catholicism and the Virgin Mary were to Tolkien. After all, we have heard from him directly how important it was that his story reflect something of his Catholic beliefs. Next, it tells us that, in a parabolic way, Tolkien wished to show how Aragorn resembles Jesus as the messiah. It was clearly important for Tolkien as a Catholic to have Mary's relationship with her son reflected in some way in his story. Catholics pray to Mary so that they can be brought into closer relationship with her son, Jesus Christ. They do not worship her but honor her. The rosary is not idolatrous; it is the gospel in prayer form.

We have concluded this chapter with an analysis of a part of Tolkien's story that was probably very close to his heart, and one which ought not to be overlooked by Protestants as much as it is. Gilraen, like Mary, brought hope into the world, hope that we, like the inhabitants of Middle-earth, all desperately need. In his essay "The Weight of Glory," Lewis spoke of this hope, calling it our "inconsolable secret." He says that "our lifelong nostalgia, our longing to be reunited with something in the universe from which we now feel cut off, to be on the inside of some door which we have always seen from the outside, is no mere neurotic fancy, but the truest index of our real situation."[537] In the next chapter, we will examine the connection between Thorin and Aragorn, especially as it relates to the overarching monarchic theme which we have seen emerge in Tolkien's parable. My main argument will be this: Thorin and his ancestors resemble the Davidic kings of Israel who adumbrate the coming of the true king. This is also the part of the book where we begin to see how *The Lord of the Rings* is related to *The Hobbit* and *The Silmarillion* in the same way that the Gospels are related to the Old Testament. With knowledge of the gospel/*The Lord of the Rings* firmly in mind, we now want to look for ways in which *The Hobbit* and *The Silmarillion* prefigure the return of the king.

4

The King Beneath the Mountain

SEEING THORIN, THINKING ARAGORN

Although Tolkien first published *The Hobbit* on September 21, 1937, he later revised it and released a second edition in 1951.[538] According to Corey Olsen, when the second edition of *The Hobbit* was published in 1951, "it was still the only story of Middle-earth available to the public."[539] Tolkien revised *The Hobbit* chiefly because he wanted to make clearer the connection between it and his upcoming sequel, *The Fellowship of the Ring*, which would be the first of three parts that would become *The Lord of the Rings*. This is the first of two chapters which will deal with the prequels to *The Lord of the Rings*. Only via retrospection can we comprehend how essential *The Hobbit*—which we discuss in this chapter—and *The Silmarillion*—in the last chapter—are to understanding Tolkien's parabolic novel. In the previous chapter we learned that the consummation of the new heaven and new earth is still far in the future, both according to the Bible and *The Lord of the Rings*. However, the return of the true king to his throne is the *beginning* of that consummation which is promised in the future. The end of the story is brought into the present by the king himself. This is the *good news* which Christ came proclaiming two thousand years ago, but as we saw, it is not every Christian's understanding of the gospel. We also learned that if we come to Tolkien's parable with a distorted understanding of the gospel, then our ability to understand it as a proper Christian story—as good news—becomes quite difficult. We began with *The Lord of the Rings* because we determined, following the insights of top biblical scholars today, that reading Tolkien's books *backwards* is the only way to see the deep, intimate intertextuality at work in his mythology, and the only way to properly discern the gospel in Middle-earth. Again, a figural, retrospective hermeneutic is, according to Hays, "the discernment of unexpected patterns of correspondence between earlier and later events or persons within a continuous temporal stream."[540] And the stream can flow in both directions, illuminating our understanding of both poles of the narrative. There is, then, a big difference between prediction and prefiguration; the former is necessarily prospective and the latter retrospective.

Both in the previous chapter and at the beginning of this book we laid out evidence that Tolkien himself seems to have had this hermeneutical approach in mind while writing *The Lord of the Rings*. Recall his comment about "part of the appeal" of the novel being the glimpses of the vast backstory we get while reading *The Lord of the Rings*, glittering like an island on the horizon just beyond our reach. As a Christian, Tolkien also seems to have been deeply influenced and shaped by the Four Evangelists' narrative styles, especially Mark's. We concluded the previous chapter with an overview of Aragorn's early life and his first encounter with the hobbits in Bree. In this chapter, we will look at how Thorin, who is a type for the Davidic kings, and the dwarves, who are one type for Israel, prefigure Aragorn and the reconstituted Israel—the church. Remember that Tolkien himself thought of the "Dwarves like Jews."[541] In this chapter, we will have several opportunities to note how all this can be understood best retrospectively, with knowledge of the antitype (Jesus/Aragorn) in mind. Once again, it is the close intertextuality between Tolkien's books, and not any intertextuality between Tolkien's books and the Bible, which accounts for one of the chief resemblances between Tolkien's mythology and the Bible.

In this chapter, we are leaving Tolkien's parabolic novel behind and getting into the bigger narrative that frames it. Parables transfigure "the story that has gone before," but without compromising the intrinsic worth of the backstory.[542] A predictive, prospective hermeneutic—which continues to dominate popular theology—is harmful to the integrity of the Old Testament. It follows, then, that this kind of approach would also be harmful to a reading of Tolkien's books. *The Hobbit*, then, is not just a text to be mined for prooftexts about *The Lord of the Rings*, but a completely worthwhile story on its own. To understand Thorin as a prefiguration of Aragorn does *not* mean that Thorin's story is a mere prooftext for the story of Aragorn, or that it is not a unique, meaningful, standalone story without the story of Aragorn. In conclusion, "seeing Thorin, thinking Aragorn," or "seeing David, thinking Jesus," only makes sense retrospectively. The rest of this chapter will continue our retrospective journey from TA 2941, which is the year *The Hobbit* takes place, all the way back to the founding of Erebor by the dwarves in 1999.

"THE HALLS OF WAITING"

When the last great king of the House of David rode out from Jerusalem in 610 BC to stop Egyptian Pharaoh Necho II from giving aid to the crumbling Assyrian empire—which was being conquered by the ascendant Babylonian Empire—he thought he would return a conquering hero. Over the last thirty years, the people and nation of Israel had been living in a golden age. King Josiah's (640–610 BC) grandfather Manasseh (687–643 BC) was a despicable king who "did what was evil in the sight of the Lord."[543] Aside from permitting the worship of false gods, children were also sacrificed during his reign. But Josiah was hailed as a new Moses. Manasseh's idols had been torn down, human sacrifices outlawed, and rival temples destroyed; he had done the will of the Lord, and yet he had massacred many of his own people in the process. Josiah was indeed the last great king of the House of David before it went into exile. As 2 Kgs 22:2 tells us—in clear contrast to Manasseh—"he did what was right in the eyes of the Lord and walked in all the ways of his father David, not turning aside to the right or to the left." Sadly, Josiah was killed in battle, and Israel's dream of independence died with him. Three and a half centuries after the death of Josiah, another messiah of the Jews—but this time not from the House of David—lost his life in defense of Jerusalem. This king's name was Judah Maccabee ("The Hammer"). At the Battle of Elasa in 160 BC, Judah and a small band of Jews defended Jerusalem from the Greeks who were trying to recapture the territory that Judah had reclaimed a few years earlier. Judah, along with his father and his brothers, had led a revolution against the Greek king Antiochus IV and, with Roman help, had established the first Jewish independent state since Josiah. This, too, would not last, for Judah's descendants failed to establish a just and prosperous kingdom and eventually lost Israel to the Romans in the decades before the birth of Jesus.[544]

In many ways, Josiah's and Judah's stories resemble the story of Thorin Oakenshield and the House of Durin. Like Josiah and Judah, all his people's hopes rested on Thorin's shoulders. Unfortunately, though Thorin reclaimed Erebor—the Lonely Mountain—from the dragon Smaug, he, too, failed to establish justice in his kingdom. Like Josiah, Thorin met a tragic end, but the reestablishment of the "Kingdom under the Mountain" would not prove to be a total loss. As a Catholic, Tolkien would have been well familiar with the story of Judah Maccabee, for 1 and 2 Maccabees are considered deuterocanonical Scriptures in the Catholic but not Protestant tradition. We begin Thorin's story, sadly, with his final words to Bilbo, whom he had had a falling out with earlier in the book after the hobbit stole the Arkenstone and brought it to Thranduil: "I go now to the halls of waiting to sit beside my fathers, until the world is renewed. Since I leave now all gold and silver, and go where it is of little worth, I wish to part in friendship from you . . . if more of us valued food and cheer and song above hoarded gold, it would be a merrier world. But sad or merry, I must leave it now. Farewell!"[545] In contrast with Aragorn's parting words to Arwen ("In sorrow we must go but not despair"), Thorin's parting words are more somber. Thorin is not living in a world where the rightful king of all the children of Iluvatar sits on the throne. That hope—Estel—has not yet been fully revealed (remember: Aragorn is only ten). There is a hint of uncertainty and more than a hint of regret in the dwarf's last words. But there is also genuine repentance. Whether the world Thorin envisions in his parting words will become a reality or not he cannot foresee, but he hopes for it. He knows that he has loved the less important things more—the Arkenstone, for instance—and the more important things less. Then there is the eschatological significance of Thorin's comment, "I go now to the halls of waiting to sit beside my fathers, until the world is renewed." This is once again clear evidence that Tolkien's eschatological views were rooted in Jewish rather than Hellenistic soil. Christian eschatology teaches that first there is life after death, and then there is what Wright calls "life *after* life after death."[546] As a Catholic, Tolkien would have believed that purgatory is that first interim state (life after death). Both Catholics and Protestants believe that at the end of history, Jesus will return, raise the dead, and then judge the living and the dead.

The books of 1 and 2 Maccabees, which are only found in a Catholic Bible, also testify to the existence of purgatory. Yet it is important that we understand that purgatory is not so much a place as it is a process. According to Jerry Walls, "the essential purpose of purgatory is sanctification."[547] There is no consensus among Christians about a person's immediate, postmortem destiny, for the Bible spends more time talking about what happens in *after* life after death. Both Catholics and Protestants believe in purgatory, but the latter sees death itself as the final purgation of a person's sins. A person's ultimate destiny is sealed in their last moments; if there is genuine repentance and a turning toward Jesus Christ, that person will be saved; if not, they will merit hell (we will return to this topic in a moment). Most Protestants do not believe that a person is consciously able to cooperate with God in the sanctification process in life after death. The tree lies where it falls, in other words. As for people who lived before Jesus, who could not, as Rom 10:9

says, confess that Jesus is Lord with their mouths, Protestants believe they are judged based on how they responded to the measure of truth which was revealed to them (think here of Abraham, Moses, David, Confucius, Buddha, etc.). Some Protestants are more uncompromising than others when it comes to discussing the salvation of pre-Christian figures like Confucius, Socrates, and Buddha. In contrast, let us look at what Catholics believe.

Catholics believe in what they call the "particular judgment," which occurs immediately after a person dies. According to Peter Kreeft, "God infallibly knows and judges each soul as either (a) able to enter heaven immediately, or (b) needing to be purified in purgatory first and then able to enter heaven, or (c) set forever (since our lifetime is over) in unrepented sin and capable only of hell."[548] When, in Luke 23:43, Jesus told the penitent thief who was on a cross beside him that "today, you will be with me in paradise," he was *not* telling him that paradise was his *ultimate* destiny, but that he has inherited a share in the *olam haba* this very day, and that he, Jesus, would be with him somehow during the interim. This must be right, since Christians believe that we all follow the pattern Jesus set; first death, then the grave, then resurrection in the new creation. Three days later, Jesus rose from the dead and walked in *this* world before ascending to heaven—the transcendent dimension of reality, not a completely separate place. Thus, heaven is not the Christian's ultimate destiny, and we will not experience a disembodied afterlife where only our souls will be saved. As Wright has argued very persuasively in his book *Surprised by Hope*, the Judeo-Christian tradition emphasizes that our bodies matter, too.[549] Catholics believe that the penitent thief, like most people, died as an imperfect human being still in need of sanctification.

Understandably, Protestants like Wright here worry that the Catholic view of purgatory can not only sound sadistic, but can also diminish the saving work of Jesus on the cross; but this is a misunderstanding. If we place too much emphasis on the doctrine of grace, a saved person could easily take advantage of this, ask forgiveness for sins directly from God, and then go out and sin again. Protestants often cite Rom 8:38-39, "And I am convinced that nothing can ever separate us from God's love. Neither death nor life, neither angels nor demons, neither our fears for today nor our worries about tomorrow—not even the powers of hell can separate us from God's love. No power in the sky above or in the earth below—indeed, nothing in all creation will ever be able to separate us from the love of God that is revealed in Christ Jesus our Lord," as evidence that one cannot lose one's salvation, but this defense overlooks the importance of "works."[550] Yes, the blood of Christ covers all sins, but even a truly penitent person's sins still offend God, and the cost of covering that person's sins was the life of

Jesus. Catholicism, properly understood, walks the tightrope between grace and works. And there is a complex case such as Thorin who repents on his deathbed. Here, a Protestant would say that because Thorin repented, God accepts him into "temporary heaven" (paradise) and he will one day rise from the dead and enjoy the new creation, reigning with Christ. A quick word on several words that are often conflated and confused in the Bible. The Hebrew word *sheol* and the Greek words *hades* and *paradeisos* all refer to the same interim, temporary reality in life after death. This author's understanding, which has been informed by both Catholics and Protestants, is that *sheol/hades/paradeisos* ought to be understood as different ways of experiencing purgatory.

Those who have died obstinately unrepentant experience purgatory not as a place of sanctification, but as the beginning of hell. When that person is raised from the dead and judged in the future, they will either cease to exist (the church calls this position *annihilationism*) or suffer eternally in hell. Now, a word on hell. Hell is something we, not God, choose. In one of his classic books, *The Problem of Pain*, C. S. Lewis, famously argued that "the doors of hell are locked on the *inside*."[551] Yes, God is love, but he also granted us free will, and both love and justice demand that God not override our free will in choosing between good and evil. God will not, in other words, coerce us to love him. If, however, a person freely and persistently rejects God, because God is love he honors their choice. Hell, then, is ultimately alienation and exile from the presence of God. Jesus spoke of hell quite frequently in the New Testament as *gehenna*, which refers both to a valley outside Jerusalem and fire.[552] What Jesus meant was this. When a person dies either an unrepentent sinner or someone who refuses to participate with God in sanctification in purgatory, that person experiences hell. Whether that person eventually ceases to exist (annihilationism) or suffers eternally is still a matter of debate among theologians. The important thing is that both views hold to the belief that this person will *forever* be alienated from the presence of God.

As a Catholic, though he would agree that someone like Thorin would enter heaven's waiting room (purgatory) because he repented and died in a state of friendship with God, Tolkien would have believed that someone like Thorin would still need to be sanctified and purged of his remaining sins before entering heaven. Whatever we call it (*sheol, hades, paradeisos*), life after death is purgatory. For some, it is a painful but blissful experience as the person prepares for heaven and the new creation with Christ. For others, it is the beginning of hell and is a miserable experience. Protestants, however, remain firm in the belief that purgatory occurs at the moment of a saved person's death. On the Catholic view of things, just about everyone except the absolutely wicked experience purgatory. Purgatory is the waiting room of heaven/hell; it is like a layover where we await our final destination. For the few if any rare persons who died in a state of near-perfection, , Catholics believe that they go straight to heaven to await the unveiling of the new creation. Protestants like Wright believe that everyone who believes in Jesus Christ, and who has therefore freely accepted the undeserved grace that God has given us through Jesus, goes straight to paradise/temporary heaven to await the new creation. Any purgation, Wright believes, happens at the moment of one's death. This view, however, overlooks many special cases such as a person who has decided in his or her heart to become a Christian and get baptized tomorrow but dies today.

This view also overlooks those people who have done some very seriously evil things in life; are we really to believe that a person is saved by uttering a proposition? This is where the Catholic view of purgatory reveals its strengths.[553] Walls agrees that confessing the name of Jesus is vital for a person's salvation, but this still does not deal with certain special cases. The Bible clearly teaches that we are all sinners, that no sin can enter heaven, and that sin and holiness are separated by a huge chasm.[554] For anyone to be in temporary heaven with God, he must do something to us when we die to transfigure us from sinners into saints. Kreeft tells a story about an argument he and his father—a Calvinist—had about purgatory once. Finally, his mother stepped in and said, in light of what we just said above, "If the Catholics want to call it Purgatory, and we don't, aren't we arguing only about words?"[555] Purgatory, then, is what Thorin is alluding to when he refers to the "halls of waiting." Then, at the end of history, there will be the resurrection and the final judgment, which is "life *after* life after death." Thorin's comment about the "renewed" world is reminiscent of Isa 25:6–8, in which the prophet envisions a time in the future when God will prepare "a feast of rich food for all peoples, a banquet of aged wine—the best of meats and the finest of wines." This is what the Jews call the *olam haba*, "the Age to Come," or the "Messianic Age." Little did Thorin know that there was a king coming who would usher in and inaugurate that age ahead of schedule. We will return to this topic again later in this chapter and in the final chapter when we discuss Aule, the creator of the dwarves.

"ALL SORROW FAIL AND SADNESS AT THE MOUNTAIN-KING'S RETURN!"

We should now turn our attention to the way in which Tolkien addresses the issue of idolatry in *The Hobbit*. Although we have not discussed it very much, the One Ring is, like the Arkenstone, an idol, a false god. Both the Arkenstone and the One Ring represent man's desire to be the center of wisdom and order instead of God. According to Timothy Keller, "a counterfeit god [idol] is anything so central and essential to your life that, should you lose it, your life would feel hardly worth living." An idol, then, "is anything more important to you than God, anything that absorbs your heart and imagination more than God, anything you seek to give you what only God can give."[556] For Thorin, the Arkenstone was his idol. In the Silmarillion, Tolkien tells us that the dwarves were created by Aule—one of Iluvatar's divine council members—who desired to bring beings like himself into existence apart from Iluvatar. This, in a sense, is how Tolkien addresses the Catholic doctrine of "original sin." According to Kreeft, "sin does not mean that we are wholly evil or more evil than good (how could that be measured?) or that our very being is evil or that we are no longer infinitely valuable and infinitely loved by God. It means that we are seriously wounded, a defaced masterpiece. The greater the masterpiece, the more terrible its defacement is."[557] Although Iluvatar ultimately blesses Aule's creations, they have been tainted by the theme of Melkor, who is the divine council member responsible for introducing the desire to create things independent of Iluvatar.

So, what is the Arkenstone and why did Bilbo steal it? Bilbo himself was drawn to the Arkenstone and thought of keeping it as part of his share of the treasure promised by Thorin at the beginning of the quest.[558] The Arkenstone was discovered in Erebor by Thrain I (r. 1934–2190), one of Thorin's ancestors. The Arkenstone was known as the "Heart of the Mountain" and clearly resembles the ark of the covenant from the Hebrew Bible. It is a beautiful jewel that wields great influence over its owner (much like the Silmarils that we will discuss in the next chapter). In fact, it does nothing but corrupt the hearts of those who possess it. It became the king's jewel and the dwarves' most precious treasure. Losing the Arkenstone to Smaug was the most grievous loss for the dwarves and was the treasure Thorin longed for more than anything. And that was the problem, just as it was for the ancient Jews. According to Jer 3:15–16, "'Then I will give you shepherds after my own heart, who will lead you with knowledge and understanding. In those days, when your numbers have increased greatly in the land,' declares the Lord, 'people will no longer say, "The ark of the covenant of the Lord." It will never enter their minds or be remembered; it will not be missed, nor will another one be made.'"[559] This is an extremely important passage because it combines two major themes we've been looking at throughout this book. First, the prophet speaks of a day in the future when he will give Israel a "shepherd" (another way of saying "king" in ancient Israel) after God's own heart. Interestingly, Jeremiah was speaking this during the reign of King Josiah, so he was essentially saying, "Even Josiah isn't a king after God's own heart." Jeremiah was looking past Josiah to the future when the true king will appear.

Second, notice that Jeremiah is looking forward to a time when Israel will not *want* the ark of the covenant, presumably because they have something better. According to Pitre, the prophet Jeremiah "took the Ark from Jerusalem and hid it in Mount Nebo, in the territory east of the Jordan River, shortly before the Temple was destroyed" c. 587 BC. Once again, this testimony is preserved in 2 Macc 2:4–8, found only in a Catholic Bible. In this fascinating and little-known passage, Jeremiah takes both the tabernacle (precursor of the Temple of Solomon from Moses's day) and the ark and "found a cave . . . and he sealed up the entrance." When people tried to come and retrieve them, Jeremiah declared that "the place shall be unknown until God gathers his people together again and shows his mercy. And then the Lord will disclose these things, and the glory of the Lord and the cloud will appear, as they were shown in the case of Moses."[560] This text helps us to better understand what the prophet meant in Jer 3:15–16. Jeremiah is telling the people that a time is coming when they will not even want the ark, because he was planning on *hiding* it. Moreover, as he would later go on to say, God would plant the law in their hearts instead of on the stone tablets of Moses that were in the ark.[561] Jeremiah's remarks in 3:15–16 tell us that Israel's loves had long been out of order, just as Thorin's were.

But what did Jeremiah mean when he said that the ark's location would not be known *until* "God gathers his people," and the "glory of the Lord and the cloud will appear"? As we discussed at the end of the previous chapter, Mary/Gilraen can be seen as the New Ark, the new dwelling place of God's *shekinah* on earth. In light of what we know about the annuciation from the Gospel of Luke, we can look back on Jeremiah's words and see them as a prefiguration of Mary as the New Ark. Moreover, Jeremiah connects the reappearance of the glory of the Lord with the ingathering of Israel. That is, when the glory of God reappears, it will also mean that the messiah has reappeared to gather the scattered people of Israel once more. It is also important to point out here that after the destruction of Jerusalem in 587 BC by the Babylonians, even when the temple was later rebuilt, the holy of holies where the ark was once kept remained *empty*. Not only that, but Jews all the way up to the time of Jesus were waiting not only for a new Moses but for the return of God's "cloud" to the temple. Jews during the first century still believed that a new Moses and a new ark had not yet appeared. That is until Mary and Jesus came along, who were the New Ark and New Moses.[562]

Bilbo stole the Arkenstone and delivered it to the men and elves camped outside Erebor because he saw what it was doing to his friend.

Obviously, when Thorin discovered Bilbo's "betrayal," he was livid and tried to kill the hobbit. To quote Gandalf, Thorin was not making a very "splendid king under the Mountain."[563] Thorin's return to Erebor made him cynical and self-absorbed. Idols corrupt our hearts and prevent us from being able to reflect the image of God in which we were made.[564] On the one hand, Thorin had good cause to be cynical. By 2941, Thorin had lived in exile for 171 years, worked for outsiders, lost his father, Thrain, to Sauron, and immediately after he had reclaimed his throne under the mountain, he was being asked to part with the wealth of his people. Except on this last issue was Thorin somewhat in the right for feeling cynical and suspicious of outsiders. Not all the wealth of Erebor belonged to the dwarves; some of it belonged to the people of Laketown, who were led by Bard (the man who would go on to slay Smaug). Gold and treasure were a weakness to Thorin, but the Arkenstone was his idol. Tolkien's description of this is reminiscent of the effect which the One Ring had on Gollum and Boromir. According to Bilbo, "he did not reckon with the power that gold has upon which a dragon has long brooded, nor with dwarvish hearts. Long hours in the past days Thorin had spent in the treasury, and the lust of it was heavy on him."[565]

There is one last resemblance between the 2 Maccabees account, Thorin, and Aragorn we should point out before moving on. Like the ark, the Arkenstone was eventually placed upon Thorin's breast and *buried* with the king beneath the mountain: "There let it lie till the Mountain falls! May it bring good fortune to all his folk that dwell here after!"[566] Recall from the previous chapter that before Aragorn departs Lorien, Galadriel gives him a green and silver brooch called "Elessar," the Elfstone. There are several connections here worth noticing. The Arkenstone is buried underneath Erebor just like Jeremiah buried the ark in a cave. The prophet Jeremiah said that the ark would only be revealed when God's people were gathered together (the Fellowship/Jesus and the twelve disciples). The Elfstone is a great jewel like the Arkenstone, and it becomes Aragorn's symbol from that point forward. Later, after his coronation, he takes the name "King Elessar." The ark/Arkenstone, then, reappears after God's people are gathered together and the glory cloud of God "overshadows" Mary/Gilraen, the mothers of the messiahs. On his deathbed, Thorin looked forward to the merrier world that Aragorn would usher in when he becomes king. Aragorn, like Jesus, would be the kind of king Jeremiah fervently hoped for.

"GOLD IN A DYING FIRE"

According to "Appendix A" of *The Return of the King*, Thorin, the "heir without hope," was in exile from 2770 until 2941, for a total of 171 years. It would then be another seventy-seven years before Frodo set out to destroy the One Ring (3018). By this point in the book, we can now begin to understand with Gimli how everything in Tolkien's mythology is "strangely woven together." On March 15, 2941, as Gandalf was nearing the village of Bree, he happened to encounter Thorin, who was then living in exile northwest of the Shire. Looking *back* on this event later after the return of Aragorn as king, Gandalf says that "it was at that moment that the tide began to turn."[567] Why was this meeting so significant? Because had it not been for Thorin and the quest of Erebor, there might have been "dragon-fire and savage swords in Eriador" and "night in Rivendell," where a ten-year-old Estel lived hidden from Sauron. Had Thorin not returned to Erebor, Smaug would probably not have been slain by Bard of Laketown. Gandalf, who set the entire quest to reclaim Erebor into motion, wanted to prevent Sauron from using Smaug "with terrible effect."[568] Isaiah 49:2 conveys beautifully the hiddenness of the messiah: "in the shadow of his hand he hid me; he made me into a polished arrow and concealed me in his quiver." In the last chapter, we discussed how the hiddenness of the messiah—the "messianic secret"—is something that the Bible and Tolkien's parable have in common. Gandalf concludes providentially, "But that has been averted—because I met Thorin Oakenshield one evening on the edge of spring in Bree. A chance-meeting, as we say in Middle-earth."[569]

In retrospect, it is quite clear that neither Jesus nor Aragorn could have become king without Israel's and Thorin's respective returns to Jerusalem and Erebor. A sense of divine providence pervades both stories. Of course, one story does not "equal" the other. Instead, the resemblance between the two stories is their intertextuality and, of course, the shared theme of the return of the king. The way that Tolkien's parable is related to *The Hobbit* and *The Silmarillion* resembles the interaction between the New Testament and the Old Testament. As Christopher Scarf has already pointed out earlier, the "relation of the Gospels in 'looking back' to the Old Testament is parallel to the necessity of 'looking back'" in *The Lord of the Rings* and Tolkien's prequels.[570] Tolkien would have absorbed this way of looking at things from long years of meditating on Scripture, especially the parables of Jesus, which are "full of echoes" that "resonated with ancient scriptural promises."[571] It seems Tolkien paid a lot of attention to the backstories of both Aragorn and Thorin in the appendices of *The Lord of the Ring* because he wanted us to see how they were related when we looked back. The real reason for this is quite obviously Tolkien's Catholic faith. As a Catholic, Tolkien believed that Israel and David prefigure the church and Jesus. Tolkien knew that Jesus spent a lot of time in the Gospels and his parables alluding to the story of Israel and specifically to King David. By claiming to be at least the Son of David in the Gospels, Jesus was expressing continuity between himself and David's line. On the other hand, as we have already seen, Jesus also claimed that something "greater than Solomon" is here, and that the messiah is not only David's son, but his Lord.[572] This is paralleled in Middle-earth by having a Numenorean man come to the throne of Middle-earth, not just an elf, ordinary man, or dwarf. In some way, Aragorn is a part of each race's story and also separate from them, just like Jesus.

The events at the end of *The Hobbit* show us the strife which Iluvatar predicted long ago would exist between his "children of my adoption" (the dwarves) and the "children of my choice" (elves and men).[573] Although we will return to why this is in the next chapter, it's important to see the Battle of Five Armies infighting in light of this prophecy. This battle, which takes place before the gate of Erebor, involves elves, men, dwarves, orcs, and wargs. The fight is almost very nearly a battle between elves, men, and dwarves, but Gandalf prevents that disaster by showing up at the eleventh hour. It is interesting to know that Gandalf has just come from Dol Guldur, where he and the White Council expelled Sauron only to learn later that he retreated to Mordor. Thorin, whom we last saw brooding angrily over the loss of the Arkenstone and Bilbo's so-called betrayal, is nowhere to be seen. Just as the battle begins to turn against Iluvatar's children, however, Thorin appears clad in magnificent armor on the battlefield. His entrance is truly awe-inspiring and is reminiscent of Josiah's final battle. If we were to read Tolkien's books in chronological order, we might think that the prophecies and songs that we hear in *The Hobbit* predict the coming of a king who will bring universal prosperity. But by that story's end, we would learn that this hope was tragically and only partially fulfilled. Thorin dies in bed shortly after the battle, accompanied by Bilbo, "wounded with many wounds" with his "rent armor and notched axe . . . cast upon the floor."[574] Salvation would not come to Middle-earth through Thorin and the dwarves, even though it looked like the narrative was heading in that direction. Why not? Because like the Jews—whom Tolkien said the dwarves remind him of—the dwarves were also in need of saving. The savior, as it were, needed salvation, too. In continuing with our interpretation of the stories of all Iluvatar's children reflecting, resembling, and paralleling the biblical story of Israel in some way, this also goes for the elves and the Numenoreans, too. One of the paradoxes of Christianity is just this: the messiah must come from within the story of Israel but also outside it so that Israel can be restored to its proper task of being a light for all nations. Nevertheless, Thorin and the dwarves, like Israel, play an indispensable role in bringing about salvation.

One of the texts which we will examine in the next chapter is a dialogue between Galadriel's brother, Finrod, and a wise-woman named Andreth, both of whom lived during the First Age, when the first dark lord, Melkor, was the enemy of Iluvatar's children. In this text, called "The Debate of Finrod and Andreth," Finrod and Andreth look forward to a time when Arda is "healed." Finrod specifically says that he has had a vision of "Arda Remade." It is no coincidence that immediately before saying this, the elf says that he believes that elves will be "delivered from death" by the "Second Children" (i.e., men).[575] Shortly after his vision of "Arda Remade," Andreth refers to some who believe in the "Old Hope [Estel]," which is the hope that "the One will himself enter into Arda, and heal Men and all the Marring from the beginning to the end."[576] Now, part of what makes this most interesting is that this text was written *after* the publication of *The Lord of the Rings* (1955) around 1959. Why is this so interesting? Because Tolkien wrote this after *looking back* on his mythology. It seems Tolkien only discovered new ways in which his mythology reflected the Christian worldview "in the revision."[577] This seems a good justification for for the figural, retrospective approach we have taken in this book. According to Birzer, "one should regard this as *the* central explanatory text of the theology of Tolkien's mythological world."[578] After the novel was finished, it seems Tolkien wanted to find ways to ensure that his mythology faithfully reflected his Christian worldview.

Many Tolkien scholars have overlooked the eschatological significance of Finrod's vision of "Arda Remade." Not only have Tolkien scholars (and many biblical ones) gotten the "place" wrong, but the "time" also. The authentic biblical picture of heaven is to see it as the "control room" of earth, or the "transcendent part of the created order," not an otherworldly place.[579] It seems most Tolkien scholars have interpreted "Arda Remade" as a place and time which has not yet arrived by the end of *The Lord of the Rings*. "Arda Remade" is, like the incarnation of Iluvatar, a far-off event. Yet as Middleton has argued, "ethics is lived eschatology," so if we get our future wrong, our present will consequently become distorted.[580] The point here is that the new creation—"Arda Remade"—is *already* a present reality through the return of the king. Yes, it is also not yet fully consummated, and so yes, there is a future aspect to the new creation as well. Thorin's role in bringing about the inauguration of that kingdom of already but not yet is indispensable. We should see the healing of Arda—"Arda Remade"—as the promise of the new creation in the future being brought *early* into the present age which has been inaugurated by the return of the king. The renewal of all things is already, but not yet. As with the renewal of all things, so with the messiah:

God is already incarnate in Middle-earth through a Numenorean king, but he must keep on reigning, as Paul says, "until he has put all his enemies under his feet."[581] The act of looking back from *The Lord of the Rings* to the "Debate" text is parallel to the act of looking back from the New Testament to the Old Testament. And this brings us back to the meaning of salvation. Many Christians have been brought up to believe that Jesus's words in John 18:36—"My kingdom is not of this world"—mean Jesus is from a completely separate place called "heaven." Furthermore, many in the church have been brought up to believe that salvation consists in being saved *from* this world rather than *for* this world, but this is a dangerous distortion of the real gospel.[582] Tolkien's parable can help us readjust our theology, even if we are not aware of it doing so.

Despite a few great kings of David's house, the kings of Israel did not honor the covenant that God made with David. Second Samuel 7:12–16 tells us about this covenant:

> When your days are over and you rest with your ancestors, I will raise up your offspring to succeed you, your own flesh and blood, and I will establish his kingdom. He is the one who will build a house for my Name, and I will establish the throne of his kingdom forever. I will be his father, and he will be my son. When he does wrong, I will punish him with a rod wielded by men, with floggings inflicted by human hands. But my love will never be taken away from him, as I took it away from Saul, whom I removed from before you. Your house and your kingdom will endure forever before me; your throne will be established forever.

David and his descendants may have failed to uphold their part of the covenant, but God did not. Even when Israel failed to be the nation of priests that God called them to be (see Exod 19:6), reflecting the image of God into the world, God remained faithful, even if the people themselves doubted this. Psalm 89:38–39 conveys this feeling of doubt powerfully: "But you have rejected, you have spurned, you have been very angry with your anointed one. You have renounced the covenant with your servant and defiled his crown in the dust." Thorin experienced this bitterness and feeling of rejection, too: "The embers in the heart of Thorin grew hot again, as he brooded on the wrongs of his House and the vengeance upon the Dragon that he had inherited."[583] Did Tolkien have Ps 137 in mind when writing this? There is a remarkable resemblance: "By the rivers of Babylon we sat and wept / when we remembered Zion / . . . if I forget you, Jerusalem, / may my right hand forget its skill."[584]

There is another important point to be made here about Israel and their struggle to obey God's words from Deut 32:35, "It is mine to avenge; I will repay." Although we are making this point slightly ahead of its introduction in the next chapter, it is an important digression. In *The Silmarillion*, Tolkien tells us of Melkor, the Satan-like figure of his mythology, that "desire grew hot within him to bring into Being things of his own, and it seemed to him that Iluvatar took no thought for the Void, and he was impatient of its emptiness."[585] In this, Tolkien gives us an excellent summary of the Christian perspective on the nature of evil. Melkor's "desire to bring into Being things of his own" is the very essence of true evil. Why? First, it is important to understand this is not what is commonly called a "dualistic" view of good and evil. The moment you put a "good god" and a "bad god" into the universe, a philosophical contradiction will plague your argument. "The moment you say that, you are putting into the universe a third thing in addition to the two Powers: some law or standard or rule of good which one of the powers conforms to and the other fails to conform to." From this, we can infer that only absolute goodness (metaphysically) exists, for who would be prepared to say that if there is a God, he is inherently evil? "But since the two powers are judged by this standard, then this standard, or the Being who made this standard, is farther back and higher up than either of them, and He will be the real God," concludes Lewis.[586] The conclusion is this: evil is the privation or lack of a good that ought to be there. Alternatively, evil can be understood as playing God. In "Appendix A" of *The Return of the King*, when we hear that "the embers in the heart of Thorin grew hot again, as he brooded on the wrongs of his House and the vengeance upon the Dragon that he had inherited," it is vital that we do not miss the similarity in wording when juxtaposing Melkor's "desire grew hot within him" with "the embers in the heart of Thorin grew hot again." As we will see in the next chapter, Aule—creator and father of the dwarves—is similar in this one regard to Melkor: he plays at being God. This may have been Tolkien's way of showing how the created beings of Arda were affected by sin—failing to be God's imagers. The significance of this connection cannot be overstated, for Thorin's desire for both vengeance and treasure goes back to the moment of his people's creation and the taint of Melkor's theme (more on this in the next chapter).

It is remarkable how much the stories of Israel and Durin's folk resemble each other. In *The Hobbit*, as in the Psalms and Prophets of the Old Testament, there are songs which speak of the greatness and the weakness of Durin's folk and Israel. As we will learn in the next chapter, the dwarves were created first, before elves and men, resembling Israel's status as God's "firstborn son."[587] But Israel's highborn status was not to be cause for boasting. According to Middleton, "God tells Abraham, Isaac, and Jacob that the long-term purpose of their election (including that of their descendants) is that through them all the nations or families of the earth will find blessing."[588] It is difficult not to be reminded of Thorin's selfishness at the end of *The Hobbit* here. Once upon a time, Erebor used to have a good relationship with the elves of Mirkwood and the men of Laketown, and it is true what Bard says to Thorin that there are treasures that belong to his people in the mountain. Not only that, but the people of Laketown helped Thorin arrive at Erebor, and now that he has reclaimed his kingdom, he is turning his back on those who have given him aid. As God's "firstborn son," Israel/the dwarves are supposed to bless the nations, not turn them away. All the great songs about Thorin in the book are at best half true, as he simply does not fulfill the task for which he was appointed, as Gandalf makes very clear. On the other hand, when Thorin is shouting at Bilbo about the Arkenstone and Gandalf tells the dwarf that he's not cutting a very royal figure, he says, "But things may change yet."[589] The Battle of Five Armies is the moment of Thorin's redemption. He gives us a brief but very powerful glimpse of what the true king will one day look like.

Peter Jackson's third film adaptation of *The Hobbit*—*The Battle of the Five Armies* (2014)—gets this poignant moment mostly right. In the film, Bombur blows a horn and a great bell smashes the dammed gate of Erebor, revealing Thorin and company charging into battle. Upon seeing this, Bilbo says, "The dwarves: They're rallying," to which Gandalf replies, "They're rallying to their king." Viewers of this film have (probably) already seen the three *Lord of the Rings* films and so Gandalf's tone and comment should resonate with us. There seems to be a twinkle in Gandalf's eye in the film that tells viewers who've seen The *Lord of the Rings* films that he's thinking of Aragorn. Since these films were made after the *Lord of the Rings* films, this is a cinematic version of the retrospective hermeneutic we have been discussing in this book. Looking back on *The Battle of the Five Armies* with knowledge of *The Return of the King* in mind is powerful, and it certainly stirs something in me. Let us see how this unfolds in the actual *Hobbit* text. After it looks like Thorin would never show up to help the beleaguered armies of men, elves, and dwarves, Tolkien tells us "out leapt the King under the Mountain, and his companions followed him. Hood and cloak were gone; they were in shining armor, and red light leapt from their eyes. In the gloom the great dwarf gleamed like gold in a dying fire."[590] Wielding his mighty axe with great skill, Thorin then shouted, "'To me! To me! Elves and Men! To me! O my kinsfolk!' He cried, and his voice shook like a horn in the valley."[591] In this rousing and beautiful moment, we get a glimpse of what it will look like when the true king returns to his throne. Thorin's call to arms brings all the children of Iluvatar together in one glorious moment, but it does not last. Thorin ultimately failed to unite dwarves, elves, and men, but the one who would come after him would not fail. Thorin did, in part, redeem himself. Thorin's hardness of heart and subsequent downfall is evocative of passages like Ezek 34:4–5 in which God says to the kings of the House of David, "You have not strengthened the weak or healed the sick or bound up the injured. You have not brought back the strays or searched for the lost. You have ruled them harshly and brutally. So, they were scattered because there was no shepherd, and when they were scattered they became food for all the wild animals."

We are in a better position now to understand the full dimensions of the Fellowship's departure from Rivendell on December 25. The Fellowship was comprised of members of all Iluvatar's children and was led by the king who would one day unite elves, dwarves, and men in one community. Aragorn later succeeds where Thorin failed. Aragorn resembles Christ as the head of the church, and the diverse members of the Fellowship resemble humanity, made in God's image, unified by Jesus the King. Thorin, like the Davidic monarchs, failed to care for his flock, but Aragorn did not. Perhaps, then, the songs about Thorin in *The Hobbit* and the prophecy of the return of the king under the mountain are, in retrospect, poetic prefigurations of Aragorn rather than predictions of the kind of king Thorin would prove to be. This is consistent with how Jesus himself reinterpreted Scripture in light of himself, as with Ps 110:1 as seen in Matt 22:41–46. Doing so does not invalidate the uniqueness or importance of Israel or the dwarves; in fact, it intensifies their importance in the greater story. The "blended quotations" seen in the Gospel of Matthew, for example, "seem to function as allusive, hermeneutically constructive compositions; they beckon the reader to recall two different scriptural contexts simultaneously and to reflect upon the way in which each one illuminates the other."[592] Similarly, the allusions to *The Hobbit* and *The Silmarillion* in Tolkien's parable achieve the same thing. When we are reading about Aragorn, we are challenged to recall Thorin and reflect on the way each one reveals something more about the other and the gospel. If we imagine Aragorn and Thorin as the two poles of our figural reading thus far, insights flow in both directions. Our knowledge of Aragorn shapes our perception of Thorin just as learning about Thorin deepens our existing understanding of Aragorn.

"THE KING IS COME UNTO HIS HALL"

Tolkien's books are filled to the brim with songs, proverbs, poems, and prophecies. Some are silly and merry—like the hobbits' song in the House of Tom Bombadil or the dwarves' kitchen song—and some are dark, serious, and important—like the "Misty Mountains" song the dwarves sing in Bilbo's home or Gimli's song in Moria about Durin the Deathless. According to James Stuart Bell, this is yet another thing Tolkien's books and the Bible have in common. According to Bell, biblical prophecies are "meant to help readers look backward as well as forward."[593] Bell also believes that prophecies and songs function the same way in Tolkien's books. In 2949, eight years after the death of Thorin, Gandalf and Balin visit Bilbo in the Shire. Balin tells the hobbit that wealth has again begun to flow out of Erebor and the relationship between dwarves, elves, and men has mended. Bilbo then says something curious: "Then the prophecies of the old songs have turned out to be true, after a fashion!"[594] "After a fashion" is appropriate, for it implies that things have not turned out quite exactly how the prophecies foretold. What prophecies and songs is Bilbo referring to?

They are far too extensive to quote in full here, but they can be found in chapters 1, 10, and 15 of *The Hobbit*. There are two features of the songs and poems in Tolkien's books which showcase his knowledge of Jewish Scripture that are worth pointing out here. First, there is parallelism. According to Timothy Keller, "the most fundamental mark of Hebrew poetry is parallelism," in which there are "two phrases, clauses, or sentences" that complement, magnify, or extend each other. Keller concludes, "in each case, the two thoughts mutually clarify each other, sharpening our understanding."[595] Parallelism is present in a psalm or proverb when two verses deliberately contrast with one another or repeat the same phrase in a different way, illuminating a new perspective that the first phrase did not have. There are various kinds of parallelism. Synonymous parallelism is when a second line of poetry repeats the first with slightly different wording but still resulting in the same overall meaning.[596] For example, the lines, "On silver necklaces they strung / the flowering stars, on crowns they hung," from the "Misty Mountains" song in chapter 1 of *The Hobbit* is a great example of this kind of parallelism. The second line repeats the first using different words and referring to different objects but results in the same meaning. Emphatic parallelism is when synonymous words are used to emphasize a point, as in Deut 6:5: "Love the Lord your God with all your heart and with all your soul and with all your strength." The words "heart" and "soul" for instance emphasize that one's *entire* person (Hebrew *nephesh*) must love God.

Emphatic parallelism is pervasive in Middle-earth. In the same song quoted above from chapter 1, take the lines "the pines were roaring on the height, / the winds were moaning in the night," for example. "Roaring" and "moaning" are words that are extremely close in meaning. Then, there is synthetic parallelism where a second line of poetry adds to the first. Using the same line, we observe that the second line about the winds "moaning in the night" adds to the meaning of the first line, which tells us that the "pines were roaring on the height." These lines speak about the coming of Smaug to Erebor in the year 1999 of the Third Age. The second line adds more detail to the already harrowing atmosphere. All this is evidence of Tolkien's intimate familiarity with the Hebrew *mashal*, or poetic form.

The second Hebraic feature of Tolkien's songs and poems is something known as "stringing pearls" in Judaism.[597] Not only is stringing pearls an ancient homiletic technique which the rabbis used to teach their students, it is also a hermeneutic device. "Stringing pearls" is the act of "bringing together passages from different places in order to explore their great truths."[598] For example, Jesus does this to great effect in Matt 5:3–12, as each of the "Blessed are . . ." statements would have reminded "the crowd of passages in the Bible in which God had promised to rescue his faithful followers."[599] In Mark 1:11, "You are my Son, whom I love; with you I am well pleased," there are *three* Scriptures from the Hebrew Bible which Mark is alluding to: Ps 2:7, Gen 22:2, and Isa 42:1. Stringing pearls occurs frequently in Jesus's parables, too, as Jesus was inclined to bring together several well-known Jewish images (kings, shepherds, widows, bridesmaids) to show what God was up to. How does Tolkien do this? The "Riddle of Strider" in book I, chapter 10 of *The Fellowship of the Ring* contains several echoes of the "Misty Mountains" song from chapter 1 and chapter 10 of *The Hobbit*. The three lines "not all those who wander are lost," "the old that is strong does not wither," and "renewed shall be blade that was broken" all speak about both the character of Aragorn and what will happen in the near future on his quest to reclaim his throne. Yet they also contain echoes of the songs about Thorin. For example, the lines "renewed shall be blade that was broken, / the crownless again shall be king" resemble "his crown shall be upholden, / his harp shall be restrung" and "all sorrow fail and sadness / at the Mountain-king's return!"

On their own, these respective songs/poems are about the character of each king. They are also about each king's respective journey to becoming king. For example, in the "Misty Mountains" song, we are told that the dwarves "must away ere break of day / to seek the pale enchanted gold" and "must away, ere break of day / to win our harps and gold from him [Smaug]." These lines tell us Thorin's identity is wrapped up with Erebor's treasure, though the mention of "harps" may allude to reclaiming the dwarves' culture from the dragon, which is a much nobler goal than gold. The lines "the King beneath the mountains, / the King of carven stone, / the lord of silver fountains / shall come into his own!" and "All that is gold does not glitter / . . . the crownless again shall be king" are also a perfect example of the contrast between the two exiled kings. Thorin's return to the throne will usher in an age of wealth and ostentation, whereas Aragorn's return is humbler—there is no promise of great wealth, only of a great man coming back to his throne. Nevertheless, there is also a similarity here which depends upon how we define "wealth" and what we consider true royalty.

It is interesting to note in passing here how the dejected description of Aragorn's appearance resembles the famous Suffering Servant song from Isa 53:2: "He had no beauty or majesty to attract us to him, nothing in his appearance that we should desire him." Despite his appearances, however, both texts—Isaiah and the "Riddle of Strider"—are talking about the true king. Although we have interpreted the song about Thorin's return as one of pomp and circumstance, it could be read similarly to the "Riddle of Strider," so long as we keep texts like Isa 25:6–8 in mind when we do. For example, another line from chapter 10 of *The Hobbit* reads, "His wealth shall flow in fountains / and the rivers golden run." This resembles the Isa 25:6 prediction that one day there will be a "banquet of aged wine" in Jerusalem. This could refer not only to material prosperity but spiritual health and prosperity as well. We may also include the eagle's proclamation about Aragorn from book VI, chapter 5 of *The Return of the King* in our analysis. The line at the end which reads "and the Tree that was withered shall be renewed" is a nice parallel to the lines "his crown shall be upholden, / his harp shall be restrung." The words "restrung" and "renewed" illuminate each other nicely. These poems are evocative of various messianic Hebrew psalms which, like in Tolkien's story, are about the return of exiled kings. In this section, we have endeavored to show through the Hebrew poetic device of parallelism and stringing pearls that Thorin's return to Erebor prefigures Aragorn's return. We shall finish this chapter on *The Hobbit* in the same way we concluded the previous chapter, by looking at Thorin's backstory all the way back to the founding of Erebor in 1999 of the Third Age. This will be a perfect segue into our final chapter, where we will be tying up our story of the return of the king by looking at how that story began in *The Silmarillion*, just as it begins in Genesis in the Bible. My hope is that this enriches and reenchants not only your appreciation of Tolkien's books but also your reading of the Bible.

"THE DWARVES OF YORE"

"Pride goes before destruction, a haughty spirit before a fall," says Prov 16:18—this is a verse to remember when we think of either the House of David or the House of Durin. Like King Josiah, Thorin not only came from an immediate family of failures but descended from a people who were known to be "stiff-necked" like the Israelites themselves (see Exod 32:9). Josiah's father, Amon, and grandfather Manasseh are not remembered as virtuous kings of the House of David. According to 2 Kgs 21:20, "He [Amon] did evil in the eyes of the Lord, as his father Manasseh had done." Amon and Manasseh were known for worshiping false gods and building holy places to them, something that ancient Jews became increasingly intolerant toward. Manasseh was even known to have sacrificed one of his own sons "in the fire."[600] And we have already heard from the prophet Ezekiel, who testified that the kings of the House of David had cumulatively failed to shepherd their people Israel. According to Tolkien in *The Silmarillion*, "Aule made the Dwarves strong to endure. Therefore, they are stone-hard, stubborn, fast in friendship and in enmity, and they suffer toil and hunger and hurt of body more hardily than all other speaking peoples."[601] Like Israel, who lost Jerusalem to the Babylonians in the sixth century BC, the dwarves of the House of Durin also failed to keep their kingdom under the mountain. In *The Hobbit*, Tolkien chooses to use the Arkenstone and the dwarves' love of treasure to allude to the issue of idolatry, which was also Israel's central problem. Once again, idolatry is loving something—even good things—more than God, or, alternatively, taking a good thing and turning it into an ultimate thing.

Josiah must have been intimidated when he inherited the throne, for he did so as a boy (eight years old).[602] Moreover, he knew what his father and grandfather's reputation was. Thorin also came from a line of kings whose reputation was less than stellar. We should pause for a moment to consider how this is important in our understanding of both the Jews and the dwarves. As we will go over in more detail in the next chapter, the dwarves were created before elves and men by the Vala Aule. The Valar have been mentioned several times throughout this book, but we have not yet discussed who they are. Since this is a major topic in the next and final chapter, let us just say for now that the Valar are (in this author's opinion) *not* angels or archangels, but members of Iluvatar's "divine council." Tolkien was definitely inspired by the Old Testament in his creation of the Valar, but it is important that we understand that the divine council/Valar are *not* equals of Iluvatar/God. According to John Walton, "in the pantheons of the ancient world, a high god usually occupied the leadership role over the other gods." The divine council/Valar are a "network and community for Yahweh."[603] This does not mean that God/Iluvatar needs the divine council, or that the divine council/Valar have their own power base, for he does not and they do not. As we will point out in the next chapter, the divine council/Valar are, among other things, the poetic expression of God's *immanent presence* in the created world which he made.

Aside from the struggle with their inordinate love of treasure, the dwarves struggled with pride. On at least two occasions, they made foolish decisions to attempt to take back either Moria or Erebor from the orcs, resulting in tragic, fatal consequences. There is nothing wrong with fighting for one's home, but the dwarves' sense of identity became inextricably bound up with particular geographical locations. This is also true of the Jews in the Old Testament, who finally learned during the Babylonian exile that "Israel was not a people because it dwelt in a particular country, but because it lived in the presence of its God, who traveled with the people wherever in the world they happened to be."[604] Interestingly, early on in their history the Jews knew and understood this, but after they settled in the land God had promised Abraham, their sense of identity fused with the promised land. It should be pointed out that, in the beginning, God designed *all* of creation to be sacred space (as in Eden). Now it is true that God's *shekinah* or "presence" came to dwell specifically in Solomon's Temple in Jerusalem, but God's original intention—and he promises to do this in the end—was to be "all in all."[605] The important point here is that even when the Jews and dwarves are living in exile, God is with them, and they still enjoy God's special favor as humanity's representatives. Yet as we have seen, neither Israel nor the dwarves fully live up to this task, which necessitates the personal intervention of God himself to both redeem the redeemers (Israel), *and* through them, to redeem all humanity. In Middle-earth, Tolkien divides allusions to Israel's story between the stories of the dwarves and the Numenoreans specifically.

In 2793, 148 years before the events of *The Hobbit*, there was a great war between the orcs of Moria and the dwarves of Erebor, who had recently gone into exile. The fire-dragon Smaug had descended on Erebor only twenty-three years before this war broke out in 2770. What caused these hostilities between orcs and dwarves? While in exile, Thorin's grandfather Thror bequeathed one of the seven rings of power that the dwarves were given by Sauron long ago to his son Thrain, and then left to search for fortune. Although he did not return to Erebor, he did foolishly go to the ancient kingdom of his people—Khazad-Dum, otherwise known as Moria. Before proceeding, we should pause to discuss the history of Moria and Erebor and how events unfolded up to the coming of Smaug in 2770. The dwarf-kingdom of Khazad-Dum was a kingdom founded by Durin I, the oldest of all the seven dwarf fathers (more on him later). The dwarves prospered there through the Third Age when, in 1981, the dwarves were driven from their kingdom by the Balrog. A Balrog is a corrupted Maia. What is a Maia? As we will see in the next chapter, the Maiar are also part of Iluvatar's divine council but are less powerful than the Valar. Gandalf and Sauron are also Maia, and so when Gandalf fights the Balrog in Moria in *The Fellowship of the Ring*, he is facing another member of God's divine council. The dwarves dug deep into the earth because their creator, Aule, implanted in them a love for all things of the earth. According to Tolkien, "the dwarves delved deep at that time, seeking beneath Baranzinbar for *mithril*, the metal beyond price."[606] After the awakening of the Balrog, Durin VI and Nain I were both slain by it and the dwarves fled to the north where Nain's son, Thrain I, founded the kingdom of Erebor and "began new works, and became King under the Mountain."[607] Erebor, the Lonely Mountain, was founded in 1999 and prospered until the coming of Smaug in 2770.

Thus, we return to the dwarves in exile, bereft of both their ancient kingdoms. Thror became restless and, after leaving his son and grandson, came to Moria with one other dwarf named Nar. Tolkien tells us that it may have been the residual corrupting influence of the ring of power—which was now aware its master Sauron had returned—that drove him to this folly. When Thror arrived, however, no orc was in sight, so he walked through the gate like a king returning home after a long campaign. The dwarf named Nar who had accompanied Thror and warned him not to enter. Not long after, an orc emerged from the darkness and threw a body on the steps. As Nar cautiously rose from his place of hiding, he saw that the body was Thror's, and that he had been decapitated and branded by Azog. Weeping, Nar brought news of Thror's death back to his son Thrain, who, after weeping for his father, remained silent for seven days. Then, Thrain arose and said, "This cannot be borne!"[608] Bereft of both their ancient kingdoms, and consigned to exile, the dwarves' plight reminds us of Israel's while they were in exile in Babylon. "By the rivers of Babylon we sat and wept / when we remembered Zion," laments the author of Ps 137:1. The prophet Jeremiah wrote a letter to the exiles in Babylon saying, "Build homes, and plan to stay. Plant gardens, and eat the food they produce. Marry and have children. Then find spouses for them so that you may have many grandchildren. Multiply! Do not dwindle away! And work for the peace and prosperity of the city where I sent you into exile. Pray to the Lord for it, for its welfare will determine your welfare."[609]

After seven days of weeping, Thrain declared war on Azog and the orcs of Moria for vengeance. A long and terrible war (six years) between dwarves and orcs followed. During the final battle, Thorin earned his nickname "Oakenshield" because after his shield was destroyed in battle, he used his axe to fell "a branch of an oak and held it in his left hand to ward off the strokes of his foes, or to wield as a club."[610] In the end, Dain Ironfoot (the dwarf who takes over Erebor after Thorin's death in *The Hobbit*) slays Azog and Thrain decides that he wants to retake Moria, but Dain and the others refuse because of the Balrog. Dain tells Thrain, "The world must change and some other power than ours must come before Durin's Folk walk again in Moria."[611] Indeed, Moria would not become safe again until after the coronation of Aragorn and the defeat of Sauron. And so it was that the House of Durin lost both their great kingdoms and became a people "scorned by everyone, despised by the people."[612] After the war, Thrain and Thorin once again became wanderers. Many more years passed, and then it was Thrain's time to grow restless. One day, without saying a word to his son Thorin, he disappeared along with the ring of power which Thror had given him.[613] Tragically, Sauron and his servants found Thrain in the wild and imprisoned him in Dol Guldur. "So Thorin Oakenshield became the Heir of Durin, but an heir without hope . . . the years lengthened. The embers in the heart of Thorin grew hot again, as he brooded on the wrongs of his House and the vengeance upon the Dragon that he had inherited."[614] This passage is rich with scriptural allusions. First, notice the monarchic language Tolkien uses here to describe Thorin. The phrase "heir without hope" also strongly resembles Scriptures that describe Israel in exile. Lamentations 3:18 says, "My splendor is gone and all that I had hoped from the Lord," and the psalmist in Psalm 13:1 asks, "How long, Lord? Will you forget me forever?" The "embers" growing hot in the "heart of Thorin" as he "brooded on the wrongs of his House" echoes exiled Israel sitting "by the rivers of Babylon." Thorin's desire for vengeance also parallels forgetful Israel, who has forgotten—or has ignored—that God has said, "It is mine to avenge; I will repay."[615]

And then, on March 15, 2941 "there came about by chance a meeting between Gandalf and Thorin that changed all the fortunes of the House of Durin, and led to other and greater ends beside."[616] Recall that in the previous chapter we learned Gandalf had entered Dol Guldur in 2850 a second time and found a dying Thrain, who gives the wizard the key of Erebor. There in Bree Gandalf and Thorin formulated their plan to retake Erebor from Smaug, hoping to prevent Sauron from meeting up with the dragon, who would have been used to take over northern Middle-earth. We now come to the beginning of *The Hobbit* when Gandalf and the dwarves visit Bilbo in the Shire and recruit him for their quest. In *The Hobbit*, Tolkien has given us a story that continues to recapitulate the monarchic theme we have been exploring in this book. We have seen how Thorin and his return to Erebor prefigures Aragorn and his return to Minas Tirith, compared both kings, and explored both kings' backstories. Hopefully it has also become clear by this point that *The Hobbit* functions very similarly to the Old Testament in serving as the crucial frame for *The Lord of the Rings*. The act of looking back from the Gospels to the Old Testament is parallel, we have argued, to looking back from Tolkien's parable to *The Hobbit*. What is the ultimate point of all this? Once again, we would do well to recall the three characteristics of Tolkien's fairy-story: Consolation, Escape, and

Restoration. Tolkien believed that sub-creation was an act of worship. If that is true, then by "dipping" the biblical myth into Tolkien's, we see the former more clearly.[617] Tolkien wanted to broaden and deepen our understanding of the biblical myth, not tell us a story we already know. Tolkien's myth *adds* to the biblical myth; indeed, it becomes an extension of it.[618]

As Christians will testify, much of the Hebrew Bible speaks of the faithfulness of God in one day becoming king again through his "firstborn son," Israel. In this chapter, we have seen parallels of this story from the Old Testament in the story of Thorin Oakenshield. We have alluded to the fact that the dwarves are, indeed, the firstborn sons of Iluvatar, but we have seen that God ultimately becomes king through a man, not a dwarf. Of course, if we were reading all this as a strict allegory, then we would expect Aragorn to be a dwarf, if the dwarves primarily resemble Israel. Yet we have not done this because Tolkien very wisely divided allusions and parallels to Israel across multiple storylines. Not only that, but we have learned that Tolkien imitated Jesus's art of the parable, which does not reflect truth in this way. Again, Tolkien's parable is about what Jesus's parables are about. That means that Tolkien's parable will reflect the gospel in the same way Jesus's parables do. This also means that Tolkien's parable will contain ancient echoes of Middle-earth's past just as Jesus's parables contain echoes of Israel's. Although we are coming to the conclusion of our retrospective journey through Tolkien's mythology, we have still yet to discuss "The Debate of Finrod and Andreth," Tolkien's most incarnational text. In the last chapter, we will discuss the ancestries of Aragorn and Thorin, "The Debate of Finrod and Andreth," and Tolkien's creation story, the "Ainulindale." Our primary goal is to show that there is clear evidence in *The Silmarillion* and "The Debate of Finrod and Andreth" that Tolkien's novel expresses the incarnation parabolically, just like Jesus himself does.

5

"Estel"

The Gothic cathedral in Cologne, Germany, is one of the most magnificent buildings in the world (I personally visited it in 2006). The building serves as an enlightening visual analogy of the character of the Judeo-Christian God. According to Father Robert Barron, "every line on the exterior of the building points dramatically upward; the logic of the structure compels the viewer's gaze skyward . . . all of this speaks of the transcendence, strangeness, and radical otherness of God . . . but the Cologne Cathedral, which speaks so compellingly of the divine transcendence, preaches just as convincingly the immanence of God."[619] The Cologne Cathedral conveys in visual terms what Tolkien has Finrod say in philosophical terms in "The Debate of Finrod and Andreth": "Even if He in Himself were to enter in, He must still remain also as He is: the Author without."[620] This, as we will see by chapter's end, is the prophecy of the messiah—the incarnation—in Middle-earth. In the great Catholic tradition to which Tolkien belonged, God is understood to be both outside (transcendent) *and* inside (immanent) his creation. In the Introduction, we discussed the importance of understanding Hebraic thought as a prerequisite for understanding Christian theology. We also learned that Hebrew language and thought is very metaphorical, concrete, and imaginative. That is why the Bible—and *The Lord of the Rings*—is filled with so many *mashalim*. Riddles, proverbs, and parables are natural expressions of a mind that is at home with metaphor, paradox, and dialectical thinking. Imaginative narratives (parables), then, play a central role in communicating who God is. These images tell—or rather *show*—us what God is like. The ancient Jews believed that after God created the world (from outside the world) he remained involved in it. This belief is made explicitly clear in "The Debate of Finrod and Andreth" when Finrod says that Iluvatar is "already in it, as well as outside" it.[621] The transcendent God is revealed in the Bible through a staggering variety of concrete images such as: a stranger visiting Abraham (Gen 18), a pillar of fire and cloud of smoke (Exod 13:21), the tabernacle (Exod 26), the temple (1 Kgs 6), a still, small voice (1 Kgs 19:11–13), a chariot (Ezek 1), a shepherd (Ezek 34), and many others. That is, God's transcendence is understood via his immanence.

We can learn about God by looking at people, animals, nature, art, and morality. Recall our discussion early in the Introduction about types and antitypes. In other words, we can learn about God by looking at the things which he made. Is it any surprise, then, that when it came to expressing himself directly in history, God chose to be "mythopoeic"? That is, even when God revealed his full glory to mankind through his Son, he still did so in a way that was considerate of our "tragic dilemma . . . either to taste and not to know or to know and not to taste."[622] The incarnation can be understood as the tension of these two characteristics of God held together in the person of Jesus of Nazareth. To symbolize the immanence of God, the cathedral's exterior is decorated with, among other things, foliage, whereas the interior's nave soars to an astonishing 142 feet, symbolizing the transcendence of God. In summary, the totality of the building is a visual illustration of Christianity's central doctrine: the incarnation. As we have learned throughout this book, Jesus did not state the incarnation propositionally but illustrated it through parables. Although they take the long way around, God seems to prefer communicating with us via parables. Parables bring together the transcendent and the immanent in a mythic literary form. According to Bradley J. Birzer, "The Debate of Finrod and Andreth" is the "central explanatory text" of Tolkien's mythology because it is the text which contains the clearest allusions to the incarnation.[623]

In the quote from "The Debate" above, Tolkien uses the image of an "author" to speak about Iluvatar (God) entering his creation, which is compared to a story. This text seems to be a meditation on the entire mythology. Indeed, "The Debate" was written in the late 1950s, right after Tolkien finished *The Lord of the Rings* (1955). Did Tolkien take a moment to look back from the end of the Lord of the Rings to the First Age? Perhaps "The Debate" was a way of ensuring that the entire narrative reflected the truth of the Christian worldview in the parabolic, allusive, Markan way that Tolkien seemed to prefer. In this final chapter of the book, we will be taking a closer look at how the incarnation—which is present in *The Lord of the Rings*—is adumbrated in *The Silmarillion* and "The Debate of Finrod and Andreth." More specifically, we will look at how Aragorn himself is prefigured in "The

Debate." There is one objection some may raise to this exclusive focus on Aragorn, which is that at least two other characters—Gandalf and Frodo—in *The Lord of the Rings*, together with Aragorn, resemble the threefold office (prophet, priest, king) of Jesus Christ.[624] One of the reasons why we have focused exclusively on Aragorn is because of the special attention Tolkien paid to his appearance and manifestations of his royal authority. While this author does agree with the many scholars who have elucidated how characteristics of the messiah are apparent in Frodo and Gandalf, the Aragorn-centric approach of this book is further justified by the contemporary biblical research of scholars such as N. T. Wright who have argued how important it is to see the incarnation as God becoming king. Furthermore, in the previous chapter, we saw how Thorin Oakenshield resembles and prefigures Jesus in the same way Israel (particularly the Davidic kings) resembles and prefigures Jesus Christ. There is, then, a monarchical theme running through the entirety of Tolkien's mythology.

In this chapter, we will see how hints of the incarnation—understood as God becoming king—are present from the very beginning of Arda's history, even back to the very moment of creation, just as they are in the Bible. Just as with Jesus's parables, the parabolic form of *The Lord of the Rings* is the very content it wishes to communicate. And, like the Gospels and the parables of Jesus in the Gospels, Tolkien prods us to look back at the ancient backstory in order to recognize this. The constant allusions to Middle-earth's past invite us to assume this retrospective stance, just as the echoes of Israel's history in the parables/Gospels do the same. In this chapter, we will take a close look at two important texts in Tolkien's mythology: the "Ainulindalë" from *The Silmarillion* and "The Debate of Finrod and Andreth" from *Morgoth's Ring*. Even though most of the chapter will focus on how these two texts contain adumbrations—detected retrospectively—of the incarnation, we will also take a brief look at the ancient history of elves, dwarves, and men along the way. By doing so, we will also finally be able to see how Tolkien buried resemblances to Israel and the disinherited nations of Deut 32:8–9 in the stories of all Iluvatar's children. Before we begin this last sojourn into Tolkien's mythology, we need to address what Tolkien himself said about the incarnation.

Recall from the Introduction that we heard from Tolkien scholar Matthew Dickerson, who wrote that his main reason for concluding that *The Lord of the Rings*—and indeed Tolkien's entire mythology—is not a fully Christian story is the absence of the incarnation. Dickerson bases his opinion on the words of Tolkien himself, who wrote, "The Incarnation of God is an *infinitely* greater thing than anything I would dare to write."[625] We heard from Dickerson earlier in the book on this point. Remember, according to

Dickerson, "there would be no real way to present the actual Incarnation in Middle-earth without it becoming allegory."[626] We argued earlier that this is a misunderstanding of the incarnation itself, which *must*, by necessity, be communicated via parables in order to become real to us. This is because God—and the incarnation—is ultimately a mystery to our finite minds. We are like Moses, who, upon asking God to see his glory in Exod 33:18–23, is only permitted to see him from the back. This means that it is only possible to see and know God *indirectly*. We also noted that Dickerson conflates the "conscious and intentional" allegory with the parable/fairy story, failing to see the nuanced difference between these two very different types of allegory. Recall that one of the crucial differences in a parable is the shift between metaphorical and allegorical language, and the ultimate breakdown of the latter. We also argued earlier in the book that if we do not understand parables, we will not understand the incarnation. Again, parables are, in form, what they wish to say in content. So, when Tolkien wrote that there was "no embodiment of the creator" anywhere in his mythology, he was not denying the presence of the incarnation in Middle-earth, he was denying an *allegorical representation of it*.[627]

Furthermore, it seems Tolkien was trying to warn us not to interpret his work as a retelling of the Gospels, for he writes in the same letter quoted above, "But though one may be in this reminded of the Gospels, it is not really the same thing at all."[628] Since Jesus himself is the gospel in person, the best way we have of experiencing the concrete presence of the messiah today is through parable. Jesus was not pointing away from himself to someone or something else; the parables are in form the very content Jesus sought to communicate. This point was as lost on Jesus's disciples and audiences as it is on modern disciples and audiences. As Bruce Young has argued, "the Gospels do not derive from the imagination of poets but instead report, and allow us to participate in, real and concrete encounters with the Son of God himself."[629] Again, Tolkien is not denying the presence of the incarnation in Middle-earth, he is denying that he has written a parody or crude allegory of it. We also need to point out here that the Four Evangelists themselves did not "dare to write" the incarnation; they merely *reported* it.

This, as we have already learned, is a very significant comment because it means that the thing which Jesus wished to communicate—God becoming king—was inseparable from the way in which he said it—parables. "What we learn from the Gospels if we read them mythically but also historically is thus something about the nature of reality," says Young.[630] Tolkien did not wish to write a rival to or a substitute of the Gospels, but an extension of them. One cannot "write" the incarnation, as that implies that the Four Evangelists, as sub-creators, dreamed it up all on their own, too. Jesus and his parables are proof that, contra Dickerson, it is possible to communicate the incarnation without turning *The Lord of the Rings* into a "conscious and intentional" allegory. As we will see, "The Debate" also contains evidence that points to the necessity of understanding *The Lord of the Rings* as a parabolic novel.

Due to the complex nature of some of the material in this chapter, we will be analyzing events in progressive chronological order unlike in our two previous chapters. We will begin with the creation of Arda and work our way up to a discussion of "The Debate of Finrod and Andreth."

THE "MUSIC OF THE AINUR"

In the beginning, there was silence and the thoughts of Iluvatar, who is also called Eru, "the One." Iluvatar is Tolkien's mythical version of Yahweh, the deity of the Bible. Springing from each thought of Iluvatar were the Ainur, "the Holy Ones," who formed a mythological version of Yahweh's divine council from the Bible. There are two categories of beings that make up the Ainur, one senior and one junior: the Valar and the Maiar. The former possesses sub-creative powers and are much more powerful than the Maiar. The Ainur are not unlike the divine beings that surround God's throne, who are mentioned frequently throughout the Old Testament.[631] This recurrent image in the Old Testament can be easily misunderstood, so we should clarify what it means for Yahweh—and Iluvatar—to have a "divine council." First, this author does not believe that Tolkien intended that the Ainur resemble pagan deities, angels from the Judeo-Christian tradition, Jewish elders, or the Christian doctrine of the Trinity.[632] So, what does it mean that Yahweh/Iluvatar has a divine council? Verlyn Flieger argues that the Valar are more comparable to *elohim* as "multiplicity," not suggesting several Gods, but "God in all his aspects." Flieger continues, saying, "Wisely, Tolkien never allows the comparison to be specific or explicit," in keeping with the art of the parable.[633] Recent research, especially the work of biblical scholar Michael Heiser, now makes this view incredulous. The "gods" of the divine council are not "aspects" or "characteristics" of Yahweh, but created, imperfect, free-will-possessing members of God's heavenly family. It is, therefore, no longer possible to understand the Ainur in *The Silmarillion* as "aspects" or "characteristics" of Iluvatar either. If *The Silmarillion* is meant to resemble the Old Testament, and scholars are supposed to interpret the Scriptures from the perspective of their ancient Israelite authors first, then it would be wrong to conclude that the authors of the Bible had the Trinity in mind when writing Gen 1:26 or Ps 82, just as it would be wrong to assume Tolkien had the Trinity in mind in writing the "Ainulindale." This is true especially with respect to his knowledge of the Old Testament and Hebrew.

The divine council also means that while God stands alone, "he does not work alone." Recall that earlier in the book, we learned that God needs neither a divine council nor a human family; he *enjoys* and *prefers* working through representatives. According to John H. Walton, "in the Old Testament the divine council is portrayed as a structural reality of Yahweh's administration of the cosmos." The first reference of the divine council comes, by the way, from Gen 1:26, the very first chapter of the Bible. According to Gen 1:26, "God said, 'Let *us* make mankind in *our* image, in *our* likeness.'"[634] This verse has often been a source of confusion for the modern interpreter because the word for "God" in Hebrew here is the plural *elohim*. God seems to be speaking to "himselves," or to what appears to be other, equally powerful deities, but this is not the case. The Hebrew word *elohim* is plural in form, but it can be either singular or plural in meaning. We can now properly understand this amazing story in *The Silmarillion*.

Like the divine council in the Bible, the Valar "each had their own divine authority composed of the realm they represented and the constellation of attributes that they possessed."[635] Throughout the Old Testament, God makes it very clear that the divine council is always held in check with a tight rein, as in Ps 82, for example. Yahweh is incomparably greater than any member of his council and any of the gods he assigned to the disinherited nations. In Ps 89:6–8, we are told exactly that. According to Walton, there are five principles we can learn about God via the divine council. First, that God has a divine council tells us that he works through servants to "carry out his will, even though, theoretically, he does not need to do so." Second, the divine council is subservient to God and only has as much power as God gives. Indeed, God can and will "judge them for their failings." Third, that God has a divine council tells us that God values "community and consultation." God loves to share his power, and even does this with Adam and Eve. Fourth, even though God is surrounded by servants "to whom he delegates tasks, Yahweh retains his status as the sole being in his class. He is not simply a high god among others." Fifth and finally, "political wrangling does not take place in Yahweh's council, and his rule is supreme." This last point is particularly important in considering the role of Satan/Melkor, for it would seem that he proves the exception to that rule. As we will see, however, that is not true: Satan/Melkor's rebellion is a part of God's overall divine plan. Let me be clear: God does not *need* evil as part of his plan to bring about the good, but any abuse of free will by either his divine or human family is worked into his overall, benevolent plan. God is not, in other words, "overpowered" by one of the members of the divine council; Satan/Melkor play right into God's hand.[636]

One question we may want to ask at this point is, "Are the Ainur/members of the divine council *created* beings, like human beings?" The answer would have to be yes, for if the Ainur or divine council were *uncreated* like God, then that would imply Yahweh/Iluvatar is not unique or supreme, and that he has rivals. This, of course, would mean that God is not God, but that is not at all the feeling we get when reading the Scriptures or *The Silmarillion*. Having said this, it is still not necessary to argue that the divine council/Ainur are archangels and angels, as some Tolkien scholars have argued. The members of God's divine council are immaterial beings—beings without bodies—but they are nevertheless created beings, just like us. Another way to understand the divine council/Ainur is that they are an expression of the *immanence* of God in his created order. We have already seen that in the Bible Yahweh is both transcendent *and* immanent, so this conclusion has traction. Tolkien assigns the Ainur the ability to sub-create, a gift which human beings also possess. Sub-creation and free will are interrelated concepts. Like human beings, the divine council/Ainur possess free will. In the beginning, Tolkien tells us that Iluvatar "propounded" a theme of music to the Ainur. Iluvatar "spoke to them, propounding to them themes of music; and they sang before him, and he was glad."[637] This moment is reminiscent of the time when Job questioned God's justice in the Old Testament. According to Job 38:4, in response God asks Job, "Where were you when I laid the earth's foundation? Tell me, if you understand." In Job's silence, God then continues to ask a series of questions that no human being could ever answer: "On what were its footings set, or who laid its cornerstone—while the morning stars sang together and all the angels shouted with joy?"[638] The "angels" (Hebrew *mal'ak*, meaning "messengers") in this verse are lower members (*elohim*) of the divine council, like the Maiar. The point of this verse from Job is that the divine council *witnessed* the creation of the world and humanity, which was solely the work of Yahweh.

In Tolkien's mythology, the world comes into being through sonorous words "like unto harps and lutes, and pipes and trumpets, and viols and organs, and like unto countless choirs and singing with words." Gradually, the theme of Iluvatar becomes, with the Ainur's assistance, a great music. Not long after the Ainur begin to sing, however, one of the Valar named Melkor decides to introduce an alternate theme of his own devising. Melkor, who is the wisest and most powerful of all the Ainur, seems to have been dissatisfied with his sub-creator status. There is more than a hint here of the story from Gen 3 when Adam and Eve eat from the Tree of the Knowledge of Good and Evil and so become "like God."[639] No explicit explanation is given either in the "Ainulindale" or Gen 1 for why God chose to create in the first place. All we are told in Gen 1:2–3 is that the "earth was formless and empty." According to Walton, the Hebrew words here, which are *tohu* and *vohu*, together mean "that the earth is described as not yet functioning in an ordered system."[640] That is, there is no assigned *purpose* yet for creation. But why did Yahweh/Iluvatar create the world in the first place? God has no needs, so why would he do such a thing? Both Tolkien and Lewis had much to say on this topic. In "On Fairy Stories," Tolkien argues that the reason why God created the world and humankind can be found in the heart of every person, but especially in that of an artist. He says that the implanted desire in each of us to create things is the clue to God's nature and motivation for creating all things. Human-beings rejoice at a finely crafted weapon, book, or painting because we, in the making of things, we find truth, beauty, love, and goodness.

In *Mere Christianity*, Lewis says, "If I find in myself a desire which no experience in this world can satisfy, the most probable explanation is that I was made for another world." All of one's desires for "earthly pleasures were never meant to satisfy" the one restless desire "but only to arouse it, to suggest the real thing" that all of us are constantly searching for.[641] We create because we were created, and God created because he *loves* making things other than himself. According to Barron, "love is not a sentiment or feeling, not merely a tribal loyalty or family devotion. Love is actively willing the good of the other as other."[642] God is a relational being, and therefore we also are relational beings. Arguably, we have children so that we can pass on the gift of enjoying the beautiful world and all the experiences it can give us. It seems God created beings like himself for the same reason. Every human being aspires to lay hold of goodness because there is no real metaphysical alternative. During the Council of Elrond, Elrond himself says of Sauron that "nothing is evil in the beginning."[643] From this it is clear Tolkien himself held the view that evil is a privation of the good, like a cavity in a healthy tooth. Evil does not have an independent existence of its own, and it cannot exist without its host.

Yet another parallel between Iluvatar and the Ainur and Yahweh and the elohim is in their use of *words* to create the world. This is not just because of Tolkien's love of language; it is also another allusion to the Christian worldview. According to Wood, "Tolkien the Christian holds that our *logoi* (words) are rooted in the *Logos* (the Word)."[644] Christians believe that the universe was made *by* the Word (one person of the Triune God) and *through* the power of words. Once again, Tolkien believed that we create stories because God is a storyteller. Our love of words, which is particularly evident through our dependence on metaphor and parable, springs from God's decision to speak the world into existence. According to Ps 78:2, God says, "I will open my mouth with a parable; / I will utter hidden things, things from of old." This psalm tells us that parables are central to understanding reality itself. Stories are the key to understanding reality. Yet this is only the beginning of the story. Every story, we learned, has four parts: creation, fall, redemption, and restoration, or alternatively, beginning, conflict, conflict resolution, and ending. In chapters 3 and 4, we looked at redemption and restoration, or the conflict resolution and ending of the story. Thus far in this chapter we have only looked at the creation and beginning of the story, so now it is time to look at what went wrong in the story.

THE THEME OF MELKOR

One of the most intriguing and instructive parallels to the biblical story in *The Silmarillion* is the introduction of evil into creation. Over the years, I have recommended that students struggling with understanding the nature of evil and God's relationship to it read what Iluvatar says to Melkor in the "Ainulindale," because it gives a very satisfying mythical answer to a question many have while studying their Bibles. It has been my experience that Tolkien's story illuminates the biblical drama in ways that can enhance our understanding and appreciation of Scripture. Before we begin to explore how, there is one very important parallel to the biblical narrative that must be identified now before we address it more fully at the end of this chapter. After Melkor's theme contests with Iluvatar's for some time, Iluvatar warns him, "And thou, Melkor, shalt see that no theme may be played that hath not its uttermost source in me, nor can any alter the music in my despite."[645] This warning is reminiscent of the one which God gives to Adam, Eve, and the Serpent in Gen 3:15, known as the *protoevangelium*, or "first gospel": "And I will put enmity between you and the woman, and between your offspring and hers; he will crush your head and you will strike his heel." Not only are these two passages important for our present analysis of what Christian apologists have called "the problem of evil," but this is also a prophetic nod toward the moment and nature of redemption in the story. It is known as the "first gospel" because it mysteriously gestures toward the good news of Jesus Christ (typologically, of course). Genesis 3:15 anticipates the moment when the "Last Adam"—Jesus Christ—restores humanity's imager vocation and disarms evil.[646] This is why later Paul can boast in 1 Cor 15:55, "O death, where is thy sting? O grave, where is thy victory?"[647] Now the most important thing that we must recall in saying all this is that these insights only make sense *retrospectively*. Only by looking back from Aragorn's hopeful final words, his marriage to Arwen, his coronation, and his successful traveling of the Paths of the Dead to this moment in *The Silmarillion* can we see how everything fits together.

All worldviews approach evil very differently, but what does Christianity say about it? Why is it that evil people often seem to get rewarded for their unjust deeds and the deeds of the just and upright are punished or left unrewarded? This is a question everyone, at some point in their lives, asks. Indeed, Jesus himself, dying on the cross, asks this question, "My God, my God, why have you forsaken me?"[648] The question does presuppose, however, that there is a God who ought not to allow this sort of thing to happen. That, in turn, presupposes the existence of an objective morality which assumes that certain things are always right and wrong, no matter what, when, or how. If one does not believe in an objective morality, however, then one has no ground to stand on. If one does not believe in a God who is omnipotent and omniscient, one does not have the right to complain about bad people being rewarded and good people being punished, because in a universe without such a God, there is no sovereign power that cares, and we just have to get used to that being the way things are. The existence of evil poses a truly difficult problem for those who believe in a God who is all-powerful, all-knowing, and good. Remember, the power of the challenge parable/fairy story is the recovery of some insight that has been lost or hidden by what Lewis called "the veil of familiarity."[649] If God is good, as both Tolkien and the biblical authors tell us, then why does he allow evil? Other questions that come to mind are: Did God create evil? What does he plan to do about it—if anything? In the opening pages of the "Ainulindale," which we have been exploring, Tolkien gives us an immensely satisfying and nuanced answer to this important question.

After Iluvatar gave themes of music to the Ainur, they began to make their own contributions. Melkor, who is the strongest of all the Ainur, decides to create his own theme from scratch rather than add to the music given by Iluvatar. There are not many passages in the Bible which explicitly mention the figure of Satan. This is especially true of Gen 3, where the serpent is not explicitly identified with the figure in the book of Job known as "the Satan." Ezekiel 28:1–19 contains probably the closest description of the Satan. "You were the seal of perfection, full of wisdom and perfect in beauty, you were in Eden, the garden of God . . . you were anointed as a guardian cherub, for so I ordained you . . . you were on the holy mount of God," God says of Satan in vv. 12–14. This figure was originally good, beautiful, and an extremely significant servant of God who watched over Eden as a guardian, but something happened which did not align with this servant's original vocation. Verse 17 says, "Your heart became proud on account of your beauty, and you corrupted your wisdom because of your splendor. . . . So I threw you to earth; I made a spectacle of you before kings." Satan became "proud" and "corrupted" *because* of his good qualities, not in spite of them. Evil, then, is not an independent entity, but a parasite which feeds and depends on good, healthy things. Finally, elsewhere, in verses 6–9, Satan is described as someone who believes he is "as wise as a god," which is to say that he believes he can be his own creator-god. His fate? For anyone who has been filled with arrogance and dangerous self-sufficiency, the consequences are eventually humility and repentance, as one witnesses the destruction of one's impeccable, best-laid plans. According to Keller, "evil carries within it the seeds of its own destruction."[650] Nevertheless, God's creations are part of his family, and he neither coerces nor compels anyone to pursue goodness. There is an extremely delicate, paradoxical balance between predestination and foreknowledge, and these concepts are *not* mutually exclusive. God foreknowing an event does not necessarily mean the event *will* happen, only that he foreknew that possible outcome.[651] According to Bradley Birzer, "Tolkien believed in the immediacy of evil" throughout his life and himself said, "For of course the Shadow will arise again in a sense, but never again will an evil daemon be incarnate as a physical enemy."[652] According to Tolkien's critics, Melkor and Sauron are not as terrifying as they could be, but perhaps this is because we have forgotten how banal evil can be.

Readers ought not to be surprised, then, that Iluvatar does nothing to stop this new theme of Melkor's from developing. Here, we see Tolkien's clearest expression of the Christian concept of free will. From the Christian perspective, objective goodness is rooted in God's nature, whereas badness is defining goodness for yourself. Evil, then, is pursuing the objective good too much or too little, or in the wrong way. Once again, "badness is only spoiled goodness," according to Lewis.[653] Whenever anyone undertakes any act, our actions are held up to the standard of a moral law. God/Iluvatar imbued all his creation with the freedom to obey or disobey the moral law. Satan/Melkor desired to become the source of wisdom and goodness unto themselves. There is a paradoxical balance between fate and free will. A world where only fate existed would be a world without moral responsibility, whereas a world where only free will existed would be a world of relativistic anarchy. We are free, but in order to live authentic, meaningful lives, we must choose to give up some of that freedom. For the Ainur to be part of the world they helped create, they freely choose to contribute to Iluvatar's theme rather than invent their own as Melkor had done. These Ainur resemble the faithful members of God's divine council after Yahweh disinherited the rebellious *elohim* and their assigned nations.

In conclusion, Iluvatar does not stop the variant theme of Melkor, but instead interweaves Melkor's theme within his own. Tolkien then tells us that it seemed like a storm raged around Iluvatar's throne. Melkor's music "essayed to drown the other music by the violence of its voice, but it seemed that its most triumphant notes were taken by the other and woven into its own solemn pattern."[654] After this, Iluvatar rises from his throne and stops the music of the Ainur. Iluvatar then reveals the music the Ainur made together in a vision of the world, Arda. He also tells the Ainur that in that world, they will each see a reflection of their contributions, while reminding them that they are not its chief architects. "Each of you shall find contained herein, amid the design that I set before you, all those things *which it may seem that he himself devised or added*," concludes Iluvatar.[655] Indeed, in the next passage, Iluvatar reveals things which the Ainur had not anticipated, such as the coming of the "children of Iluvatar," whom we already know to be elves and men. But what of the dwarves? Unfortunately, the tainting influence of Melkor not only affected Arda, but his fellow Valar as well.

THE "CHILDREN OF MY ADOPTION"

Tolkien tells us that the Vala Aule created the dwarves in the darkness of Middle-earth because he longed for beings that he could relate to and because he grew impatient for the arrival of elves and men, which the Valar glimpsed in the vision of Arda.[656] It is intriguing how Aule resembles Adam in Gen 3. It has been customary for quite some time for Christians to interpret Adam and Eve as humanity's literal parents, but according to John Walton and Peter Enns, this is not what the authors of Genesis meant. Enns believes that we can learn a lot about the Adam and Eve story by looking ahead to the exodus story, when God creates the nation of Israel. Like Adam, Israel is "created" by God during the exodus "through a cosmic battle," given a "lush land flowing with milk and honey," and meant to "remain in the land as long as they obey the Mosaic law." Ultimately, however, like Adam and Eve, Israel persists in a pattern of disobedience and is exiled to Babylon. According to Enns, Adam is also created after God tames the primordial waters of chaos, just as in the Moses story.[657] Thus it may be insightful to interpret the Aule–dwarves story as a story which resembles the story of the creation of Israel rather than the creation of the first human beings. According to Walton, Adam and Eve are considered by both the Old and New Testament authors as "archetypal" rather than biological. "Consequently," Walton says, "to contend that some treatment of Adam is archetypal is not to suggest that he is not historical. Jesus is also treated archetypally by Paul, yet he is historical."[658] Recall that Israel is later called through Abraham so that through Israel all humanity could eventually be redeemed. The call of Israel is the answer to the sin of Adam and Eve, and the incarnation is the answer to the persistent disobedience of Israel. Through Jesus, God himself redeems the redeemers so that they can carry on with the original task for which they were called.

"Did God reject his people? By no means," writes Paul in Rom 11:1. Paul is telling us that, despite some of Israel's rejection of Jesus, Israel will not be forgotten in the messiah. Israel does not cease to be important because of the coming of Jesus. On the contrary, Paul tells us that salvation comes "first to the Jew, then to the gentile."[659] Similarly, despite Aule's error in creating the dwarves before Iluvatar's children of "choice" came into the world, Iluvatar nevertheless blessed Aule's work and adopted his children as his own. This is reminiscent of God's decision to allow Adam and Eve to still maintain their imager status while simultaneously making it more difficult for them to carry out that vocation. When all this is understood retrospectively, we can see that there is more than a hint here of the calling of Abraham by God and his promise to Abraham that through him "all peoples on earth will be blessed."[660] In other words, the dwarves' role in bringing salvation into the world is, like Israel's, absolutely central. We have seen this come to fruition especially in the figure of Thorin Oakenshield, whose return to Erebor was instrumental in preparing the way for Aragorn. After the creation of the elves (more on this soon), Durin I, one of the seven fathers of the dwarves, awoke from his slumber and wandered across Middle-earth, eventually founding the kingdom of Khazad-Dum (Moria). In book II, chapter 4 of *The Fellowship of the Ring*, Gimli sings a song about this important event: "The world was young, the mountains green, / no stain yet on the Moon was seen, / no words were laid on stream or stone, / when Durin woke and walked alone. / He named the nameless hills and dells; / he drank from yet untasted wells; / he stooped and looked in Mirrormere, / and saw a crown of stars appear / . . . above the shadow of his head."[661] This whole song has a messianic tone that gestures to a future salvific dwarf-king from the line of Durin who will restore the fortunes of his people. This is further reinforced by the fact that it is Gimli, the son of Gloin—who was one of the dwarves in Thorin's company in *The Hobbit*—who is singing the song in a ruined Khazad-Dum. Gimli is singing not only to recall the age of Durin I, but also to look forward to the time when the fortune and welfare of his people will be made secure. But as we know, this would not happen through the return of another king from the line of Durin (because Thorin failed), but through a Numenorean man.

So, was it wrong for Aule to create the dwarves? The answer seems to be both yes and no. Yes, because Tolkien is clearly warning us against the abuse of sub-creation in the story of Aule. Sub-creation in and of itself is not necessarily sinful, but it can be. If a sub-creator wishes to transcend their creaturely, sub-creative vocation, then it is wrong, for only God himself can create *ex nihilo*. In the story of Aule's creation of the dwarves, Tolkien may also have been alluding to the divine rebellion of some of the Sons of God from God's council as told in Gen 6:1–4. According to Heiser, the rebellious Sons of God were guilty of trying to create their own imagers as God did with humanity in Gen 1:26–27. The offspring of these rebellious council members and human women—the Nephilim—as well as their later descendants—the various giant clans—would become a "lethal threat to Yahweh's children, the Israelites."[662] That is why Iluvatar is initially angry with Aule: as a member of Iluvatar's council, Aule's decision to create the dwarves resembles the rebellious Sons of God's decision to create their own imagers as rivals to God's own. Just as with the Serpent in Eden, it is the corrupting influence of Melkor that implants the desire in Aule's heart to "be like God." In one sense, as the first to be created in Arda, the dwarves resemble Israel as God's "firstborn Son" (Exod 4:22). In another sense, in Tolkien's story, the Numenoreans also resemble Israel, since it is ultimately through them that the messiah comes to Middle-earth. Although Aule did initially follow Melkor's example of abusing sub-creation, he remained a faithful member of Iluvatar's council because of his repentance. Indeed, Aule offered to destroy his imagers, but Iluvatar showed mercy and instead put the dwarves into a deep sleep. Although Yahweh/Iluvatar does not require his imagers' evil choices to bring about a greater good, he nevertheless incorporates Aule's rebellious decision to create the dwarves into his great plan to bring the messiah to Middle-earth. As we have already seen, Thorin's later return to Erebor was a crucial event that helped ensure Aragorn's survival and eventual return to his throne. In the story of Aule and the dwarves, one is also reminded of Adam and Eve's shame in being naked in Eden. Aule's children live because he created them out of love, just like Iluvatar will go on to create elves and men out of love. Melkor, on the other hand, desired mastery of his creations, not relationship. Melkor's desire to "bring into Being things of his own" grew out of his impatience with Iluvatar concerning the Void, the potential to create.[663] It is interesting to note here that Tolkien tells us that "the Children of Iluvatar were conceived by him alone ... and none of the Ainur had part in their making."[664] This is analogous to the biblical truth from Gen 1:26–27 that humanity is only made in Yahweh's image—not in any member of the divine council's. Iluvatar seems to have foreseen the effects which Melkor's theme would have upon Aule, and so prepared children in his own image in secret. The dwarves, like Israel, produce the king that will pave the way for the messiah who will not only be a "son" of that family, but also its Lord.

"THE CHILDREN OF MY CHOICE"

After the creation of the dwarves, Iluvatar not only puts them to sleep, but he also grants permission to willing members of the Ainur to enter Arda so that they can continue shaping it. Careful readers will see that Tolkien makes it clear that without the Ainur's help, Arda will not take full shape. This may be an allusion to God's desire to work with both his human and divine family as partners in the creation project. Apparently, the other Ainur were not aware of Aule's transgression, and we are told that many of the Ainur begin to yearn for companionship with Iluvatar's Firstborn, the elves, and the Atani (humankind), later called the "Followers." These, Iluvatar tells Aule, are the "children of my choice," whereas the dwarves are the "children of my adoption."[665] Iluvatar keeps the details of their arrival unknown to most of the Ainur, except for Manwe, Iluvatar's viceroy in Middle-earth, but even he is not completely aware of the details of their coming. If any being resembles the "angel of Yahweh" and therefore Jesus Christ in *The Silmarillion*, it is Manwe, who is unique in the divine council. According to Heiser, the "angel of Yahweh" is a being which manifested the presence of Yahweh on earth. He is the "second Yahweh" who also often appears with the heavenly Yahweh throughout the Old Testament.[666] In Tolkien's mythology, Manwe rules from within Arda, just as the "angel of Yahweh" in the Old Testament frequently interacts with many famous characters in the Old Testament.[667]

Not long after some of the Valar decide to enter Arda, Melkor builds the fortress of Utumno and begins to corrupt the beauty of Yavanna—who loves all that is green—while simultaneously frustrating the labors of the other Valar. We are told about the two great lamps which were called Illuin and Ormal that gave continuous light throughout the Earth until Melkor destroyed them. As a result, "the shape of Arda and the symmetry of its waters and lands was marred," Tolkien writes.[668] That passing period was known as the "Spring of Arda." This first battle between Melkor and the Valar resulted in the retreat of the Valar to Aman, the "westernmost of all lands upon the borders of the world." After fortifying the region known as Valinor, we are told that Yavanna created two trees—Telperion and Laurelin. These trees replaced the previously destroyed lamps, and after their creation, the "hour appointed by Iluvatar for the coming of the Firstborn" finally arrived.[669] At this time the Vala Varda began the great work of the creation of the stars, whose light would cause the awakening of the elves at a place called Cuivienen, the "Water of Awakening."[670] Melkor began to abduct and corrupt some of the elves at this time and twisted them into orcs, a deed which we are told was the most hated by Iluvatar. After this, a great battle between Melkor and the other Valar took place which resulted in his imprisonment in Valinor.

At that time, the Quendi (the elves) were summoned to Valinor, yet some were unwilling to go. Those that went to Valinor were called the Eldar, whereas those that remained behind became known as the Avari, or the "Unwilling." Underneath the general designation of the Eldar are the Vanyar, or the "First Elves," and the Noldor, who became friends of Aule and would come to be known for their crafts. There were the Teleri also, called the "Sea-Elves" because of the music they made beside the sea. In the tale entitled "Of Feanor and the Unchaining of Melkor," readers learn that eventually Melkor was set free by the Valar with the condition that he must remain in Valinor under his fellow Valar's supervision. But Melkor hated the Eldar because the Valar loved the elves dearly. It is at this point in the story that we learn of Feanor's creation of the three Silmarils, which are jewels that contain the light of the Two Trees of Valinor. This was a secret labor. Melkor began to crave the light contained in these jewels and thus began the corruption of the Eldar, who eventually have a falling out. Melkor turns the Eldar against each other by telling them that Manwe—and Iluvatar—concealed the awakening of humankind from them, which caused strife between the Eldar and the Valar. Both Feanor and Melkor had an inordinate, idolatrous love for the Silmarils. Melkor succeeds in sowing strife among the elves and eventually, Feanor is exiled. Since Finwe loved his eldest son, he followed him into exile. Melkor grew brazen enough to demand the Silmarils from Feanor, and after being rebuffed, returned while Feanor was away, killed Finwe, and stole the Silmarils. This took place shortly after Melkor and Ungoliant destroyed the Two Trees, thus depriving the world of the trees' beautiful light. After the Two Trees were destroyed, their light remained in the Silmarils, and Yavanna created the moon and the sun from the last flower of Telperion and the last fruit of Laurelin, respectively. This entire storyline resembles the Gen 3 narrative, especially with regards to Melkor/the Serpent. Melkor, like the Serpent, is cunning and manipulative, and Valinor is quite reminiscent of the garden of Eden. Quite obviously there is also the fact that there are two trees in Valinor and two trees in Eden.

After Melkor slew Feanor's father, Finwe, king of the Noldor, and stole the Silmarils, he forever became known as "Morgoth," "the Black Foe of the World."⁶⁷¹ After this, Feanor becomes utterly consumed with a desire for vengeance and the recovery of the Silmarils. Feanor then convinces some of the Eldar to go into exile in pursuit of Morgoth and the Silmarils, which eventually leads to the terrible massacre of the Teleri at Alqualonde. Feanor needed ships to pursue Morgoth, and the Teleri were unpersuaded by Feanor's crusade. This event Tolkien named the *Noldolante*, "the Fall of the Noldor."⁶⁷² A biblical parallel to this event would be Cain's decision to murder his own brother Abel in Gen 4. Cain's punishment is not death, but permanent exile and unending frustration. God also forbids anyone from killing Cain, so that he must live with the shame of fratricide. Tolkien tells us in the tale "Of the Beginning of Days" that the "Elves remain until the end of days," and that "the Elves die not till the world dies," which resembles Cain's status as "a restless wanderer on the earth" (Gen 4:12).⁶⁷³ The elves—like Cain—must live with the knowledge of what they have done. Eventually, the Noldor fragment and settle throughout Middle-earth.

In the "Valaquenta," which is Tolkien's account about the Valar and Maiar, we are told that the Vala Manwe "is dearest to Iluvatar and understands most clearly his purposes." It is also said that Manwe "was appointed to be, in the *fullness of time*, the first of all Kings: lord of the realm of Arda and ruler of all that dwell therein."⁶⁷⁴ This passage reminds one of Gal 4:4, where Paul says, "When the fullness of time had come, God sent forth his Son, born of woman, born under the law, to redeem those who were under the law, so that we might receive adoption as sons." It also reminds us of Aragorn's coronation when Gandalf proclaims, "May the thrones of the Valar endure!" There is a deep theological connection between Iluvatar, Manwe, and Aragorn. If Manwe is essentially an expression of Iluvatar's immanence in the world, and the enthronement of Aragorn prompts Gandalf to make a connection between this Numenorean king and Manwe, then the conclusion is clear: Aragorn is Iluvatar become king. According to Birzer, "Tolkien made it quite clear in his letters that the king was Iluvatar's reprentative on Earth. If Manwe was Iluvatar's regent of the whole earth, Aragorn was Iluvatar's regent of Middle-earth."⁶⁷⁵ Although Iluvatar works through all his children to save Arda, it is ultimately through Aragorn that he inaugurates Iluvatar's kingdom on earth. The Numenoreans, as we will learn soon, were Elros's descendants, and his ancestors were elves, men, and a Maia named Melian. "And from these brethren alone has come among Men the blood of the Firstborn and a strain of the spirits divine that were before Arda," writes Tolkien of the Numenoreans.⁶⁷⁶ The Numenorean bloodline springs from a member of the Maiar and therefore can be traced back to Iluvatar himself.

Manwe's destiny to be "first of all Kings" of Arda is fulfilled through the return of the king to Minas Tirith. Iluvatar accomplishes this plan by working through all his children—and then supremely through Aragorn—who collectively resembles Israel in Middle-earth. It is now time to discuss Aragorn's ancestors, the Numenoreans. Although the appendices of *The Lord of the Rings* are helpful, today readers can go online and find Aragorn's family tree quite easily. Any good family tree will show that there were several marital unions between elves and men which ultimately produced Elrond and his brother Elros. At the end of the First Age, there was a terrible battle called the War of Wrath. The War of Wrath was the final conflict between all three races of the children of Iluvatar and Morgoth. Eventually, due to the pleading of Earendil (the father of Elrond and Elros), the Valar went to war with their fallen brother Melkor and emerged triumphant. After the War of Wrath was concluded and Melkor was imprisoned in the Void, Manwe granted the sons of Earendil a choice between the bloodlines: they could remain elves or become men. Elrond chose to remain with the elves whereas Elros chose the life of a mortal man. Although Elros and his descendents were mortal, the Valar granted them extraordinarily long lives and an island called Numenor, a gift for man's faithfulness during the War of Wrath. We should pause here momentarily to look at Aragorn's ancestry, for it is an important part in our argument that the incarnation is present in Middle-earth.

As we already know, the Numenoreans were not ordinary men; they descended from Elros, the son of Earendil and Elwing. If you have gone online to find Aragorn's family tree, you will notice that Aragorn's distant ancestor is Melian, who is one of the Maiar.[677] Melian was married to Thingol, an elf, and together they had a daughter named Luthien Tinuviel, one of Tolkien's most cherished characters. Luthien falls in love with a man named Beren, who sees her dancing in the forest. Yet because Thingol did not think Beren to be worthy of his daughter's hand in marriage, the elven king gave him the impossible task of retrieving one of the Silmarils from the crown of Morgoth. Interestingly, Finrod, who owed a debt to Beren's father, Barahir, because he saved his life, accompanied Beren in his quest only to later to die in helping Beren escape from the dungeon of Sauron. Importantly, Beren is an ancestor of Aragorn. Is it a coincidence, then, that Finrod, who foretold the coming of the messiah in Middle-earth, helped save the man whose family would later sire Aragorn? Moving on, Dior, the son of Beren and Luthien, would go on to marry Nimloth, an elf-princess, and they would have a daughter named Elwing. This comprises the half of Aragorn's family tree which originates in one of the Maiar. On the other side of his family tree, Aragorn's ancestors are once again half-elf and half-human. Tuor, a human, marries Idril, an elf and the only daughter of King Turgon of Gondolin.[678] Together, they have a son named Earendil, who will go on to marry Elwing, the daughter of Dior, the son of Beren and Luthien. Earendil and Elwing go on to have two sons named Elros and Elrond. One will notice that there is a total of *three* unions between elves and men in Aragorn's family tree. All this to say that Tolkien, using myth, wanted to show that Aragorn, like Jesus, "hasn't come from within the story as it was—though, strangely, those with eyes to see will recognize that it is where the story *ought* to have gone all along" but from *outside* the story.[679] Aragorn is, like Jesus, an outsider-insider. He does not emerge from the part of the story in which we might expect. Aragorn is not just an elf, man, or dwarf, but the lord of them all, something we later see reflected in the Fellowship of the Ring. All Iluvatar's children have a part to play in preparing the way for the messiah. Is it possible that Iluvatar foresaw the crucial role which the dwarves would have in preparing the way for his chosen king, and that is why he accepted Aule's creation?

Since Numenor was near Valinor, the Valar gave Elros and his people one prohibition: never attempt to sail to Valinor and take immortality by force. After a very long history of peace and stability throughout the Second Age, the Numenorean kings fall into idolatrous practices because of the Maia Sauron, who becomes an advisor to the last kings of Numenor. Sauron was once a lieutenant in Morgoth's army. He convinces them to stop worshiping Iluvatar and to sail with a great armada to Valinor, which results in the destruction of both the armada and Numenor. At that time, the path to Valinor is hidden from all except the elves. This is indeed an allusion to the loss of sacred space—Eden—from the book of Genesis. After the destruction of Numenor, man lost the ability to fellowship with God intimately and directly, just like Adam and Eve. The earth is still God's sacred space, but it is much less so after the fall/Akallabeth.[680] Creation itself now begins to yearn for renewal. Man will tirelessly search for immortality, but will never find it within the circles of the world. Fortunately, one man, named Elendil, along with his two sons, Isildur and Anarion, escape the destruction of Numenor and arrive safely in Middle-earth.

By the end of *The Silmarillion*, all Iluvatar's children—adopted and chosen—have become exiles, just as it is in the Bible. Israel is adrift and the nations under the other *elohim* have been disinherited by God. Tolkien himself once commented on this, saying, "We all long for it [Eden], and we are constantly glimpsing it: our whole nature at its best and least corrupted, its gentlest and most humane, is still soaked with the sense of 'exile.'"[681] The end of the Second Age is no less violent and sorrowful than the end of the First Age, for it, too, ends in a cataclysmic battle. This time, the Last Alliance of men and elves fight against Sauron and his armies, and though the Last Alliance prevails, their victory brings new perils. Perhaps the greatest is the taking of the One Ring by Isildur, who defeated Sauron after the Dark Lord killed his father, Elendil. And yet one can see Iluvatar weaving the theme of Melkor into his own mighty theme here once again, for Smeagol comes by the One Ring because of Isildur, which in turn leads to Bilbo's winning of it in a riddle contest, which in turn leads to Frodo's inheriting of the One Ring and its subsequent destruction. Evil does indeed carry within it the seeds of its own destruction. By the end of the Second Age, the elves are divided and scattered and are skeptical of both man and dwarf, the dwarves have retreated into their mountains, and the Numenorean kingdoms of Arnor in the north and Gondor in the south slowly begin to decline after Isildur's acquisition of the One Ring. All the children of Iluvatar are in need of salvation, but who among them is capable? This question begs another: did Tolkien himself conceive a savior for Middle-earth? This brings us to the final topic of the book: the prophecy of "Estel" from "The Debate of Finrod and Andreth."

"THE DEBATE OF FINROD AND ANDRETH"

According to Christopher Tolkien's commentary on "The Debate of Finrod and Andreth," this text is a "manifest challenge to my father's view in his letter of 1951 on the necessary limitations of the expression of 'moral and religious truth (or error)' in a 'Secondary World.'"[682] So, the answer to the question asked at the end of the previous section is *yes*, Tolkien did intend a savior for Middle-earth, but not in the way we might think. The answer to this question, however, depends on how we understand the incarnation. Throughout this book, a case has been made that the incarnation is best understood as the return of the king. According to Wright, "the gospels were all about God becoming king, but the creeds are focused on Jesus being God."[683] If we read the Gospels expecting them to be stories about Jesus being God, we will, paradoxically, miss *how* they are ultimately about this. The parables simultaneously gesture toward and participate in the mystery of the incarnation. This means that there does not need to be an explicit "savior" accompanied by the theological talk of that savior dying for sins in Jesus's parables or *The Lord of the Rings* in order for these stories to be "about" the incarnation. By being stories about the return of the king and the downfall of evil, they are stories about the incarnation. Ultimately, the result of meditating and reflecting on Jesus's and Tolkien's parables should be that God has really taken charge of the world and that everything is being put to rights.

Once again, Tolkien's comment that "the Fall of Man is in the past and off stage; the Redemption of Man in the far future" does not mean there is no incarnation in Middle-earth, it only means that there is nowhere any allegorical embodiment of the Creator in Middle-earth.[684] Tolkien knew his theology. By referring to the redemption of man in "the far future," Tolkien is speaking of the *final and ultimate* redemption of man, which will only take place after the resurrection and final judgment at the end of history. Therefore, it is not implausible to suggest that the historical atmosephere of *The Lord of the Rings* resembles neither an explicitly Christian nor explicitly non-Christian period, making it analogous to Jesus's parables. When Tolkien wrote of the historical atmosphere of Middle-earth, saying, "We are in a time when the One God, Eru, is known to exist by the wise, but is not approachable save by or through the *Valar*," Tolkien might have even been referring to the doctrine of general revelation, the notion that God's existence can be inferred from the created universe.[685] This does not mean, as most Tolkien scholars have argued, that Middle-earth is set *literally* during a pre-Christian period. It *could* refer to a pre-Christian time period, but it could just as easily be read as a description of the first century in which Jesus lived, which was a simultaneously Christian *and* non-Christian historical period. It is surprising that these alternatives have not been explored or touched on in other scholarly treatments of Tolkien's books. This seems to be an ideal setting in which to show how Christianity can flourish in any historical period while avoiding coming across as an explicitly Christian story.

Of course, it is always possible to fall back on the traditional explanation that Tolkien is telling us that by novel's end, the incarnation is still a far-off reality. But this does not fit with all the other evidence we have examined in this book. If *The Lord of the Rings* is a parable, it has a very unique way of reflecting the truth of the incarnation that is different from other literary forms. Parables simultaneously are and point toward the truth they seek to communicate. Once again, by adopting the allusive, understated tone of the Gospel of Mark in *The Lord of the Rings*, Tolkien was not adopting a so-called "low Christology," but speaking parabolically. The low christological view adopted by scholars such as Bart D. Ehrman promotes the notion that Jesus does not claim to be God in the Synoptic Gospels as much as he does in the "high Christology" found in the Gospel of John.

There is one final reason why Tolkien's comment does not exclude the possibility of the incarnation in Middle-earth: the comment, "approachable save by or through the *Valar*." The Valar closely resemble God's divine council in the Bible, which, among other things, is how God's immanence—involvement in the world—is understood. Tolkien's comment, then, might simply point out that we can best understand God's transcendence via his immanence. It is ultimately through the most unique member of the divine council, Jesus Christ—the one who is considered one with and distinct from Yahweh—that human beings come to know God. In *The Silmarillion*, the Vala Manwe is presented in a way that closely resembles the "angel of Yahweh" in the Bible. This mysterious angel, who appears in many Old Testament stories—perhaps most famously the story of Abraham and the binding of Isaac in Gen 22—is often blurred together with descriptions of Yahweh himself.[686] According to Tolkien, Manwe is described as the "dearest" to Iluvatar and understands the mind of Iluvatar the most clearly. Moreover, Tolkien describes Manwe as the "king" of Arda using language very similar to Paul's language about Jesus in Gal 4:4–5: "When the fullness of time had come, God sent forth his Son, born of woman, born under the law, to redeem those who were under the law, so that we might receive adoption as sons."[687] Moreover, according to Birzer, Tolkien had made it very clear that the king (Aragorn) was not only Iluvatar's representative on earth, but somehow one with Manwe, and thus with Iluvatar himself: "If Manwe was Iluvatar's regent of the whole earth, Aragorn was Iluvatar's regent of Middle-earth."[688] Birzer also comments that Gandalf identifies Aragorn *with* the Valar, which is an important detail that I believe shows us Tolkien was familiar with the divine council and how the incarnation relates to it. We now need to turn to "The Debate of Finrod and Andreth," a text which provides more clues that we are on the right track.

When does this dialogue take place in the history of Middle-earth, and what is it about? Tolkien originally wanted "The Debate" to be a part of the appendices of *The Silmarillion*, which itself was originally meant to be published alongside *The Lord of the Rings*. Tolkien's publisher thought this was a bad idea, so it was later published by Christopher Tolkien in *Morgoth's Ring*, volume 10 of The History of Middle-earth. "The Debate" never made it into the mainstream publication of *The Silmarillion*, which was first published in 1977. The dialogue between Finrod and Andreth took place in the First Age of Arda during the Siege of Angband, Morgoth's fortress. There was a total of six major battles between the children of Iluvatar and Morgoth during the First Age, and this debate took place during the third battle, the Dagor Aglareb ("Glorious Battle"). In the previous section we learned that Morgoth was eventually defeated in the sixth and final battle, the War of Wrath, which subsequently ended the First Age of Arda. Although Tolkien finished "The Debate of Finrod and Andreth" in the mid to late 1950s after *The Lord of the Rings* was published, it was not published until after his death when his son Christopher Tolkien included the text in *Morgoth's Ring* (1993). This text contains two important theological topics which, with this background information in mind, provide evidence that the incarnation is present in Middle-earth through the parabolic form of *The Lord of the Rings* in the same way that Jesus is present through his parables.

The text begins as a conversation about the metaphysical condition of the Atani ("men") between Finrod—an elven king, philosopher, and brother of Galadriel—and Andreth—a somewhat skeptical female loremaster among the Atani. The conversation begins when Finrod laments the "swift passing" of the Atani. Andreth agrees and then goes on to explain that men are never content and always restless. After the elves awoke in the far east of Middle-earth, many of them took the journey to Valinor, where they dwelt for untold years, while men, who awoke with the creation of the sun, were not permitted to come to Valinor. At several points in the dialogue, Andreth appears to be bitter, for she seems to imply that men were left to fend for themselves against Morgoth, who corrupted many of the first men. Andreth is also bitter because she feels that the so-called "gift of men"—death—causes the elves to look down on the Atani as little children. She says that Finrod—and many other elves besides—have never had to live in constant fear of the Enemy since they dwelt for so long in the land of light—Valinor. Finrod seems to possess a perspective on the *hroa* ("body") and *fea* ("soul") of the Atani that Andreth's bitterness may prevent her from seeing. He believes that the Atani's "swift passing" is indeed a gift, a purposeful part of their design by Iluvatar. This is a very Job-like dialogue, for Finrod is essentially trying to persuade Andreth to see that even though the Enemy told men that death is a curse on the Atani, because Iluvatar is ultimately sovereign, suffering and death are in actuality a gift.

According to Andreth, "men are not by nature short-lived, but have become so through the malice of the Lord of the Darkness whom they do not name." That is, had it not been for the theme of Melkor, there would have been no "marring of Arda" and thus no diminishment of the body/soul of men, for they were originally intended to be immortal. In anger, Andreth tells Finrod that death constantly haunts the Atani and they feel like restless exiles. In response to her anger, Finrod says, "These words are strange and terrible. And you speak with the bitterness of one whose pride has been humiliated, and seeks therefore to wound those to whom she speaks." Tolkien clearly had the book of Job in mind when writing this, for Andreth's parts show her wrestling with the problem of evil. In the next segment of the debate, Finrod's speech resembles one of Job's friends'. Finrod rebukes Andreth's anger, saying, "Beware of the chaff with your corn, Andreth! For it may be deadly: lies of the Enemy that out of envy will breed hate. Not all the voices that come out of the darkness speak truth to those minds that listen for strange news." Finrod also explains to Andreth that death "is but the name we give to something that he [Morgoth] has tainted, and it sounds therefore evil: but untainted, its name would be good." Mortality is supposed to be a gift because it prompts us to yearn for eternity (Ecc 3:16), but the Enemy has obfuscated this truth. The Enemy created in the Atani a fear that this physical world and body is all there is. Throughout the rest of their conversation on this topic, we learn that while the *fea* ("souls") of elves and men are the same, the elves' souls are bound to Arda whereas men's souls are not. This is Tolkien the Christian alluding to the belief that after death, the faithful dead will receive new bodies at the resurrection and be permitted to live in the new creation. From the debate we can deduce that men alone are able to perceive that the present state of the world is not permanent. That is why Finrod says that men look at "no thing for itself . . . if they study it, it is to discover something else."[689] The Christian position on death is that while it is "the last enemy to be destroyed," it nevertheless brings us closer to God, ultimately paving the way for the resurrection bodies we will one day receive.[690] Despite Finrod's persuasive argument, and despite the fact that he tells Andreth that the elves know and fear death, too, Andreth cynically asks him, "What know ye of death?" It is at this point in the debate that Andreth reveals that elves do not really die because they are given a new *hroa* after death, whereas for men, "Death is an uttermost end, a loss irredeemable."[691] Finrod assures Andreth that though death comes to elves much more slowly than it comes to men, it comes nonetheless. Finrod also tells Andreth that she has given far too much credit to Morgoth, who could not be the source of the "gift of men."

Finrod believes that Andreth is mistaken about man's original nature, which she thinks was immortal from the beginning. This may be an allusion to the Christian belief that before the fall, Adam and Eve had access to the Tree of Life, and thus immortality. Andreth seems to believe that Iluvatar withheld or retracted the gift of immortality from men after men had dealings with Morgoth. Finrod seems to hint that the elves envy the Atani for their "gift," which may explain why Finrod occasionally became frustrated with Andreth's insistence that the Atani were originally immortal like the elves. In other words, immortality in the elvish sense is not something to be envied. In conclusion, Finrod illustrates the difference between elves and men thusly: "To me the difference seems like that between one who visits a strange country, and abides there a while (but need not), and one who has lived in that land always (and must). To the former all things that he sees are new and strange, and in that degree lovable. To the other all things are familiar, the only things that are his own, and in that degree precious." Men are pilgrims and exiles, or "guests" as Andreth calls them, but the elves were only meant for Arda in its current state. Whether he knew it or not, Tolkien is speaking here of the Jewish belief that history is divided into two ages: *olam hazeh* and *olam haba*.[692] The *olam hazeh*—"present age"—corresponds here with Arda in its current state, whereas the *olam haba*—"the age to come"—corresponds to the promise of "Arda Remade."[693]

Although Andreth does not fully understand how all this will work out, she recognizes the truth in Finrod's words: "'You speak strange words, Finrod,' said Andreth, 'which I have not heard before. Yet my heart is stirred as if by some truth that it recognizes even if it does not understand it. But fleeting is that memory, and goes ere it can be grasped; and then we grow blind.'" This passage is redolent with allusions to the inaugurated eschatology which Tolkien seemed to believe in, and which we explored in chapter 3. It is not so much that we used to have immortality in the garden of Eden as it is that we *had access* to it through direct fellowship with our Creator. When Adam and Eve ate from the Tree of the Knowledge of Good and Evil, they set themselves up as the arbiters of their own meaning. You will recall that God's original plan for humanity was to make them members of his divine council. The command that God gave to Adam and Eve not to eat from the Tree of the Knowledge of Good and Evil was a test of loyalty: will humanity exercise their freedom to trust God or decide that they know better than him? They chose to believe God was holding out on them somehow and disobeyed God, thus violating their innocence, which is really what the Gen 3 story is all about.

According to Heiser, the serpent tells Eve that if she violates God's command, she and Adam will become as *elohim* "knowing good and evil . . . not *will be capable of good and evil.*" Adam and Eve, like God's divine family, already possessed free will but had not yet "experienced evil—either by their own commission or as bystanders."[694] Adam and Eve were influenced by the serpent to love God only for what he gave them, not for who he is. They were tempted to use their freedom to build a kingdom for themselves rather than to cooperate with God and his providential plan for creation. God chose not to intervene and prevent the fall, for then he would prevent an even greater good that would come "in due course."[695] Yes, God foreknew the fall, but "foreknowledge did not propel the event."[696] The choice of Adam and Eve was incorporated into God's cosmic plan, which would culminate in the incarnation; it could have gone differently, but it did not. The coming of God into creation will be the answer to the sin of Adam and Eve. God becoming king is the reestablishment of God as the epicenter of truth, wisdom, goodness, and order. God does not inhibit our freedom, for it would be a violation of his loving nature to force us to obey him. God wants us to do good, but we are free to abstain from being his imagers if we so choose.

Our mortality is supposed to remind us that we are meant for so much more, but more often than not, it is a source of fear and anxiety. Recall that Finrod said of mankind "that they look at no thing for itself; if they study it, it is to discover something else." What are men searching for? Perhaps, Finrod says, men are searching for that place where there is no division of the *hroa* and *fea*, where all things are one. With a clear allusion to the resurrection, Finrod says that the *fea* is "wedded indissolubly to a *hroa* of Arda," and that in time, "the *fea* shall have the power to uplift the *hroa*."[697] Before proceeding, we need to clarify what Tolkien is *not* saying here. Tolkien rejected the spirit/matter dualism of Platonism and gnostic Christianity with its belief that the material world is evil and secondary whereas the immaterial world is good and primary. To overemphasize the importance of the *fea* would degrade the importance of the *hroa*, and so Tolkien concludes through his characters here that the proper view is that of an eventual integrated, *renewed hroa* and *fea*. Christians believe that the body (and the material world) is good; it is not a mere wrapper to be discarded upon death. God will one day raise our perishable bodies and replace them with imperishable bodies. Tolkien therefore rejected the idea of "souls in transit" to a disembodied reality after we die.[698] According to Rom 8:17, our ultimate destiny is to be "co-heirs with Christ" in the "new heaven and new earth."[699] Neither Finrod nor Andreth, living in a marred Arda, can say with certainty when or how this redemption will take place, but it is clear from the text that they hope for it. The next part of the dialogue turns to the issue of how this redemption would come about.

At this point in the debate, Finrod proclaims that he thinks men are not the "followers" of the elves or the "little children" that Andreth thought the elves saw the Atani as, but instead the "heirs and fulfillers of all." This is quite a compliment. In other words, Finrod believes that it will be through *men* that salvation comes to Middle-earth. Finrod then says something that once again gives us a glimpse of Tolkien's eschatological views: "For that Arda Healed shall not be Arda Unmarred, but a third thing and a greater, and yet the same." Nowhere in Tolkien's entire mythology is there such a clear example of inaugurated eschatology, sometimes expressed in biblical scholarship by the phrase "already, but not yet." This is yet another reason why "The Debate of Finrod and Andreth" is *the* central explanatory text of Tolkien's mythology: in it we see Tolkien's clearest expression of the theology which undergirds his entire mythology, especially *The Lord of the Rings*. Unfortunately, Andreth despairs at this point because she does not share Finrod's eschatological optimism. She sees no point in "Estel"—"hope"—as Finrod does. Indeed, she seems to see no escape from the evil of Morgoth.

Now the debate turns to the topic of the means by which Arda might one day be healed, and thus to the topic of the incarnation—the return of the king.

"ESTEL"

Something of the whole experience of reality is glimpsed in Tolkien's mythology. Earlier in the book, we heard from Peter Kreeft, who argued that that is precisely why *The Lord of the Rings* "bears endless rereading: it is heavy enough to bear the mind's journeys into it, like our world."[700] As we learned in the Introduction, this is arguably because of the presence of the Christian worldview within the text. Tolkien's parable is about what Jesus's parables are about—and Jesus's parables are about reality itself. From the Christian perspective, that reality is that the true king has returned and is making all things new again—this is the good news. We have argued throughout this book that this is something which can only be discerned by reading Tolkien's books backwards, just as we should read Scripture. Now we have arrived at the key text in Tolkien's mythology which introduces the hope of the incarnation in Middle-earth. Interestingly, "The Debate" was written in the late 1950s *after* Tolkien finished *The Lord of the Rings*. Was "The Debate" Tolkien's meditation on the presence of the incarnational tone of his mythology which he only discovered "in the revision"? It certainly seems that Tolkien wanted to ensure that "The Debate" reflected his ultimate desire to "deliberately" tell a story built out of "certain religious ideas." Perhaps after revising *The Lord of the Rings*, Tolkien recognized that the central theme of his mythology was also the central theme of the gospel and therefore of reality itself. Whether he was consciously or unconsciously aware of it, "The Debate" is the legend of the entire mythology; it is the musical key that the rest of the mythology is played in. Indeed, with regards to both Tolkien's books and the Bible, "we have mistaken key for tune." According to Wright, we have "read as the main text what the gospels treated as presupposition."[701] As with the Bible, so with Tolkien's books; in looking for a divine messiah in Middle-earth, we have ironically missed him.

This tale from the First Age of Middle-earth both explains and foreshadows the four themes of the biblical metanarrative. In "The Debate," there are various allusions to the "Ainulindalë," in which we learn not only how the world came to be, but why Finrod and Andreth feel a taint upon their existence (creation). We also learn about the effects which Melkor's rebellion have had on all creation (fall). The themes of redemption and restoration, which we have already seen hints of in the first part of the debate, become ever clearer in the second part of the debate. The fact that Andreth refers to the idea of Iluvatar entering Arda as the "Old Hope" suggests that this was already an ancient idea during the First Age. This is once again revealing, for Christians believe that Jesus is both God and the preexistent Son of God; Jesus has been part of the place since the beginning. According to Pitre, "Jesus . . . is not just a descendant of David; he is David's 'Lord' . . . and most staggering of all, Jesus is implying that he himself was 'begotten' by the Lord from 'the womb of the dawn.'"[702] If this hope is already ancient by the time of Finrod and Andreth, is it possible it was known from the very beginning? It seems Tolkien may be hinting at this. Moreover, Finrod's explanation of how this will happen is parabolic in nature. Finrod's comment that Eru must "enter in" to his story while still remaining the "Author without" is not only a *mashal* itself, it also points to the *parabolic nature* of the coming messiah. As we learned in the Introduction, in the ancient Middle East, knowledge of God was glimpsed through his "son" and "shadow," the king. The king was the shadow of the transcendent God who is beyond his creation (Tolkien's "Author without"). When Andreth asks Finrod how the "singer" can "enter into his tale or the designer into his picture," Finrod responds almost rabbinically, saying, "He is already in it, as well as outside. But indeed the 'in-dwelling' and the 'out-living' are not in the same mode."[703] Not only is this Tolkien the theologian speaking about God's transcendence ("out-dwelling") and immanence ("in-dwelling"), it is also a poetic description of a parable, and thus the incarnation understood as the return of the king. The image of an author "entering" his story is on the same metaphorical level as "God becoming king." Moreover, the form of the parable allows for God to "enter in" while still remaining the "Author without."[704] God writes himself into his own story while still remaining its author, just as he rules in and through his "shadow," the king on earth, without vacating his throne in heaven.

Once again, all this reveals what kind of story *The Lord of the Rings* is. In the Gospels, God is incarnate through a king from the House of David. Through Manwe, Iluvatar can enter his story through the promised Numenorean king while still remaining the "Author without." God is immanent within his creation without compromising his transcendence. This is good Christian theology. According to Wright, "there is a sense in which it isn't an either/or choice, *either* God *or* David. Somehow it seems to be both."[705] Doesn't this sound exactly like Finrod's description of the incarnation? In being a story about an exiled king whose return has long been foretold, *The Lord of the Rings* most resembles the parables of Jesus, many of which have some kind of monarchic theme.[706] All this is communicated to us as a concrete experience, as *mythos*. When we look back at "The Debate of Finrod and Andreth" from the end of the Third Age, it becomes even clearer that this is so, for that text puts forth the hope that one day Iluvatar will enter his creation in the *form of a man* who will redeem all of Iluvatar's children. And that is exactly the story that we see unfolding in *The Lord of the Rings*.

After all, Tolkien did once say that "Man the story-teller would have to be redeemed in a manner consonant with his nature: by a moving story."[707] And what better way to reflect this great truth than to have the savior of Middle-earth be a man who represents all the children of Iluvatar? Finrod is quite clear that the savior will be a man, not an elf: "This then, I propound, was the errand of Men, not the followers, but the heirs and fulfillers of all: to heal the Marring of Arda, already foreshadowed before their devising."[708] Like Jesus, who came to redeem all humankind, this coming redeemer will redeem "sheep that are not of this sheep pen"—that is, the other children of Iluvatar, elves and dwarves.[709] Paul's comment that salvation comes to "everyone who believes: first to the Jew, then to the gentile" is later glimpsed in the Fellowship, which Aragorn leads.[710] The Fellowship contains members from all the children of Iluvatar, each of which has borne some resemblance to Israel throughout Arda's history. In the previous chapter we saw how closely the story of the House of Durin resembles Israel's story at several points, but her story is also alluded to in the story of the Numenoreans. When Elendil and his two sons arrived on the shores of Middle-earth toward the end of the Second Age, they founded two kingdoms, just as Israel did in the Bible. After Sauron's defeat and the end of the Second Age, both kingdoms declined and the bloodline of Numenor dwindled. Tolkien's parable—indeed, his entire mythology—is pervaded by this monarchic theme just as Jesus's parables are "dominated by the figure of a father, master, or king, who is generally an archetype of God."[711]

Some Tolkien scholars argue that despite the fact that Aragorn—who has the power to command the dead and to heal—becomes king and ushers in an era of peace, *The Lord of the Rings* still lacks the presence of the incarnation. To justify this stance, scholars such as Matthew Dickerson and Bradley Birzer have argued that evidence for this exists in Finrod's comment that "even if Melkor . . . could in any way be thrown down or thrust from Arda, still his Shadow would remain, and the evil that he has wrought and sown as a seed would wax and multiply."[712] But again, this is not evidence *against* the incarnation, it is evidence *for* it. As we have already argued, the persistence of evil is not evidence of the absence of a redeemer-king. Another piece of evidence that is cited is the exchange between Sam and Gandalf toward the end of the novel when Sam asks Gandalf, "Is everything sad going to come untrue?" To which the wizard replies, "A great Shadow has departed."[713] Despite the eventual defeat of both Melkor and Sauron, evil, suffering, and death still exist; therefore, the incarnation must still be in the future. Dickerson and others have also cited *The New Shadow* as further proof that Aragorn's return does not resemble the incarnation. While it is true that all these examples confirm what Finrod told Andreth would happen, this does not at all prove the absence of the incarnation in *The Lord of the Rings*. In fact, all this evidence only points more to the presence of the incarnation and goes to show how deeply Christian Tolkien's mythology really is.

So instead of seeing Finrod's prophecy as looking past *The Lord of the Rings* to a far-off event that has not happened yet, we should understand it as a prophecy of the messiah's first advent. Finrod's prophecy first looks forward to the proclamation of the good news in Middle-earth, which we hear from the eagle at the end of *The Return of the King* ("Sing and be glad, all ye children of the West, for your King shall come again, and he shall dwell among you all the days of your life"), *then* it looks forward to the further event that will happen as a result of the return of the king.[714] But if Iluvatar really became king through Aragorn, wouldn't there have been more fanfare? As Andreth says, "Would it not shatter Arda?" Finrod reminds Andreth that this would only be true of a finite being, which God is not; indeed, Iluvatar is "Measureless."[715] That depends on what we are looking for, which depends on our theology.

Then there is the issue of the absence of the death and resurrection of the messiah in *The Lord of the Rings*. If there is no death and resurrection of the messiah in Middle-earth, then there is no incarnation, and if there is no incarnation and death and resurrection of the messiah, then redemption has not yet come to Middle-earth, and if redemption has not yet come to Middle-earth, then *The Lord of the Rings* is not a fully Christian story. At least, that is what Dickerson has argued in his book *A Hobbit Journey*. As Wright has sadly noted, however, many Christians "have reduced the kingdom of God to private piety, the victory of the cross to comfort for the conscience and Easter itself to a happy, escapist ending after a sad, dark tale."[716] Tragically, Christianity has (for some) become all about what *we* get out of Jesus. This is not to say that one's personal relationship with Jesus and one's salvation are unimportant, because they are, but they are not the most important things. It seems that many Christians care about what we are saved *from* instead of what we have been saved *for*. We want "a religious leader, not a king! We want someone to save our souls, not rule our world!"[717] But if *The Lord of the Rings* is a parable modeled on the parables of Jesus like we have been arguing, then the former is not a story primarily about "private piety" and "comfort for the conscience," but about *God becoming king*. Tolkien wanted "to re-transplant" the *logos* of Christianity "back into the original, mythic soil from which it first took root" so that we can see the true meaning of the good news.[718]

Just as we cannot have a full understanding of the New Testament without an understanding of the Old Testament, neither can we fully understand *The Lord of the Rings* without first understanding "The Debate," *The Silmarillion*, and *The Hobbit*. This is one of the many reasons why interpretations of *The Lord of the Rings* like Dickerson's are unconvincing. If we fail to understand Hebraic thought—with its affection for *mashalim*—and the larger Jewish backstory of the New Testament, we will be left with a distortion of the good news. So, depending on what Christianity we are looking for, we will either conclude along with Dickerson that *The Lord of the Rings* is not a fully Christian story, or we will see it, like Jesus's parables, as good news. Nevertheless, Dickerson holds on to his thesis that *The Lord of the Rings* is ultimately not a Christian story, but this conclusion is unpersuasive. Nowhere is this made clearer than when he says,

> There would be no real way to present the actual incarnation in Middle-earth without it becoming allegory. Unless, of course, Tolkien were to fully connect Middle-earth to our world. But while that might be in some way possible, the moment that final step was made, not only would Middle-earth cease being Middle-earth (as we know it in the stories), but the incarnation itself would simply be the event in our world as it has already been described in the Gospels; it would not be an incarnation in Middle-earth.[719]

This interpretation fails to give enough credit to the central role parables play in conveying who Jesus is. In Dickerson's other book, *From Homer to Harry Potter*, he does, however say "part of what makes Jesus's parables so rich is that they are *not* exhausted by a single reading but often function as illustrations of the gospel on many levels."[720] Ultimately, it does seem as if Dickerson overlooks the parabolic nature of *The Lord of the Rings* because he does not address the central role which parables have in imagining the incarnation indirectly and suggestively. It also seems as if Dickerson assumes a high christological view is necessary for the incarnation to be present in Middle-earth, looks for it in the novel, and then concludes that it is not there. Dickerson writes, "There is no presence of the Creator, Eru Iluvatar, as an incarnate being within his creation," and "Christianity rests fundamentally on a set of historical events: the birth, life, death, and especially the resurrection of the first-century Jew named Jesus."[721] No Christian would contest this, but it seems that Dickerson is mistaking key for tune. According to Wright, "the key in which the gospels are set is that of incarnational

Christology," but the melody "is that of the kingdom and of 'Christology' in the much stricter sense of 'Jesus as Messiah.'"[722] If one grasps this distinction, then it becomes clear that the "return of the king" *means* the incarnation is present in Middle-earth. Lastly, in suggesting that if "Tolkien were to fully connect Middle-earth to our world," the story would become an allegory, Dickerson misunderstands how Jesus communicated the incarnation to begin with. This suggests that for Tolkien to write a fully Christian story, he would have had to essentially copy the Gospels and compromise the integrity of the mythical world he had created. I understand how important it is to maintain the integrity of Tolkien's mythological world, but did not Jesus tell myths to communicate who he is to people? If *The Lord of the Rings* is a parabolic novel as this book has argued, then it would connect with the real world in the same way that Jesus's parables did. Jesus told stories about how things were not, in order to speak about how things were; Tolkien did the same thing. There are other reasons why this is an unconvincing argument.

First, as a parable, the incarnation is already a type of allegory. Dickerson assumes that there is a way of presenting the incarnation that is not allegorical, which is impossible. Recall that Lewis once said that we are free to try to "restate our belief in a form free from metaphor and symbol . . . the reason we don't is that we can't."[723] Second, according to Dickerson, since there is no incarnation in Middle-earth, "it is not surprising that the stories are so full of sorrow and sadness."[724] Yet here is another misunderstanding of Christian theology. *The Lord of the Rings* is not a sad story because the incarnation is still far off in the future, it is a sad story because "the New Testament tells us we will know full satisfaction only in the new heavens and new earth (Revelation 22:2)."[725] While it makes sense to say that *The Silmarillion* and *The Hobbit* are filled with sorrow and sadness because the incarnation has not yet occurred, *The Lord of the Rings* is "full of sorrow and sadness" precisely *because* the incarnation has occurred (we explored this in chapter 3). God's victory on the cross and on Easter morning was the beginning of the new creation that the Bible promises throughout its pages, not its consummation. Jesus promised that there would be trials and much persecution before the kingdom was fully consummated and that we would not "know the hour" of its consummation.[726] The reason *The Lord of the Rings* is so sad is not because redemption has not yet come to Middle-earth, but because its complete redemption is not yet at hand. The complete redemption of man and creation is still far-off by novel's end. Aragorn and Arwen die, and a new evil appears in Middle-earth only a century after the king's death. In *The Lord of the Rings*, Tolkien has written a story that is "painful and wonderful at once," like the gospel.[727] According to Humphrey Carpenter, Tolkien cast his mythology in this form because he wanted it to be remote and strange, and yet at the same time *not to be a lie*. He wanted the mythological and legendary stories to express his own moral view of the universe; and as a Christian he could not place this view in a cosmos without the God that he worshipped. At the same time, to set his stories "realistically" in the known world, where religious beliefs were explicitly Christian, would deprive them of imaginative color. So while God is present in Tolkien's universe, He remains unseen.[728]

As we have learned throughout this book, the only way he could do this was through parables, which are "linguistic incarnations."[729] Author Joseph Loconte has argued that perhaps the reason why Tolkien went to such great pains to create an entire mythological world consonant with Christianity was because of his horrific experience in the Great War. Tolkien, who witnessed the death of the "myth of progress" which Europeans were living in up to 1914, saw in his horrific experiences a call to baptize the imaginations of Europe by presenting them with the true myth.[730] Rather than returning to England to join "the ranks of the rootless and disbelieving," Tolkien and Lewis (who also fought in WWI) "became convinced there was only one true, one singular event, that could help the weary and brokenhearted find their way home: the Return of the King."[731] For inspiration both men turned, in their own unique ways, to Jesus's parables for guidance. Parables are the only kind of story which can confront a people who, after seeing so much death and destruction, have understandably had their hearts and minds hardened. The Great War drove Lewis deeper into his pre-war atheism, and we should not think that it had no effect on Tolkien's Catholicism, for it certainly did. But Tolkien learned sooner than Lewis that without the kind of God presented in the Bible, they would be complaining to no one when they said that the Great War was horrific, wasteful, and unfair. Both men understood that a worldview without the biblical God would only plunge Europe deeper into depression. By becoming a parable and speaking in parables, God was able to sneak "past those watchful dragons" which guard hardened hearts and minds.[732]

We can no longer accept the conclusion that *The Lord of the Rings* cannot be a fully Christian story because this would mean it is an allegory, or because this would mean Tolkien had a religious agenda, or because it would exclude the other religious influences in the novel. We have learned how complex Tolkien's relationship to his book was. *The Lord of the Rings* is a parabolic novel, which is a type of allegory, and while Tolkien did not have a conscious, intentional agenda to defend and preach the Christian worldview, he "deliberately" wrote this story out of certain religious ideas.

We can also no longer accept the argument that the incarnation, death, and resurrection are missing from *The Lord of the Rings*. They are present in ways which defy how we think they ought to be, just like they are in Jesus's parables. And like Jesus's parables, they point to the historical reality of who Jesus is, what he did, what he is doing, and what he will one day finish doing. The good news surprised the original disciples and it continues to challenge and surprise us today.

Throughout this book, we have argued that Tolkien adopted a retrospective hermeneutic because both Jesus and the Four Evangelists did in their approach to Scripture. We have also argued that the act of "looking back" in *The Lord of the Rings* is parallel to the necessity of "looking back" from the Gospels to the Old Testament. Just as we catch glimpses of Israel's ancient history in the background of Jesus's parables and the Gospels, we are also meant to catch glimpses of Middle-earth's ancient history in the background of Tolkien's parabolic novel. And then there is the following passage from "The Debate of Finrod and Andreth," which reads like a mythical defense of the supremacy of parables:

> As may a master in the telling of tales keep hidden the greatest moment until it comes in due course. It may be guessed at indeed, in some measure, by those of us who have listened with full heart and mind; but so the teller would wish. In no wise is the surprise and wonder of his art thus diminished, for thus we share, as it were, in his authorship. But not so, if all were told us in a preface before we entered in![733]

In this passage, Finrod is likening Iluvatar to a storyteller who surreptitiously waits for the perfect moment to reveal the climax of his story. Perhaps the real reason why Jesus kept his identity concealed was because he wanted people to discover that parables were the key to understanding it. Perhaps the same could be said of Tolkien, who did a tremendous job as narrator of standing out of the way and letting God—whom Tolkien said was the true author anyway—do the narrating. In the passage above, Tolkien also seems to be reminding us to heed Jesus's words to "consider carefully what you hear," for "with the measure you use, it will be measured to you—and even more."[734]

In "The Debate of Finrod and Andreth," Tolkien shows us that his theology and way of writing heavily relied on the parables of Jesus Christ. A parabolic theology challenges us to focus on how parables function in bringing people to belief rather than a theology which focuses on "explaining and systematizing concepts about the kingdom." According to McFague, "parabolic theology would attempt to unite form and content, to be in genre what it claims to be about."⁷³⁵ Parable "is not simply a way of embellishing something we can know in some other way. There is no other way."⁷³⁶ It has been my hope that this book has shown that *The Lord of the Rings* does indeed stand on its own as a parable of the kingdom.⁷³⁷ At the beginning of the book, we learned that Lewis credited Tolkien for helping him return to Christ. Tolkien, too, had reason to be grateful to Lewis, for in 1961, two years before Lewis died, Tolkien wrote of his gratitude to Lewis saying, "C. S. Lewis is a very old friend and colleague of mine, and indeed I owe to his encouragement the fact that in spite of obstacles (including the 1939 war!) I persevered and eventually finished *the Lord of the Rings*."⁷³⁸ It is fitting, then, that we conclude this book with what Lewis thought about *The Lord of the Rings*. No one was better equipped to understand *The Lord of the Rings* than Lewis, who was brought to faith in Jesus Christ through the theology which undergirds Tolkien's parable. Of The Lord of the Rings, Lewis wrote, "a great romance is like a flower whose smell reminds you of something you can't quite place...I've never met Orcs or Ents or Elves--but the feel of it, the sense of a huge past, of lowering danger...of distance, vastness, strangeness, homeliness (all blended together) is so exactly what living feels like to me." When we read *The Lord of the Rings*, we smell "the scent of a flower we have not found, the echo of a tune we have not heard, news from a country we have never yet visited."⁷³⁹ This is indeed good news.

Endnotes

[1] McDermott, *Everyday Glory*, 33.
[2] McDermott, *Everyday Glory*, 24–25.
[3] McDermott, *Everyday Glory*, 34.
[4] McDermott, *Everyday Glory*, 36, quoting Edward Pusey.
[5] Sire, *Apologetics Beyond Reason*, 13.
[6] McDermott, *Everyday Glory*, 37.
[7] McGrath, *Narrative Apologetics*, 108.
[8] Olson, *Essentials of Christian Thought*, 11.
[9] McGrath, *Intellectual World of C. S. Lewis*, 62.
[10] McGrath, *Lunch with C. S. Lewis*, 63.
[11] Groothuis, *Christian Apologetics*, ch. 3, para. 12.
[12] I am not the first scholar to argue this. See Sallie McFague's book *Speaking in Parables* and Father Robert Murray's essay, "J. R. R. Tolkien and the Art of the Parable," in Pearce, *Tolkien: A Celebration*.
[13] Lewis, "Myth Became Fact," in Hooper, *God in the Dock*, 66.
[14] McGrath, *Lunch with C. S. Lewis*, 64.
[15] McGrath, *Narrative Apologetics*, 14.
[16] Tolkien, "On Fairy Stories," Epilogue, para. 3.
[17] Tolkien, *Letters of J. R. R. Tolkien*, Letter 89.
[18] Dickerson and O'Hara, *From Homer to Harry Potter*, page 49.
[19] Starr, *The Faun's Bookshelf*, ch. 10, sect. "Myth as Concrete Thought."
[20] Markos, *From Achilles to Christ*, Introduction, para. 3.
[21] Koukl, *The Story of Reality*, 31.
[22] Tolkien, "On Fairy Stories," sect. "Fairy Story," para. 5.
[23] Tolkien, "On Fairy Stories," sect. "Fairy Story," para. 7.
[24] Starr, *The Faun's Bookshelf*, ch. 10, sect. "Myth, Reality, and Truth," para. 4.
[25] Gould, *Cultural Apologetics*, 146.
[26] Kreeft, *The Philosophy of Tolkien*, ch. 1.3.
[27] McGrath, *Lunch with C. S. Lewis*, 64.
[28] Keller, *Making Sense of God*, 173.
[29] Lewis, "Letter to Arthur Greeves from the Kilns, 18 October 1931," in Lewis and Hooper, *Letters*, 368.
[30] Markos, *Apologetics*, ch. 7, sect. "Myth Made Fact," para. 4.
[31] Carpenter, *J. R. R. Tolkien: A Biography*, part 4: "Jack," para. 14.
[32] Starr, *The Faun's Bookshelf*, ch. 10, sect. "Myth, Reality, and Truth," para. 1.
[33] Markos, *Apologetics*, ch. 7, sect. "Myth Made Fact," para. 4.
[34] McGrath, *Intellectual World of C. S. Lewis*, 60.

35 Lewis, "Myth Became Fact," in Hooper, *God in the Dock*, 66.
36 Groothuis, *Christian Apologetics*, ch. 6, sect. "The Truth Question," para. 2.
37 Armstrong, *The Case for God*, Introduction, para. 4.
38 Myers, *Understanding the Faith*, ch. 5, para. 11.
39 Olson, *Essentials of Christian Thought*, 30.
40 Myers, *Understanding the Times*, 5.
41 Myers, *Understanding the Faith*, ch. 1.
42 Lewis, "Tolkien's Lord of the Rings," in Lewis, *On Stories*, 136.
43 Starr, *The Faun's Bookshelf*, ch. 7, para. 14.
44 Tolkien, "On Fairy Stories," Epilogue, para. 5
45 Lewis, "Myth Became Fact," in Hooper, *God in the Dock*, 67.
46 Lewis, "Myth Became Fact," in Hooper, *God in the Dock*, 67.
47 Tolkien, *Letters of J. R. R. Tolkien*, Letter 253.
48 See Pearce's foreword in Birzer, *Tolkien's Sanctifying Myth*, para. 5.
49 Bird and Wright, *New Testament in Its World*.
50 Marshall, *The Crucified Rabbi*, 18.
51 I am following Michael Heiser's lead on this. For a few examples of what I mean, consider Gen 1:26–27; 6:1–4; and Deut 32:8–9.
52 More on this in chapter 5. I am indebted to Michael Heiser's book *The Unseen Realm* for pointing this out.
53 Herman, *Cave and the Light*, ch. 10, loc. 3053.
54 Herman, *Cave and the Light*, ch. 10, loc. 5313.
55 Ferry, *Brief History of Thought*, 59.
56 McGrath, *Lunch with C. S. Lewis*, 64.
57 Wright, *Simply Good News*, 76.
58 Wright, *Simply Good News*, 76.
59 Wilson, *Our Father Abraham*, 145.
60 Piper, "C. S. Lewis, Romantic Rationalist," 32.
61 Pearce's foreword in Birzer, *Tolkien's Sanctifying Myth*, para. 5.
62 Justin Martyr quoted in Wilson, *Our Father Abraham*, 89.
63 Herman, *Cave and the Light*, ch. 11, loc. 3273.
64 Wright, *Simply Jesus*, 45. See Pss. 10:16–18; 47:1–9; 95:3–7; 96:10–13; Isa 52:7–10; and Ezek 34:2–6, 11–12, 14–16, and 23–24 for just a few examples of this.
65 Heiser, *The Unseen Realm*, 114.
66 This whole paragraph is indebted to Heiser, *The Unseen Realm*, chs. 9–14.
67 Heiser, *The Unseen Realm*, 261.
68 Birzer, *Tolkien's Sanctifying Myth*, ch. 3, loc. 1253, quoting Tolkien, *Letters of J. R. R. Tolkien*, Letter 306.
69 Tolkien, *Letters of J. R. R. Tolkien*, Letter 183.
70 Park, *Journey towards Home*, 69.
71 Lewis, "De Descriptione Temporum," 5.
72 For one example, see Hutton, "The Pagan Tolkien."
73 McGrath, *Intellectual World of C. S. Lewis*, 65.
74 Tolkien, "On Fairy Stories," sect. "Fantasy," final para.
75 Markos, *From Achilles to Christ*, Introduction, sect. "Christ Over Culture," para. 9.
76 Lewis, "Religion without Dogma," in Hooper, *God in the Dock*, 132.
77 Ferry, *Brief History of Thought*, 59.
78 Ferry, *Brief History of Thought*, 60.
79 Wright, *How God Became King*, 74.
80 McFague, *Speaking in Parables*, ch. 3.

[81] McFague, *Speaking in Parables*, ch. 2.
[82] See Wright, *How God Became King*.
[83] Tolkien, *The Lord of the Rings*, 963.
[84] Tolkien, *The Lord of the Rings*, Foreword, para. 10.
[85] Murray, "J. R. R. Tolkien and the Art of the Parable," in Pearce, *Tolkien: A Celebration*, 41.
[86] Lewis, "Myth Became Fact," in Hooper, *God in the Dock*, 66.
[87] McIntosh, *The Flame Imperishable*, 42.
[88] Lewis, "Myth Became Fact," in Hooper, *God in the Dock*, 66.
[89] Snodgrass, *Stories with Intent*, 7.
[90] Wilson, *Our Father Abraham*, 150.
[91] Clyde Kilby as cited in Chance, *Tolkien's Art*, ch. 1, loc. 430.
[92] Clyde Kilby as cited in Chance, *Tolkien's Art*, ch. 1, loc. 430.
[93] Wilson, *Our Father Abraham*, 152.
[94] Tolkien, *Letters of J. R. R. Tolkien*, Letter 156.
[95] Tolkien, *Letters of J. R. R. Tolkien*, Letter 328.
[96] McFague, *Speaking in Parables*, ch. 4.
[97] McFague, *Speaking in Parables*, ch. 4.
[98] McFague, *Speaking in Parables*, ch. 4.
[99] Godawa, *Imagination of God*, 81.
[100] Godawa, *Imagination of God*, 81.
[101] Young, *The Parables*, 5.
[102] Young, *The Parables*, 5.
[103] McFague, *Speaking in Parables*, chs. 2–3.
[104] Tolkien, "On Fairy Stories," Epilogue, para. 2.
[105] McFague, *Speaking in Parables*, ch. 4.
[106] McFague, *Speaking in Parables*, ch. 6.
[107] Tolkien, "On Fairy Stories," sect. "Fantasy," para. 5.
[108] McFague, *Speaking in Parables*, ch. 6.
[109] Tolkien, *Letters of J. R. R. Tolkien*, Letter 156.
[110] Kreeft, *The Philosophy of Tolkien*, ch. 1.1.
[111] Tolkien, "On Fairy Stories," sect. "Recovery, Escape, and Consolation," para. 1.
[112] McFague, *Speaking in Parables*, ch. 6.
[113] Godawa, *Imagination of God*, 81.
[114] Tolkien, "On Fairy Stories," Epilogue, para. 3.
[115] Peter Kreeft's lecture delivered at the Undergraduate Chapel at Biola University on November 18, 2013, comes to mind for a thorough treatment on this specific subject. You can easily find this on YouTube.
[116] Keller, *Making Sense of God*, 173. See also Tolkien, *Letters of J. R. R. Tolkien*, Letter 96.
[117] See Tolkien, *Letters of J. R. R. Tolkien*, Letter 96 .
[118] Tolkien, "On Fairy Stories," sect. "Recovery, Escape, and Consolation," para. 14.
[119] Lewis, *Surprised by Joy*, 19.
[120] Tolkien, "On Fairy Stories," sect. "Recovery, Escape, and Consolation," para. 14.
[121] McFague, *Speaking in Parables*, ch. 2.
[122] Piper, "C. S. Lewis, Romantic Rationalist," 31.
[123] Piper, "C. S. Lewis, Romantic Rationalist," 32.
[124] Lewis, "Is Theology Poetry?" in Lewis, *The Weight of Glory*, 120.
[125] Lewis, *Pilgrim's Regress*, 205.
[126] Lewis, "Myth Became Fact," in Hooper, *God in the Dock*, 67.
[127] Kreeft, *The Philosophy of Tolkien*, ch. 2, loc. 914.
[128] Sennett, "Worthy of a Better God," 235.

[129] Starr, *The Faun's Bookshelf*, ch. 10, loc. 1978. For source of reference to "Great Tongue," see also Lewis, *That Hideous Strength*, ch. 10.
[130] McFague, *Speaking in Parables*, ch. 3.
[131] Starr, *The Faun's Bookshelf*, ch. 9, loc. 1676.
[132] Lewis, "Myth Became Fact," in Hooper, *God in the Dock*, 67.
[133] See Isaiah 61:1 and Luke 4:18, NIV.
[134] Tolkien, *The Lord of the Rings*, Foreword, para. 8.
[135] Tolkien, *Letters of J. R. R. Tolkien*, Letter 186.
[136] Kreglinger, *Storied Revelations*, 44.
[137] Hays, *Echoes of Scripture*, 3.
[138] Tolkien, *Letters of J. R. R. Tolkien*, Letter 247.
[139] Tolkien, *Letters of J. R. R. Tolkien*, Letter 142.
[140] Hays, *Echoes of Scripture*, 3.
[141] Hays, *Echoes of Scripture*, 3.
[142] McDermott, *Everyday Glory*, 18.
[143] Heiser, *The Unseen Realm*, 242.
[144] Auerbach, *Mimesis*, 73.
[145] McDermott, *Everyday Glory*, 17.
[146] Hays, *Echoes of Scripture*, 2.
[147] Hays, *Echoes of Scripture*, 2.
[148] Scarf, *The Ideal of Kingship*, 121.
[149] Murray, "J. R. R. Tolkien and the Art of the Parable," in Pearce, *Tolkien: A Celebration*.
[150] Hays, *Echoes of Scripture*, 2.
[151] Birzer, *Tolkien's Sanctifying Myth*, ch. 3, loc. 1436.
[152] Pearce, *Frodo's Journey*, 3.
[153] Crossan, *The Power of Parable*, Epilogue, loc. 24053.
[154] For more details, see Pearce, *Frodo's Journey*, ch. 1, and Crossan, *The Power of Parable*, Prologue.
[155] Kreglinger, *Storied Revelations*, 46.
[156] Kreglinger, *Storied Revelations*, 34.
[157] Lewis, "Letter to Mrs. Hook from the Kilns," in Lewis and Hooper, *Letters*, 608.
[158] Middleton, *New Heaven and New Earth*, 24.
[159] See Isa 25:6-8; 65:17-25; Matt 6:9-10; Luke 17:20-21; and Rev 21, just to cite a few examples.
[160] Middleton, *New Heaven and New Earth*, 31.
[161] Wright, *Simply Jesus*, ch. 8, loc. 1562.
[162] Lewis, "Is Theology Poetry?" in Lewis, *The Weight of Glory*, 134.
[163] Tolkien, *The Lord of the Rings*, Foreword, para. 8.
[164] Tolkien, *Letters of J. R. R. Tolkien*, Letter 131.
[165] Crossan, *The Power of Parable*, 18.
[166] Murray, "J. R. R. Tolkien and the Art of the Parable," in Pearce, *Tolkien: A Celebration*, 47-48.
[167] Murray, "J. R. R. Tolkien and the Art of the Parable," in Pearce, *Tolkien: A Celebration*, 45.
[168] McFague, *Speaking in Parables*, ch. 4.
[169] Kreeft, *The Philosophy of Tolkien*, Introduction, loc. 260.
[170] Murray, "J. R. R. Tolkien and the Art of the Parable," in Pearce, *Tolkien: A Celebration*, 47-48.
[171] Tolkien, *Letters of J. R. R. Tolkien*, Letter 131.
[172] Duriez, *Tolkien and C. S. Lewis*, ch. 9, loc. 56.

[173] Wood, *Gospel According to Tolkien*, loc. 118.
[174] Wood, "Confronting the World's Weirdness," 146.
[175] Koukl, *The Story of Reality*, 27.
[176] Tolkien, *Letters of J. R. R. Tolkien*, Letters 151 and 183.
[177] Tolkien, *Letters of J. R. R. Tolkien*, Letter 269.
[178] Kreeft, *The Philosophy of Tolkien*, Introduction, loc. 260.
[179] Tolkien, *Letters of J. R. R. Tolkien*, Letter 186.
[180] Dickerson, *A Hobbit Journey*, 13.
[181] Tolkien, *Letters of J. R. R. Tolkien*, Letter 131.
[182] Tolkien, *Letters of J. R. R. Tolkien*, Letter 159.
[183] Murray, "J. R. R. Tolkien and the Art of the Parable," in Pearce, *Tolkien: A Celebration*, 43.
[184] Snodgrass, *Stories with Intent*, 4.
[185] Tolkien, *Letters of J. R. R. Tolkien*, Letter 131.
[186] Snodgrass, *Stories with Intent*, 15.
[187] Murray, "J. R. R. Tolkien and the Art of the Parable," in Pearce, *Tolkien: A Celebration*, 45.
[188] Krelinger, *Storied Revelations*, 41.
[189] Kreglinger, *Storied Revelations*, 41.
[190] Pitre, *The Case for Jesus*, 119.
[191] Tolkien, *Letters of J. R. R. Tolkien*, Letter 109.
[192] Snodgrass, *Stories with Intent*, 21.
[193] McFague, *Speaking in Parables*, Introduction.
[194] Murray, "J. R. R. Tolkien and the Art of the Parable," in Pearce, *Tolkien: A Celebration*, 47.
[195] Lewis, "Tolkien's *Lord of the Rings*," in Lewis, *On Stories*, 130.
[196] Lewis, "Letter to Lucy Barfield, 11 September 1958," in Lewis, *Letters to Children*.
[197] Kreeft, *The Philosophy of Tolkien*, Introduction, loc. 310.
[198] Tolkien, "On Fairy Stories," Epilogue, para. 3.
[199] Tolkien, "Mythopoeia."
[200] See Isa 6:10.
[201] Mark 4:24–25, translated by Hays in Hays, *Echoes of Scripture*, 15.
[202] Tolkien, *The Hobbit*, 11.
[203] Birzer, *Tolkien's Sanctifying Myth*, Foreword, loc. 44, quoting Tolkien, *Letters of J. R. R. Tolkien*, Letter 213.
[204] Tolkien, *Letters of J. R. R. Tolkien*, Letter 153. Emphasis mine.
[205] McFague, *Speaking in Parables*, Introduction.
[206] Tolkien, *Letters of J. R. R. Tolkien*, Letter 181.
[207] Tolkien, *Letters of J. R. R. Tolkien*, Letter 181.
[208] Ordway, *Apologetics and Christian Imagination*, ch. 6, loc. 1574.
[209] Levine, *Short Stories by Jesus*, 4.
[210] Levine, *Short Stories by Jesus*, 3.
[211] Tolkien, *Letters of J. R. R. Tolkien*, Letter 142.
[212] Birzer, *Tolkien's Sanctifying Myth*, Foreword, loc. 107.
[213] McFague, *Speaking in Parables*, ch. 4.
[214] Lewis, "Letter to Mrs. Hook from the Kilns," in Lewis and Hooper, *Letters*, 608.
[215] Birzer, *Tolkien's Sanctifying Myth*, ch. 4, loc. 1929.
[216] Lewis, Letter dated August 14, 1954, in Hooper, *Collected Letters*, 488.
[217] McFague, *Speaking in Parables*, ch. 4.
[218] 1 Cor 2:8.

219 For further reading, see Wright, *Simply Jesus*, ch. 8; Murray, "J. R. R. Tolkien and the Art of the Parable," in Pearce, *Tolkien: A Celebration*; and Hays, *Echoes of Scripture*, ch. 1, for just a few examples.
220 Tolkien, "On Fairy Stories," sect. "Fairy Story," para. 7.
221 Tolkien, "Beowulf," 112.
222 Kreeft, *The Philosophy of Tolkien*, Introduction, loc. 101.
223 Tolkien, "On Fairy Stories," sect. "Fantasy," para. 4.
224 Tolkien, *Letters of J. R. R. Tolkien*, Letter 192.
225 Murray, "J. R. R. Tolkien and the Art of the Parable," in Pearce, *Tolkien: A Celebration*, 48.
226 Tolkien, "On Fairy Stories," sect. "Recovery, Escape, and Consolation," para. 14.
227 Tolkien, "On Fairy Stories," sect. "Recovery, Escape, and Consolation," para. 14.
228 Pearce, *Frodo's Journey*, 82.
229 Pearce, *Frodo's Journey*, 81.
230 Tolkien, "On Fairy Stories," Epilogue, para. 4.
231 This is actually the title of one of C. S. Lewis's essays collected in *On Stories*.
232 Lewis, "Myth Became Fact," in Hooper, *God in the Dock*, 67.
233 Lewis, *Reflections on the Psalms*, "Introductory," 6.
234 Lewis, "Is Theology Poetry?" in Lewis, *The Weight of Glory*, 129.
235 Dickerson, *A Hobbit Journey*, 237.
236 Dickerson *A Hobbit Journey*, 239.
237 Ryken, *Messiah Comes to Middle-Earth*, 30.
238 Tolkien, *Letters of J. R. R. Tolkien*, Letter 142.
239 McFague, *Speaking in Parables*, ch. 4.
240 I am indebted to Wright's *The Challenge of Jesus*, 116–17, for this insight.
241 Wright, *The Challenge of Jesus*, 116–17.
242 Please see Paul M. Gould and Holly Ordway's books in the Bibliography especially.
243 Tolkien, "On Fairy Stories," sect. "Fantasy," para. 10.
244 Tolkien, "On Fairy Stories," sect. "Recovery, Escape, and Consolation," para. 1.
245 Matt 18:3, NIV.
246 Kreeft, *The Philosophy of Tolkien*, loc. 101. Kreeft's citation appears to be inaccurate.
247 Lewis, "Tolkien's Lord of the Rings," in Lewis, *On Stories*, 127–38.
248 1 Cor 13:11, NIV, and Lewis, "On Three Ways of Writing for Children," in Lewis, *On Stories*, xxiv.
249 Tolkien, *Letters of J. R. R. Tolkien*, Letter 131.
250 Tolkien, *Letters of J. R. R. Tolkien*, Letter 131.
251 Dickerson, *A Hobbit Journey*, 240.
252 Kreeft, *The Philosophy of Tolkien*, ch. 2, loc. 706.
253 Lewis, "Is Theology Poetry?" in Lewis, *The Weight of Glory*, 130.
254 Tolkien, *Letters of J. R. R. Tolkien*, Letter 165.
255 Snodgrass, *Stories with Intent*, 20.
256 McFague, *Speaking in Parables*, ch. 3.
257 Tolkien, *Letters of J. R. R. Tolkien*, Letter 153.
258 Tolkien, *Letters of J. R. R. Tolkien*, Letter 156.
259 Mark 4:12, NIV.
260 Mark 8:29, NIV.
261 Levine, *Short Stories by Jesus*, 4.
262 Tolkien, *Letters of J. R. R. Tolkien*, Letter 159.
263 Middleton, *New Heaven and New Earth*, 79.
264 Tolkien, "On Fairy Stories," sect. "Recovery, Escape, and Consolation," para. 7.

[265] Tolkien, "On Fairy Stories," sect. "Recovery, Escape, and Consolation," para. 6.
[266] Lewis, "Myth Became Fact," in Hooper, *God in the Dock*, 66.
[267] Lewis, "Myth Became Fact," in Hooper, *God in the Dock*, 66. Emphasis mine.
[268] Starr, *The Faun's Bookshelf*, ch. 10, loc. 1902.
[269] Starr, *The Faun's Bookshel*, ch. 10, loc. 1912.
[270] McFague, *Speaking in Parables*, ch. 4.
[271] Lewis, "Myth Became Fact," in Hooper, *God in the Dock*, 66.
[272] Tolkien, "On Fairy Stories," Epilogue, para. 4.
[273] Lewis, "Myth Became Fact," in Hooper, *God in the Dock*, 66.
[274] Lewis, "Myth Became Fact," in Hooper, *God in the Dock*, 66.
[275] McFague, *Speaking in Parables*, ch. 2.
[276] This section is indebted to Heiser, *The Unseen Realm*, 50.
[277] Lewis, *George MacDonald*, loc. 517.
[278] Tolkien, *Letters of J. R. R. Tolkien*, Letter 153.
[279] Levine, *Short Stories by Jesus*, 302.
[280] Kreglinger, *Storied Revelations*, 41.
[281] Tolkien, *Letters of J. R. R. Tolkien*, Letter 131.
[282] McFague, *Speaking in Parables*, ch. 4.
[283] Kreglinger, *Storied Revelations*, 22.
[284] Kreeft, *The Philosophy of Tolkien*, Introduction, loc. 284.
[285] Tolkien, *Letters of J. R. R. Tolkien*, Letter 165.
[286] McFague, *Speaking in Parables*, ch. 4.
[287] Tolkien, *Letters of J. R. R. Tolkien*, Letter 142.
[288] Snodgrass, *Stories with Intent*, 20.
[289] Snodgrass, *Stories with Intent*, 20.
[290] Tolkien, *Letters of J. R. R. Tolkien*, Letter 181.
[291] Tolkien, *The Lord of the Rings*, Foreword, para. 8.
[292] Tolkien, *The Lord of the Rings*, Foreword, para. 9.
[293] Bird and Wright, *New Testament in Its World*, 63.
[294] Snodgrass, *Stories with Intent*, 24.
[295] Tolkien, "On Fairy Stories," para. 1.
[296] McGrath, *Mere Apologetics*, 141.
[297] Wood, *Gospel According to Tolkien*, ch. 5, loc. 2015.
[298] Rev 21:5.
[299] Keller, *God's Wisdom*, 108.
[300] Lewis, "5 November 1959," in Lewis and Hooper, *Letters*, 565.
[301] Kreglinger, *Storied Revelations*, 16.
[302] Kreglinger, *Storied Revelations*, 46.
[303] Kreglinger, *Storied Revelations*, 40, 48.
[304] Kreglinger, *Storied Revelations*, 40.
[305] Middleton, *New Heaven and New Earth*, 79.
[306] Wright, *Simply Jesus*, 87.
[307] Heiser, *The Unseen Realm*, ch. 36.
[308] Tolkien, "On Fairy Stories," Epilogue, final para.
[309] Middleton, *New Heaven and New Earth*, 71.
[310] Kreglinger, *Storied Revelations*, 44.
[311] Kreglinger, *Storied Revelations*, 46.
[312] Kreglinger, *Storied Revelations*, 47.
[313] Crossan, *The Power of Parable*, ch. 3, loc. 20774.
[314] Crossan, *The Power of Parable*, ch. 3, loc. 20814.

[315] Yes, this is my attempt at a bit of humor. If you are a fan of Peter Jackson's *Lord of the Rings* films, you will get it.
[316] Kreglinger, *Storied Revelations*, 48.
[317] Crossan, *The Power of Parable*, ch. 6, loc. 21833.
[318] Kreglinger, *Storied Revelations*, 22.
[319] Tolkien, "On Fairy Stories," sect. "Fantasy," para. 10.
[320] Crossan, *The Power of Parable*, ch. 5, loc. 21527.
[321] Crossan, *The Power of Parable*, ch. 4.
[322] Kreglinger, *Storied Revelations*, 33.
[323] Kreglinger, *Storied Revelations*, 23.
[324] Tolkien, *Letters of J. R. R. Tolkien*, Letter 144.
[325] Tolkien, *Letters of J. R. R. Tolkien*, Letter 192.
[326] Tolkien, "On Fairy Stories," Epilogue, para. 2.
[327] Kreglinger, *Storied Revelations*, 48.
[328] Kreglinger, *Storied Revelations*, 49.
[329] Tolkien, "On Fairy Stories," sect. "Fairy Story," para. 4.
[330] Bassham, "Lewis and Tolkien on the Power of the Imagination," in in Bassham et al., *Chronicles*, 301.
[331] Tolkien, *The Hobbit*, 277.
[332] Tolkien, *The Lord of the Rings*, 171.
[333] Kreglinger, *Storied Revelations*, 53.
[334] Crossan, *The Power of Parable*, ch. 5, loc. 21891.
[335] Tolkien, *Letters of J. R. R. Tolkien*, Letter 165.
[336] Tolkien, *Letters of J. R. R. Tolkien*, Letter 163.
[337] McFague, *Speaking in Parables*, ch. 2.
[338] Mark 1:15, NIV.
[339] McGrath, *Intellectual World of C. S. Lewis*, 64.
[340] Pearcey, *Finding Truth*, 273.
[341] Koukl, *The Story of Reality*, 30.
[342] Wright, *Simply Good News*, 18.
[343] Wright, *Simply Good News*, 16.
[344] Wright, *Simply Good News*, 17.
[345] Wright, *Simply Good News*, 4.
[346] Wright, *Simply Good News*, 4.
[347] Wright, *Simply Good News*, 3–4.
[348] Ryken, *Messiah Comes to Middle-earth*, ch. 3.
[349] Tolkien, *The Lord of the Rings*, 972.
[350] See Matt 19:28, for one famous example.
[351] Tolkien, *The Lord of the Rings*, 1028–29.
[352] Tolkien, "Debate of Finrod and Andreth."
[353] 1 Cor 15:3.
[354] Wright, *Simply Good News*, 3.
[355] Tolkien, *Letters of J. R. R. Tolkien*, Letter 247.
[356] Tolkien, *Letters of J. R. R. Tolkien*, Letter 247.
[357] Drout, "Tolkien and *Beowulf*: Medieval Materials for the Modern Audience," in Dickerson, *A Hobbit Journey*, 209.
[358] Tolkien's Letters, Letter 176.
[359] Heiser, *The Unseen Realm*, ch. 4.
[360] Exod 4:22 and Luke 3:38 both come to mind.
[361] Remember that Luke places Adam in his genealogy of Jesus, as we just pointed out

in the previous endnote.
[362] Exod 4:22, NIV.
[363] Tolkien, *The Silmarillion*, 39.
[364] See Matt 22:41–46.
[365] Wright, *How God Became King*, 72.
[366] Lewis, *Pilgrim's Regress*, 147.
[367] Lewis, *Pilgrim's Regress*, 147.
[368] Tolkien, "The Quest of Erebor," in Tolkien, *Unfinished Tales*, 314.
[369] Scarf, *The Ideal of Kingship*, 121.
[370] See Rom 1:16; Acts 3:25–26; Matt 10:5–8a; and Matt 15:24 for a few examples of this line of thinking.
[371] Hays, *Echoes of Scripture*, 344.
[372] Hays, *Echoes of Scripture*, 2–3.
[373] Hays, *Echoes of Scripture*, 358.
[374] Tolkien, "On Fairy Stories," sect. "Recovery, Escape, and Consolation," para. 1.
[375] Tolkien, *Letters of J. R. R. Tolkien*, Letter 247.
[376] Kreeft, *The Philosophy of Tolkien*, ch. 1, loc. 458.
[377] Wright, *Simply Good News*, 60.
[378] Tolkien, *Letters of J. R. R. Tolkien*, Letter 131.
[379] Murray, "J. R. R. Tolkien and the Art of the Parable," in Pearce, *Tolkien: A Celebration*, 50.
[380] Wright, *Simply Good News*, 61.
[381] For all dates above, see "Appendix B" of *The Lord of the Rings*. The Red Book is a conceit of Tolkien's to explain the source of his mythology.
[382] Tolkien, *The Lord of the Rings*, 1026–29; also see the apocryphal "Acts of St. Peter," section 35, for this Christian legend.
[383] Tolkien, *The Lord of the Rings*, 1026–29.
[384] Tolkien, *The Lord of the Rings*, 1026–29
[385] Tolkien, *The Lord of the Rings*, 1028–29.
[386] Young, *The Parables*, 5.
[387] Young, *The Parables*, 6.
[388] Wright, *Simply Jesus*, 93.
[389] Tolkien, *Letters of J. R. R. Tolkien*, Letter 156.
[390] See Isa 6:9 and Mark 4:12.
[391] McDermott, *Everyday Glory*, 39.
[392] Godawa, *The Imagination of God*, 81.
[393] Godawa, *The Imagination of God*, 82.
[394] Kreeft, *The Philosophy of Tolkien*, ch. 1, loc. 586.
[395] Wright, *How God Became King*, 33.
[396] Matt 20:25–28, NIV.
[397] Kreeft, *The Philosophy of Tolkien*, ch. 1, loc. 586.
[398] Birzer, *Tolkien's Sanctifying Myth*, ch. 4. Birzer is also quoting Letter 156 in Tolkien, *Letters of J. R. R. Tolkien*.
[399] Ehrman, *How Jesus Became God*.
[400] Pitre, *The Case for Jesus*, 139.
[401] Pitre, *The Case for Jesus*, 139.
[402] Tolkien, *Letters of J. R. R. Tolkien*, Letter 144.
[403] Wright, *How God Became King*, 92.
[404] Wright, *How God Became King*, 55.
[405] Ryken, *Messiah Comes to Middle-Earth*, 98.
[406] Hays, *Echoes of Scripture*, 98.

[407] Williams, *Christ On Trial*, 6.
[408] Hays, *Echoes of Scripture*, 98.
[409] Pitre, *The Case for Jesus*, 139.
[410] See Matt 17:1–8; Mark 9:2–8; and Luke 9:28–36. Matt 17:2 is quoted here, NIV.
[411] In 2012, three years prior to signing a contract for this book, I kept a journal where I noted no less than *fourteen* episodes where Aragorn's *exousia* was on display in the text. Although we will look at a few in this chapter, here is a list of where interested readers can find all the episodes I noticed: in the *Fellowship of the Ring*, book I: chs. 10 and 11, book II: chs. 8 and 9; in *The Two Towers*, book III: chs. 2, 5, 7 and 11; in *The Return of the King*, book V: chs. 2, 6, 8, and 9; finally, book VI: ch. 5 has perhaps the best moments in the entire novel.
[412] Wright, *The Challenge of Jesus*, 116–17.
[413] Markos, *On the Shoulders of Hobbits*, ch. 8. I should hastily add that Professor Markos is well-aware of inaugurated eschatology and seems to hold it as part of his own beliefs.
[414] Tolkien, "The Quest of Erebor," in Tolkien, *Unfinished Tales*, 314.
[415] Tolkien, *The Lord of the Rings*, 963.
[416] Tolkien, *Letters of J. R. R. Tolkien*, Letters 183 and 144 respectively.
[417] Wright, *Simply Good News*, 1.
[418] Wright, *Simply Good News*, 63. Emphasis Wright's.
[419] This is Wright's humorous image from *Simply Good News*.
[420] Wright, *How God Became King*, 34.
[421] Kreeft, *The Philosophy of Tolkien*, ch. 2, loc. 914.
[422] Wright, *Simply Good News*, 60.
[423] Tolkien, *Letters of J. R. R. Tolkien*, Letter 144.
[424] Wright, *Simply Jesus*, 92.
[425] Tolkien, *Letters of J. R. R. Tolkien*, Letter 211.
[426] Wright, *Simply Jesus*, 99.
[427] Tolkien, *The Lord of the Rings*, 951.
[428] Wright, *How God Became King*, 73.
[429] Sennett, "Worthy of a Better God," 235.
[430] Levine, *Short Stories by Jesus*, 297.
[431] Tolkien, *The Peoples of Middle-earth*, 409.
[432] 1 Cor 15:25, NIV.
[433] Bart D. Ehrman's book *How Jesus Became God* comes to mind here.
[434] Tolkien, *Letters of J. R. R. Tolkien*, Letter 256.
[435] Tolkien, *Letters of J. R. R. Tolkien*, Letter 256.
[436] Tolkien, *Letters of J. R. R. Tolkien*, Letter 256.
[437] See Acts 15:2–35.
[438] See Marvin R. Wilson's book *Our Father Abraham* for more details.
[439] Keller, *Making Sense of God*, 66.
[440] Wright, *Surprised by Hope*, 129.
[441] Wright, *Surprised by Hope*, 129.
[442] Tolkien, *The Lord of the Rings*, 966.
[443] Dickerson, *A Hobbit's Journey*, 239.
[444] Wright, *How God Became King*, 240.
[445] Wright, *How God Became King*, 175.
[446] Ehrman, *How Jesus Became God*, 125; cf. 269–70.
[447] Tolkien, "On Fairy Stories," Epilogue, final para.
[448] Keller, *God's Wisdom*, April 18.

[449] Wood, *Gospel According to Tolkien*, ch. 5, loc. 2015.
[450] 1 Cor 15:26, NIV.
[451] Tolkien, *The Lord of the Rings*, 1063.
[452] Wright, *Simply Good News*, 54.
[453] Ryken, *Messiah Comes to Middle-earth*, 113–14.
[454] Tolkien, *The Lord of the Rings*, 1063.
[455] Wright, *Surprised by Hope*, 47.
[456] Tolkien, *The Lord of the Rings*, 1097.
[457] Tolkien, *The Silmarillion*, 38.
[458] Tolkien, "The Quest of Erebor," in Tolkien, *Unfinished Tales*, 311.
[459] Tolkien, "The Quest of Erebor," in Tolkien, *Unfinished Tales*, 314. Emphasis mine.
[460] Isa 51:9, NIV.
[461] Tolkien, *The Lord of the Rings*, book II ch. 2, book V, ch. 2, and book III, ch. 2, respectively.
[462] Tolkien, *The Lord of the Rings*, book II, chs. 8 and 9 respectively (p. 375, 393).
[463] Nicholas, *Aragorn*, ch. 1.10, sect. "Appearance," loc. 4416.
[464] Birzer, *Tolkien's Sanctifying Myth*, ch. 2, loc. 785.
[465] Ryken, *Messiah Comes to Middle-earth*, 35.
[466] Lewis, "Myth Became Fact," in Hooper, *God in the Dock*, 67.
[467] Nicholas, *Aragorn*, ch. 1.10, loc. 4418.
[468] Tolkien, *The Lord of the Rings*, 170.
[469] Isa 53:3, NIV.
[470] Tolkien, *The Lord of the Rings*, 951.
[471] Tolkien, *The Lord of the Rings*, 951.
[472] Pitre, *Jesus the Bridegroom*, ch. 4.
[473] Keller, *The Meaning of Marriage*, 40.
[474] 1 Cor 15:23.
[475] Wood, *Gospel According to Tolkien*, ch. 5, loc. 2128.
[476] Wood, *Gospel According to Tolkien*, ch. 5, loc. 2138.
[477] Mark 2:19 and Pitre, *Jesus the Bridegroom*, ch. 4.
[478] Tolkien, *Letters of J. R. R. Tolkien*, Letter 181.
[479] John 10:18.
[480] Pitre, *Jesus the Bridegroom*, 117.
[481] Tolkien *The Lord of the Rings*, 971.
[482] Middleton, *New Heaven and New Earth*, 164.
[483] Tolkien *The Lord of the Rings*, 971.
[484] Wright, *How God Became King*, 162.
[485] Mark 10:9, NIV.
[486] Wright, *How God Became King*, 172.
[487] Phil 2:6–7, NIV.
[488] Ryken, *Messiah Comes to Middle-earth*, 4.
[489] All quotes above from Tolkien, *The Lord of the Rings*, 967.
[490] Tolkien, *The Lord of the Rings*, 963.
[491] Tolkien, *The Lord of the Rings*, 865.
[492] Tolkien, *The Lord of the Rings*, 875.
[493] Tolkien, *The Lord of the Rings*, 775.
[494] Matt 26:39, NIV.
[495] Tolkien, *The Lord of the Rings*, 778.
[496] Tolkien, *The Lord of the Rings*, 780.
[497] Mark 9:2–3, NIV.

[498] Middleton, *New Heaven and New Earth*, 26.
[499] Tolkien, *The Lord of the Rings*, 591.
[500] Tolkien, *The Lord of the Rings*, 594.
[501] Greek *hora*, meaning a "short period of time." See John 2:4; 4:21, 23; 5:25, 28; 7:6, 30; 8:20; 12:23, 27; 13:1; 16:2, 4, 21, 25, 32; 17:1; and 19:27.
[502] Pitre, *Jesus the Bridegroom*, 46. Emphasis Pitre's.
[503] For a few examples, see "The Council of Elrond" chapter in *The Fellowship*, "The Palantir" chapter in *The Two Towers*, two instances in "The Passing of the Grey Company" chapter in *The Return of the King*, and finally in "The Steward and the King" chapter of *The Return of the King*.
[504] Resnick, "An Interview with Tolkien."
[505] John 2:4.
[506] John 10:18.
[507] Isa 53:3.
[508] Tolkien, *The Lord of the Rings*, 540.
[509] Ryken, *Messiah Comes to Middle-earth*, 106.
[510] See Tolkien, *The Lord of the Rings*, book III, ch. 10.
[511] Tolkien, *The Lord of the Rings*, 393.
[512] Luke 15:11–32 and Mark 12:1–12.
[513] Birzer, *Tolkien's Sanctifying Myth*, ch. 5, loc. 2309.
[514] Tolkien, *The Lord of the Rings*, 375.
[515] Tolkien, *The Lord of the Rings*, 968.
[516] Rutledge, *Battle for Middle-earth*, ch. 2, loc. 1471.
[517] Tolkien, *The Lord of the Rings*, 248.
[518] All dates taken from "Appendix B" of *The Lord of the Rings*.
[519] Tolkien, *The Lord of the Rings*, 250.
[520] Tolkien, *The Lord of the Rings*, 250.
[521] Tolkien, *The Lord of the Rings*, 1088.
[522] Tolkien, "Debate of Finrod and Andreth."
[523] Tolkien, *The Lord of the Rings*, 1089.
[524] Tolkien, *The Lord of the Rings*, 1089.
[525] This alias was bestowed by working with Theoden's and Denethor's fathers.
[526] Tolkien, *The Lord of the Rings*, 194.
[527] Pitre, *Jewish Roots of Mary*, Introduction.
[528] Pitre, *Jewish Roots of Mary*, Introduction.
[529] See Matt 3:13–17; Mark 1:9–11; Luke 3:21–23; and John 1:29–33, NIV.
[530] Tolkien, *The Lord of the Rings*, "Appendix A," 1059.
[531] Pitre, *Jewish Roots of Mary*, 23.
[532] See also 2 Cor 5:17 and Rev 21:5, NIV.
[533] See 1 Kgs 1:16–17; 2:19–20; 15:13; 2 Chr 15:16; and Jer 13:18; 29:2; and Psalm 45 for just a few examples.
[534] Pitre, *Jewish Roots of Mary*, 168.
[535] Pitre, *Jewish Roots of Mary*, 166. See also Jer 31:15, NIV.
[536] Tolkien, *The Lord of the Rings*, 1061.
[537] Lewis, *The Weight of Glory*, 43.
[538] The 1951 second edition is the one most people read, though copies of the first edition still exist.
[539] Olsen, *Exploring J. R. R. Tolkien's* The Hobbit, 11.
[540] Hays, *Echoes of Scripture*, 347.
[541] Tolkien, *Letters of J. R. R. Tolkien*, Letter 176.

542 Hays, *Echoes of Scripture*, 188.
543 See 2 Kgs 21:1–26, NIV. Verse 2 is quoted.
544 See any good Catholic Bible, which includes 1 and 2 Maccabees, for more details.
545 Tolkien, *The Hobbit*, 290.
546 Wright, *Surprised by Hope*, 168.
547 Walls, *Heaven, Hell, and Purgatory*, 96.
548 Kreeft, *Catholic Christianity*, 136.
549 Wright, *Surprised by Hope*, ch. 3.
550 Jas 2:14–26, NIV.
551 Lewis, *The Problem of Pain*, 131.
552 Wright, *Surprised by Hope*, ch. 11.
553 Walls, *Heaven, Hell, and Purgatory*, 188.
554 See 1 John 1:8; Rev 21:27; and 1 John 1:5.
555 Kreeft, *Forty Reasons*, "Reason #35," loc. 1009.
556 Keller, *Counterfeit Gods*, Introduction, loc. 86.
557 Kreeft, *Catholic Christianity*, 64.
558 Tolkien, *The Hobbit*, ch. 1.
559 Jer 3:15–16, NIV.
560 Pitre, *Jewish Roots of Mary*, ch. 3. See 2 Macc 2:4–8.
561 Jer 31:33, NIV.
562 All insights above from Pitre, *Jewish Roots of Mary*, ch. 3.
563 Tolkien, *The Hobbit*, 277.
564 Gen 1:26–27, NIV.
565 Tolkien, *The Hobbit*, 265.
566 Tolkien, *The Hobbit*, 292.
567 Tolkien, "The Quest of Erebor," in Tolkien, *Unfinished Tales*, 307.
568 Tolkien, *The Lord of the Rings*, 1080.
569 Tolkien, *The Lord of the Rings*, 1080.
570 Scarf, *The Ideal of Kingship*, 123.
571 Wright, *Simply Jesus*, 87.
572 See Matt 12:42 and 22:41–46.
573 Tolkien, *The Silmarillion*, 38.
574 Tolkien, *The Hobbit*, 289.
575 Tolkien, "Debate of Finrod and Andreth."
576 Tolkien, "Debate of Finrod and Andreth."
577 Tolkien, *Letters of J. R. R. Tolkien*, Letter 142.
578 Birzer, *Tolkien's Sanctifying Myth*, ch. 3, loc. 1442.
579 Wright, *How God Became King*, 269; and Middleton, *New Heaven and New Earth*, 72.
580 Middleton, *New Heaven and New Earth*, 23.
581 1 Cor 15:25.
582 Wright, *How God Became King*, 79.
583 Tolkien, *The Lord of the Rings*, 1077.
584 Ps 137:1, 5, NIV.
585 Tolkien, *The Silmarillion*, 4.
586 Lewis, *Mere Christianity*, 43.
587 Exod 4:22, NIV.
588 Middleton, *New Heaven and New Earth*, 61.
589 Tolkien, *The Hobbit*, 277.
590 Tolkien, *The Hobbit*, 285.
591 Tolkien, *The Hobbit*, 285.

ENDNOTES

[592] Hays, *Echoes of Scripture*, 186.
[593] Bell, *Spiritual World of* The Hobbit, 127.
[594] Tolkien, *The Hobbit*, 305.
[595] Keller, *God's Wisdom*, ix.
[596] Ps 19:1-2 is a good example.
[597] Spangler and Tverberg, *Rabbi Jesus*, 48.
[598] Spangler and Tverberg, *Rabbi Jesus*, 48.
[599] Spangler and Tverberg, *Rabbi Jesus*, 48.
[600] 2 Kgs 21:6, NIV.
[601] Tolkien, *The Silmarillion*, 39.
[602] 2 Kgs 22:1, NIV.
[603] Walton, *Old Testament Theology*, 32.
[604] Armstrong, *The Great Transformation*, ch. 5, loc. 3511.
[605] 1 Cor 15:28, NIV.
[606] Tolkien, *The Lord of the Rings*, 1071.
[607] Tolkien, *The Lord of the Rings*, 1072.
[608] Tolkien, *The Lord of the Rings*, 1073.
[609] Jeremiah 29:5-7, NIV.
[610] Tolkien, *The Lord of the Rings*, 1179.
[611] Tolkien, *The Lord of the Rings*, 1075.
[612] Ps 22:6, NIV.
[613] If anyone wishes to learn more about the Rings of Power, see "Of the Rings of Power and the Third Age," in Tolkien, *The Silmarillion*, 294-314.
[614] Tolkien, *The Lord of the Rings*, 1077.
[615] Deut 32:35, NIV.
[616] Tolkien, *The Lord of the Rings*, 1077.
[617] Lewis, "Tolkien's *The Lord of the Rings*," in Lewis, *On Stories*, 138.
[618] Birzer, *Tolkien's Sanctifying Myth*, ch. 3, loc. 1440, quoting Christopher Tolkien.
[619] Barron, *Catholicism*, 73-74.
[620] Tolkien, "Debate of Finrod and Andreth."
[621] Tolkien, "Debate of Finrod and Andreth."
[622] Lewis, "Myth Became Fact," in Hooper, *God in the Dock*, 66.
[623] Birzer, *Tolkien's Sanctifying Myth*, ch. 3, loc. 1442.
[624] This ancient idea is based on Deut 18:14-22 (prophet); Ps 110:1-4 (priest); and Ps 2 (king) in the Hebrew Bible. I recommend Philip Ryken's book *The Messiah Comes to Middle-earth* for more information on this important topic.
[625] Tolkien, *Letters of J. R. R. Tolkien*, Letter 181.
[626] Dickerson, *A Hobbit Journey*, 237.
[627] Tolkien, *Letters of J. R. R. Tolkien*, Letter 181.
[628] Tolkien, *Letters of J. R. R. Tolkien*, Letter 181.
[629] Young, "Lewis on the Gospels as True Myth," last line and para. of essay.
[630] Young, "Lewis on the Gospels as True Myth," fourth to last para.
[631] See Exod 24:9-10; Job 1:6-12; 1 Kgs 22:19-23; Isa 6; Jer 23:18-22; and Pss 82:1; 89:5-7; and 103:19-22 for just a handful of examples.
[632] Most biblical scholars advance the theory that the council in Ps 82 and the plural of Gen 1:26-27 are a reference either to the other members of the Trinity or a council of Jewish elders. The rest of the Bible and Dead Sea Scroll literature, however, contradict this view, especially since in Ps 82 these council members are sentenced to death. Can Christians really believe that this psalm refers to the other members of the Trinity?
[633] Flieger, *Splintered Light*, ch. 6, loc. 1238.

[634] Emphasis mine.
[635] Walton, *Old Testament Theology*, 32.
[636] All quotations above from Walton, *Old Testament Theology*, 32.
[637] Tolkien, *The Silmarillion*, 3.
[638] Job 38:7.
[639] Gen 3:5.
[640] Walton, *Lost World of Genesis One*, 49.
[641] Lewis, *Mere Christianity*, 136.
[642] Barron, *Catholicism*, 47.
[643] Tolkien, *The Lord of the Rings*, 267.
[644] Wood, *Gospel According to Tolkien*, ch. 1, loc. 454.
[645] Tolkien, *The Silmarillion*, 6.
[646] 1 Cor 15:45–49.
[647] KJV translation.
[648] Mark 15:34 quoting Ps 22:1, NIV.
[649] Lewis, "Tolkien's *The Lord of the Rings*," in Lewis, *On Stories*, 138.
[650] Keller, *The Songs of Jesus*, January 11.
[651] This topic could take us into a very long digression, so I highly recommend reading Heiser's treatment of it in *The Unseen Realm*, ch. 9.
[652] Birzer, *Tolkien's Sanctifying Myth*, ch. 5, loc. 2016.
[653] Lewis, *Mere Christianity*, 44.
[654] Tolkien, *The Silmarillion*, 5. Emphasis mine.
[655] Tolkien, *The Silmarillion*, 6. Emphasis mine.
[656] Tolkien, *The Silmarillion*, ch. 2.
[657] Enns, "Adam Is Israel."
[658] Walton, *Lost World of Adam and Eve*, 96.
[659] Rom 1:16, NIV.
[660] Gen 12:3, NIV.
[661] Tolkien, *The Lord of the Rings*, 316.
[662] Heiser, *Demons*, ch. 5, loc. 2324.
[663] Tolkien, *The Silmarillion*, 4.
[664] Tolkien, *The Silmarillion*, 35.
[665] Tolkien, *The Silmarillion*, 38.
[666] Most famously Gen 22:10–18.
[667] See Heiser, *The Unseen Realm*, ch. 17. First reference to the "angel of Yahweh" is Gen 16:7–11.
[668] Tolkien, *The Silmarillion*, 29.
[669] Tolkien, *The Silmarillion*, 32.
[670] Tolkien, *The Silmarillion*, 45.
[671] Tolkien, *The Silmarillion*, 85.
[672] Tolkien, *The Silmarillion*, 95.
[673] Tolkien, *The Silmarillion*, 29.
[674] Tolkien, *The Silmarillion*, 16. Emphasis mine.
[675] Birzer, *Tolkien's Sanctifying Myth*, ch. 4. Birzer does not provide the numbers of the letter, but see Tolkien, *Letters of J. R. R. Tolkien*, Letter 156.
[676] Tolkien, *The Silmarillion*, 306.
[677] See Aragorn's family tree here: http://lotrproject.com/character/1#!open.
[678] The tale of Gondolin will not be told in this book. For that, please see Christopher Tolkien's latest publication entitled *The Fall of Gondolin*.
[679] Wright, *How God Became King*, 72.

[680] This is the word which means the "Downfall of Numenor." The previous paragraph is indebted to a reading of that chapter of *The Silmarillion*.
[681] Tolkien, *Letters of J. R. R. Tolkien*, Letter 96.
[682] Tolkien, commentary on "Debate of Finrod and Andreth," in *Morgoth's Ring*.
[683] Wright, *How God Became King*, 20.
[684] Tolkien, *Letters of J. R. R. Tolkien*, Letter 297.
[685] Tolkien, *Letters of J. R. R. Tolkien*, Letter 297.
[686] Heiser, *The Unseen Realm*, ch. 17.
[687] See the "Valaquenta" in *The Silmarillion* for Tolkien's description of Manwe and his role in the council.
[688] Birzer, *Tolkien's Sanctifying Myth*, ch. 4. Birzer also adds that Gandalf "identifies" Aragorn *with* the Valar of Arda.
[689] Tolkien, "Debate of Finrod and Andreth."
[690] 1 Cor 15:26, NIV.
[691] This is an extremely complex subject that Tolkien never finished explicating. In the edition of the text which I have cited from The History of Middle-earth, Tolkien may be hinting that elves are given the opportunity to be reincarnated should they desire it. This is much debated.
[692] Wright, *How God Became King*, 44.
[693] Tolkien, "Debate of Finrod and Andreth."
[694] Heiser, *The Unseen Realm*, 62.
[695] Tolkien, "Debate of Finrod and Andreth."
[696] Heiser, *The Unseen Realm*, 66.
[697] Tolkien, "Debate of Finrod and Andreth."
[698] Wright, *Surprised by Hope*, 88.
[699] Rev 21:1, NIV.
[700] See Tolkien, *Letters of J. R. R. Tolkien*, Letter 247, again for the phrase "unattainable vistas," and Kreeft, *The Philosophy of Tolkien*, ch. 1.1, for the rest of the quoted material.
[701] Wright, *How God Became King*, 240.
[702] Pitre, *The Case for Jesus*, 147.
[703] Tolkien, "Debate of Finrod and Andreth."
[704] Tolkien, "Debate of Finrod and Andreth."
[705] Wright, *Simply Jesus*, 43.
[706] Snodgrass, *Stories with Intent*, 20.
[707] Tolkien, *Letters of J. R. R. Tolkien*, Letter 89.
[708] Tolkien, "Debate of Finrod and Andreth."
[709] John 10:16, NIV.
[710] Rom 1:16, NIV.
[711] Snodgrass, *Stories with Intent*, 20.
[712] Tolkien, "Debate of Finrod and Andreth."
[713] Tolkien, *The Lord of the Rings*, 951.
[714] Based on Wright's breakdown of how "news" works, as previously discussed.
[715] Tolkien, "Debate of Finrod and Andreth."
[716] Wright, *Simply Jesus*, 5.
[717] Wright, *Simply Jesus*, 5.
[718] McIntosh, *The Flame Imperishable*, 264.
[719] Dickerson, *A Hobbit Journey*, 237.
[720] Dickerson and O'Hara, *From Homer to Harry Potter*, page 60.
[721] Dickerson, *A Hobbit Journey*, 216.
[722] Wright, *How God Became King*, 240.

[723] Lewis, "Is Theology Poetry?" in Lewis, *The Weight of Glory*, 134.
[724] Dickerson, *A Hobbit Journey*, 240.
[725] Keller, *God's Wisdom*, April 16.
[726] Matt 25:13, NIV.
[727] Keller, *The Meaning of Marriage*, 44.
[728] Carpenter, *J. R. R. Tolkien: A Biography*, 128.
[729] McFague, *Speaking in Parables*, ch. 4, quoting Gerhard Ebeling.
[730] Loconte, *A Hobbit, a Wardrobe*, 2.
[731] Loconte, *A Hobbit, a Wardrobe*, 193.
[732] Lewis, "Sometimes Fairy Stories May Say Best What's to Be Said," in Lewis, *On Stories*, 70.
[733] Tolkien, "Debate of Finrod and Andreth."
[734] Mark 4:24, NIV.
[735] McFague, *Speaking in Parables*, ch. 4.
[736] McFague, *Speaking in Parables*, ch. 3.
[737] Murray, "J. R. R. Tolkien and the Art of the Parable," in Pearce, *Tolkien: A Celebration*, 50.
[738] Tolkien, *Letters of J. R. R. Tolkien*, Letter 227.
[739] Lewis, *The Weight of Glory*, 32.

Bibliography

Armstrong, Karen. *The Case for God*. Kindle ed. New York: Knopf, 2009.

———. *The Great Transformation: The Beginning of Our Religious Traditions*. New York: Knopf, 2006.

Auerbach, Erich. *Mimesis: The Representation of Reality in Western Literature*. Princeton University Press, 1953.

Baggett, David, et al. *C. S. Lewis as Philosopher: Truth, Goodness, and Beauty*. 2nd ed. Lynchburg: Liberty University Press, 2017.

Barron, Robert. *Catholicism: A Journey to the Heart of the Faith*. Kindle ed. New York: Image, 2011.

Bassham, Gregory, et al., eds. *The Chronicles of Narnia and Philosophy: The Lion, the Witch, and the Worldview*. Kindle ed. Chicago: Carus, 2005.

Bell, James Stuart. *The Spiritual World of* The Hobbit. Kindle ed. Bloomington: Whitestone Communications, 2013.

Bird, Michael F., and N. T. Wright. *The New Testament in Its World: An Introduction to the History, Literature, and Theology of the First Christians*. Kindle ed. Grand Rapids: Zondervan Academic, 2019.

Birzer, Bradley J. *J. R. R. Tolkien's Sanctifying Myth: Understanding Middle-earth*. Kindle ed. Wilmington: ISI, 2009.

Blomberg, Craig L. *Interpreting the Parables*. 2nd ed. Kindle ed. Downers Grove: InterVarsity, 2012.

Carpenter, Humphrey. *J. R. R. Tolkien: A Biography*. Kindle ed. New York: Houghton Mifflin, 1977.

———, ed. *The Letters of J. R. R. Tolkien*. Kindle ed. New York: Houghton Mifflin Harcourt, 2013.

Chance, Jane. *Tolkien's Art: A Mythology for England*. Kindle ed. Lexington: University of Kentucky Press, 2001.

Clark, Mark. *The Problem of God: Answering a Skeptic's Challenges to Christianity*. Kindle ed. Grand Rapids: Zondervan, 2017.

Crossan, John Dominic. *The Power of Parable: How Fiction by Jesus Became Fiction about Jesus*. Kindle ed. New York: HarperOne, 2012.

Dickerson, Matthew. *A Hobbit Journey: Discovering the Enchantment of J. R. R. Tolkien's Middle-earth*. Kindle ed. Grand Rapids: Brazos, 2012.

Dickerson, Matthew, and David O'Hara, *From Homer to Harry Potter: A Handbook of Myth and Fantasy*. (Grand Rapids: Brazos, 2006).

Dickinson, Emily. *The Poems of Emily Dickinson: Reading Edition*. Belknap Press of Harvard University Press, 1998.

Drout, Michael. "Tolkien and *Beowulf*: Medieval Materials for the Modern Audience." Lecture at J. R. R. Tolkien: Fantasist and Medievalist, University of Vermont, Burlington, VT, March 6, 2003.

Duriez, Colin. *Tolkien and C. S. Lewis: The Gift of Friendship*. Kindle ed. Mahwah, NJ: Hidden Spring, 2003.

Ehrman, Bart D. *How Jesus Became God: The Exaltation of a Jewish Preacher from Galilee*. Kindle ed. New York: HarperCollins, 2014.

Enns, Peter. "Adam Is Israel." Biologos.org, March 2, 2010. https://biologos.org/articles/adam-is-israel.

Ferry, Luc. *A Brief History of Thought: A Philosophical Guide to Living*. Translated by Theo Cuffe. Kindle ed. New York: Harper Perennial, 2011.

Flieger, Verlyn. *Splintered Light: Logos and Language in Tolkien's World*. Kindle ed. Kent: Kent State University Press, 2002.

Funk, Robert W. *Funk on Parables: Collected Essays*. Edited by Bernard Brandon Scott. Kindle ed. Santa Rosa, CA: Polebridge, 2006.

Godawa, Brian. *The Imagination of God: Art, Creativity, and Truth in the Bible*. Kindle ed. Los Angeles: Embedded Pictures, 2016.

Gould, Paul M. *Cultural Apologetics: Renewing the Christian Voice, Conscience, and Imagination in a Disenchanted World*. Kindle ed. Grand Rapids: Zondervan, 2019.

Groothuis, Douglas. *Christian Apologetics: A Comprehensive Case for Biblical Faith*. Kindle ed. Downers Grove: InterVarsity, 2011.

Hays, Richard B. *Echoes of Scripture in the Gospels*. Kindle ed. Waco: Baylor University, 2016.

Heiser, Michael. *Demons: What the Bible Really Says about the Powers of Darkness*. Kindle ed. Bellingham: Lexham, 2020.

———. *The Unseen Realm*. Kindle ed. Bellingham: Lexham, 2015.

Herman, Arthur. *The Cave and the Light: Plato Versus Aristotle and the Struggle for the Soul of Western Civilization*. Kindle ed. New York: Random House, 2013.

Hooper, Walter, ed. *Christian Reflections*. Kindle ed. New York: HarperOne, 2017.

———, ed. *The Collected Letters of C. S. Lewis*. Vol. 3: "Narnia, Cambridge and Joy, 1950–1963." Kindle ed. New York: Harper San Francisco, 2007.

———, ed. *God in the Dock: Essays on Theology and Ethics*. Kindle ed. Grand Rapids: Eerdmans, 2001.

Hutton, Ronald. "The Pagan Tolkien." In *The Ring and the Cross: Christianity and The Lord of the Rings*, edited by Paul E. Kerry, 57–70. Kindle ed. Madison: Fairleigh Dickinson University Press, 2011.

Keller, Timothy. *Counterfeit Gods: The Empty Promises of Money, Sex, and Power, and the Only Hope That Matters*. Kindle ed. New York: Penguin, 2009.

———. *God's Wisdom for Navigating Life: A Year of Daily Devotions in the Proverbs*. Kindle ed. New York: Viking, 2017.

———. *Making Sense of God: An Invitation to the Skeptical*. Kindle ed. New York: Viking, 2016.

———. *The Meaning of Marriage: Facing the Complexities of Commitment with the Wisdom of God*. Kindle ed. New York: Dutton, 2011.

———. *The Songs of Jesus: A Year of Daily Devotions in the Psalms*. Kindle ed. New York: Viking, 2015.

Koukl, Gregory. *The Story of Reality: How the World Began, How It Ends, and Everything Important That Happens in Between*. Kindle ed. Grand Rapids: Zondervan, 2017.
Kreeft, Peter. *Catholic Christianity*. Kindle ed. San Francisco: Ignatius, 2001.
———. *Forty Reasons I am a Catholic*. Kindle ed. Manchester: Sophia Institute, 2018.
———. *The Philosophy of Tolkien: The Worldview Behind The Lord of the Rings*. Kindle ed. San Francisco: Ignatius, 2005.
Kreglinger, Gisela H. *Storied Revelations: Parables, Imagination, and George MacDonald's Christian Fiction*. Kindle ed. Eugene, OR: Pickwick, 2013.
Levine, Amy-Jill. *Short Stories by Jesus: The Enigmatic Parables of a Controversial Rabbi*. Kindle ed. New York: HarperCollins, 2014.
Lewis, C. S. "De Descriptione Temporum." In *Selected Literary Essays*, edited by Walter Hooper, 350–51. Kindle ed. New York: Cambridge University Press, 2013.
———. *George MacDonald: An Anthology 365 Readings*. Kindle ed. New York: HarperCollins, 2009.
———. *Letters to Children*. New York: Macmillan, 1985.
———. *Mere Christianity*. Kindle ed. New York: HarperCollins, 1952.
———. *On Stories: And Other Essays on Literature*. Kindle ed. New York: HarperCollins, 2017.
———. *The Pilgrim's Regress*. Kindle ed. New York: HarperCollins, 1933.
———. *The Problem of Pain*. Kindle ed. New York: HarperCollins, 1940.
———. *Reflections on the Psalms*. Kindle ed. New York: HarperOne, 2017.
———. *Selected Literary Essays*. New York: HarperOne, 2013.
———. *Surprised by Joy: The Shape of My Early Life*. Kindle ed. New York: HarperOne, 2017.
———. *The Weight of Glory*. Kindle ed. New York: HarperCollins, 2017.
Lewis, W. H., and Walter Hooper, eds. *Letters of C. S. Lewis*. Kindle ed. New York: HarperOne, 2017.
Loconte, Joseph. *A Hobbit, a Wardrobe, and a Great War: How J. R. R. Tolkien and C. S. Lewis Rediscovered Faith, Friendship, and Heroism in the Cataclysm of 1914–1918*. Kindle ed. Nashville: Nelson, 2015.
Markos, Louis. *Apologetics for the 21st Century*. Kindle ed. Wheaton: Crossway, 2010.
———. *From Achilles to Christ: Why Christians Should Read the Pagan Classics*. Kindle ed. Downers Grove: InterVarsity, 2007.
———. *On the Shoulders of Hobbits: The Road to Virtue with Tolkien and Lewis*. Kindle ed. Chicago: Moody, 2012.
Marshall, Taylor R. *The Crucified Rabbi: Judaism and the Origins of Catholic Christianity*. Vol. 1. Kindle ed. Saint John, 2009.
McDermott, Gerald R. *Everyday Glory: The Revelation of God in All of Reality*. Kindle ed. Grand Rapids: Baker Academic, 2018.
McFague, Sallie. *Speaking in Parables: A Study in Metaphor and Theology*. Philadelphia: Fortress, 1975.
McGrath, Alister E. *C. S. Lewis: A Life*. Kindle ed. Carol Stream: Tyndale House, 2013.
———. *If I Had Lunch with C. S. Lewis: Exploring the Ideas of C. S. Lewis on the Meaning of Life*. Kindle ed. Colorado Springs: Tyndale, 2014.
———. *The Intellectual World of C. S. Lewis*. Kindle ed. Chichester: Wiley, 2014.
———. *Mere Apologetics*. Kindle ed. Grand Rapids: Baker, 2012.
———. *Narrative Apologetics: Sharing the Relevance, Joy, and Wonder of the Christian Faith*. Kindle ed. Grand Rapids: Baker, 2019.

McIntosh, Jonathan. *The Flame Imperishable: Tolkien, St. Thomas, and the Metaphysics of Faerie*. Kindle ed. Kettering, OH: Angelico, 2017.

Middleton, J. Richard. *A New Heaven and a New Earth: Reclaiming Biblical Eschatology*. Kindle ed. Grand Rapids: Baker Academic, 2014.

Miller, Donald G., and Dikran Y. Hadidian, eds. *Jesus and Man's Hope*. 2nd ed. Pittsburgh: Pittsburgh Theological Seminary, 1971.

Myers, Jeff. *Understanding the Faith*. Kindle ed. Colorado Springs: Summit Ministries, 2016.

———. *Understanding the Times*. Kindle ed. Colorado Springs: Summit Ministries, 2015.

Nicholas, Angela P. *Aragorn: J. R. R. Tolkien's Undervalued Hero*. Kindle ed. Edinburgh: Luna, 2017.

Olsen, Corey. *Exploring J. R. R. Tolkien's* The Hobbit. Kindle ed. New York: Mariner, 2012.

Olson, Roger E. *The Essentials of Christian Thought: Seeing Reality through the Biblical Story*. Kindle ed. Grand Rapids: Zondervan, 2017.

Ordway, Holly. *Apologetics and the Christian Imagination: An Integrated Approach to Defending the Faith*. Kindle ed. Steubenville: Emmaus Road, 2017.

Park, S. Steve. *Journey towards Home: The Christian Life According to C. S. Lewis*. Kindle ed. Eugene, OR: Wipf & Stock, 2017.

Pearce, Joseph. *Frodo's Journey: Discovering the Hidden Meaning of* The Lord of the Rings. Kindle ed. Charlotte: Saint Benedict, 2015.

———, ed. *Tolkien: A Celebration*. San Francisco: Ignatius, 1999.

Pearcey, Nancy. *Finding Truth: 5 Principles for Unmasking Atheism, Secularism, and Other God Substitutes*. Kindle ed. Colorado Springs: David C. Cook, 2015.

Piper, John. "C. S. Lewis, Romantic Rationalist." In *The Romantic Rationalist: God, Life, and Imagination in the Work of C. S. Lewis*, edited by John Piper et al., 21–38. Kindle ed. Wheaton: Crossway, 2014.

Pitre, Brant. *The Case for Jesus: The Biblical and Historical Evidence for Christ*. Kindle ed. New York: Image, 2016.

———. *Jesus and the Jewish Roots of Mary: Unveiling the Mother of the Messiah*. Kindle ed. New York: Image, 2018.

———. *Jesus the Bridegroom: The Greatest Love Story Ever Told*. Kindle ed. New York: Image, 2014.

Resnick, Henry. "An Interview with Tolkien [March 2, 1966]." *Niekas* 18 (1967).

Rutledge, Fleming. *The Battle for Middle-earth: Tolkien's Divine Design in* The Lord of the Rings. Kindle ed. Grand Rapids: Eerdmans, 2004.

Ryken, Philip. *The Messiah Comes to Middle-earth: Images of Christ's Threefold Office in* The Lord of the Rings. Kindle ed. Downers Grove: InterVarsity, 2017.

Sayers, Dorothy L. *The Letters of Dorothy L. Sayers*. Kindle ed. St. Martin's, 2014.

Scarf, Christopher. *The Ideal of Kingship in the Writings of Charles Williams, C. S. Lewis, and J. R. R. Tolkien: Divine Kingship Is Reflected in Middle-Earth*. Kindle ed. Cambridge: James Clarke, 2013.

Snodgrass, Klyne. *Stories with Intent: A Comprehensive Guide to the Parables of Jesus*. Kindle ed. Grand Rapids: Eerdmans, 2008.

Spangler, Ann, and Lois Tverberg. *Sitting at the Feet of Rabbi Jesus: How the Jewishness of Jesus Can Transform Your Faith*. Kindle ed. Grand Rapids: Zondervan, 2009.

Starr, Charlie W. *The Faun's Bookshelf: C. S. Lewis on Why Myth Matters*. Kindle ed. Kent: Black Squirrel, 2018.

Tolkien, Christopher, ed. "The Debate of Finrod and Andreth." In *Morgoth's Ring*. Boston: Houghton Mifflin, 1993.
———. *The Fall of Gondolin*. Kindle ed. New York: Houghton Mifflin Harcourt, 2018.
———. *The Peoples of Middle-earth*. The History of Middle-earth 12. New York: Houghton Mifflin Harcourt, 1996.
———. *The Silmarillion*. Kindle ed. New York: Houghton Mifflin, 1977.
———. *The Unfinished Tales of Numenor and Middle-earth*. Kindle ed. New York: Houghton Mifflin Harcourt, 1980.
Tolkien, J. R. R. "Beowulf: The Monsters and the Critics." In *Beowulf: A Verse Translation*, translated by Seamus Heaney, edited by Daniel Donoghue. New York: Norton, 2002.
———. *The Hobbit*. Kindle ed. New York: Houghton Mifflin Harcourt, 1937.
———. *The Lord of the Rings*. Fiftieth anniversary one-volume ed. Kindle ed. New York: Houghton Mifflin Harcourt, 2002.
———. *The Monsters and the Critics: And Other Essays*. London: HarperCollins, 2013.
———. *Tree and Leaf: Including Mythopoeia*. Kindle ed. London: HarperCollins, 2001.
Walls, Jerry L. *Heaven, Hell, and Purgatory: A Protestant View of the Cosmic Drama*. Kindle ed. Grand Rapids: Brazos, 2015.
Walton, John H. *The Lost World of Adam and Eve: Genesis 2–3 and the Human Origins Debate*. Kindle ed. Downers Grove: InterVarsity, 2015.
———. *The Lost World of Genesis One: Ancient Cosmology and the Origins Debate*. Kindle ed. Downers Grove: InterVarsity, 2010.
———. *Old Testament Theology for Christians: From Ancient Context to Enduring Belief*. Kindle ed. Downers Grove: InterVarsity, 2017.
Williams, Rowan. *Christ On Trial: How the Gospels Unsettle Our Judgment*. Grand Rapids: Eerdmans, 2003.
Wilson, Marvin R. *Our Father Abraham: Jewish Roots of the Christian Faith*. Kindle ed. Grand Rapids: Eerdmans, 1989.
Wood, Ralph C. "Confronting the World's Weirdness: J. R. R. Tolkien's *The Children of Hurin*." In *The Ring and the Cross: Christianity and* The Lord of the Rings, edited by Paul E. Kerry, 145–51. Kindle ed. Madison: Fairleigh Dickinson University Press, 2011.
———. *The Gospel According to Tolkien: Visions of the Kingdom in Middle-earth*. Kindle ed. Louisville: Westminster John Knox, 2003.
Wright, N. T. *The Challenge of Jesus: Rediscovering Who Jesus Was and Is*. Kindle ed. Downers Grove: InterVarsity, 2015.
———. *How God Became King: The Forgotten Story of the Gospels*. Kindle ed. New York: HarperOne, 2012.
———. *Simply Good News: Why the Gospel Is News and What Makes It Good*. Kindle ed. New York: HarperOne, 2015.
———. *Simply Jesus: A New Vision of Who He Was, What He Did, and Why He Matters*. Kindle ed. New York: HarperOne, 2011.
———. *Surprised by Hope: Rethinking Heaven, the Resurrection, and the Mission of the Church*. Kindle ed. New York: HarperCollins, 2008.
Young, Brad H. *The Parables: Jewish Tradition and Christian Interpretation*. Kindle ed. Grand Rapids: Baker Academic, 1998.
Young, Bruce W. "Lewis on the Gospels a True Myth." In *Inklings Forever* 4 (2004) art. 26. https://pillars.taylor.edu/cgi/viewcontent.cgi?article=1091&context=inklings_forever.
Zimbardo, Rose A., and Neil D. Isaacs. *Understanding* The Lord of the Rings: *The Best of Tolkien Criticism*. Boston: Mariner, 2005.

www.ingramcontent.com/pod-product-compliance
Lightning Source LLC
Chambersburg PA
CBHW062021220426

43662CB00010B/1418